THE
RELIGION
OF
FREEMASONRY.

BY

BRO. HENRY JOSIAH WHYMPER,

PAST DEPUTY DISTRICT GRAND MASTER, PUNJAB.

WITH AN INTRODUCTION

BY

BRO. WILLIAM JAMES HUGHAN,

PAST SENIOR GRAND DEACON OF ENGLAND.

EDITED BY

BRO. GEORGE WILLIAM SPETH, P.M.

LONDON:
GEORGE KENNING,
16 & 16a GREAT QUEEN STREET, LINCOLN'S INN FIELDS, W.C.

MDCCCLXXXVIII.

FREEMASON PRINTING WORKS, LONDON, W.C.

CONTENTS.

INTRODUCTION.

O N agreeing to write a short introduction to Bro. Whymper's work, I had no idea the latter was to be of such an extensive character. As it is, however, nothing appears to be needed to ensure its careful perusal, for the volume tells its own tale in unmistakeable language, and requires no sponsor. This is fortunate, as it is rather awkward for my part to be done when not quite in full sympathy with the author on the general question.

It is quite clear that my friend has every confidence in the stand he has taken and fears no opposition, so that my task is certainly the easier under such happy circumstances, and the more so, when it is noted how thoroughly Bro. Whymper has treated this confessedly difficult subject. His industry and perseverance have been unbounded, and no researches or enquiries appear to have been spared to make the work thoroughly comprehensive and authentic. The result is an invaluable repertory of facts, which constitute an excellent and trustworthy foundation on which to build our theories and opinions, whether favourable or otherwise to the views propounded by the enthusiastic and distinguished author, besides furnishing us with the matured observations and convictions of a zealous Masonic Student.

One of the chief objects of the work is to illustrate

" the circumstance that the original principles of Free-masonry were based on Christian Catholicity," as evidenced by the premier " Constitutions " of 1723, and more distinctly by the 2nd edition of 1738 ; several portions of which, submitted for that purpose, are given in parallel columns, with some later variations, to 1884. To my mind, however, they all tend in the direction of Cosmopolitanism and Religious Univer-sality, save the copy of 1722 (which is scarcely suitable for comparison with the *Modern* Speculative Regula-tions), that of 1723 particularly, being indicative of the altered conditions of the Society of that period.

That English Freemasonry was Christian prior to the organisation of the premier Grand Lodge cannot be doubted by those who are familiar with the " Old Charges " used by the Craft during the preceding centuries. Iu this respect, as in several others, I entirely concur with Bro. Whymper, and am, moreover, bound to admit that no record exists of any express agreement to change the Fraternity from an exclusively Christian to a Religious or Theistic organisation.

But if the original Christian basis of the Society should be continued, because never expressly altered by the " Revivalists," it appears to me that logically such a condition could not be observed by favouring the platform of *Catholicity,* inasmuch as Freemasonry until the era of Grand Lodge was distinctly *Trinitarian,* and hence Unitarians were but little more suitable as members under the old system than Jews or men of other faiths. Precisely when other candidates than Jews were admitted into the Brotherhood with pro-fessed Christians, it is not easy to determine, but as respects our Israelitish members, we shall not be far

wrong if we date their first welcome into the Fraternity as far back as one hundred and fifty years, or even more.

The R.W. Bro. McIntyre, Q.C., P.G.W. (as Grand Registrar), declared in Grand Lodge (5th Dec., 1877) that " up to 1813, the two Grand Lodges of England were *Christian* Grand Lodges. In 1813 we became a *Universal* Grand Lodge, and Jews were admitted amongst us." I am not aware of any facts to corroborate such an assertion, the simple truth being that they are all in the opposite direction, the less exclusive Constitution having been in force long before the " Union."

The lamented Lord Tenterden, K.C.B. (Prov. G.W. Essex), declared at the same Communication that " when Freemasonry was *introduced* into Germany last century, it was constituted on the Christian system of St. John. . . . . The Three Globes Lodge was constituted in 1740 as a Christian Lodge." According to Bro. Gould, P.G.D. (and there is no better guide), this Lodge was started by the sole authority of Frederick the Great, so that we are not much concerned with what was done under those circumstances ; but in reference to the *introduction of Freemasonry* into that country, we may be assured that, so far as England was concerned, there was no departure from the ordinary usage of that period, and that no Warrants of Constitution were granted of a different character to those authorised for other countries by the premier Grand Lodge.

It must be conceded that even now Freemasonry is " simply and purely Christian " under some Grand Lodges, but so long as such organisations are willing to admit visitors from England and other countries, where

the Craft is established on broader lines, it is not for us to object to their narrower system. The late Earl of Zetland, as Grand Master, obtained all necessary concessions from such Grand Lodges during the fifth decade of this century by securing the recognition of all regular brethren as visitors, without regard to their Religious Faith and Creed. More than this we cannot fairly require; though it leaves much to be desired.

It was distinctly announced by authority of the M.W.G.M. in 1865 that there was nothing to prevent anyone "who believes in the Omnipotent, Omniscient, and Omnipresent God, and who in private life practises the sacred duties of morality, from being initiated into the secrets and mysteries of our Order." This decision was officially communicated, because the then Dist. G.M. of Bengal objected to Hindoos being proposed as candidates for initiation, notwithstanding one of that number had offered to make a declaration that " he was not a Pantheist or Polytheist, and did not identify the Creator with any of his creatures, but believed in T.G.A.O.T.U."

Lord Zetland but followed in the steps of his illustrious predecessor, H.R.H. the Duke of Sussex, M.W.G.M., who aided in the arrangements for the initiation of a Mahommedan in 1836, and was in full sympathy with those who desired to extend rather than curtail the foundation on which Freemasonry rests.

It is clear, however, that such authoritative decisions presuppose that candidates cherish or have adopted some particular form of Religious Faith, and are not simply Deists, because the obligation to Secrecy and Fidelity is to be taken on those " Sacred Writings" which to them are binding on their consciences.

Still, with all the predilections for a comprehensive and cosmopolitan basis, nothing can obliterate the evidences of the Christian origin of our Fraternity, and hence, whilst prepared to the fullest extent possible to accept worthy neophytes without respect to their creed, colour, or clime, one cannot but feel that those brethren who are neither professed Christians, nor Jews, will meet with numerous references in our ceremonies founded on the Old and New Testament Scriptures, which will not favour their own notions of theology.

The Bible should always be " the Great Light of the Craft," and never be closed in open Lodge, whatever volumes else may be at times essential for the purposes of reception. I have never heard of any objections to such a rule, and trust that none will ever be urged, for unless other religionists are prepared to practise as well as expect toleration by thus maintaining the actual and obligatory foundations of the Society, the continuity and identity of the Institution cannot be permanently and uniformly preserved.

Bro. Whymper evidently favours separate Jewish, Parsee, Hindoo, and Mahommedan Lodges, but would such a plan really meet his objections to the present régime ? He emphatically states that " It is impossible for any man, *no matter what his former religion may have been,* to become a Fellow-Craft Mason in English Masonry and refuse to accept both the Old and the New Testaments." How, then, would those distinctive combinations provide for such a contingency ? If we cannot do with these religionists in our Lodges, I do not see how we can do without them—*i.e.,* in separate Lodges. We meet on the *Level* or not at all, and therefore, if we cannot as votaries of various Faiths

become members together in Lodge, and thus illustrate the "Brotherhood of Man," better far to refrain from all attempts at Universality, and revert to an exclusively Christian Constitution, as in the olden time.

I am anxious to look at the question in all its aspects, and do not mention difficulties because of any fondness for them, but simply to suggest that if a return to the old system is to be recommended, and primarily because it prevailed prior to the inauguration of Grand Lodges, it is well we should understand what is involved in such a course.

At all events, it seems to me that we are at the present time observing the old rule of 1723, in promoting the "*Religion in which all men agree, leaving their particular opinions to themselves,*" as well as respecting some of the usages and customs of our Grand Lodge. Besides which, by thus extending the scope of our Ancient and Honourable Society, we are adding immensely to its beneficial influence and practical usefulness, especially abroad.

Holding this view, and bearing in mind the esteemed Brethren who hold and advocate otherwise, I am prepared to accept the opinion and advice of the revered Brother, the Rev. A. F. A. Woodford, M.A., P.G. Chap., who maintained that " the Christian School and the Universal School can co-exist in Freemasonry. Though their views are necessarily antagonistic, yet they need not be made the subject of contention ; they can be held in peace and consideration, and all fraternal goodwill. Indeed, we think, upon the whole, that Freemasonry has, curiously enough, a two-fold teaching in this respect."

According to Bro. Whymper's convictions, the

spread of the Craft in India amongst Parsees, Hindoos, and Mahommedans calls for serious consideration, and increasingly so when Brethren of each of those Faiths become sufficiently numerous to support Lodges composed mainly of members of their own persuasion.

Should difficulties arise in consequence, we may yet have to try the ingenious suggestion of chartering Lodges for each particular Faith, subject to the rights of mutual visitation ; but I confess to the feeling that, should ever such be deemed requisite, an element of religious distinction and classification will be of necessity introduced, which will considerably modify or weaken the unsectarian character of the Institution.

Clearly, then, this important subject deserves—in fact, demands—our earnest attention and careful consideration, and our hearty thanks are due to Bro. Whymper for having so fraternally introduced the matter to our notice in the following pages.

WM. JAMES HUGHAN.

TORQUAY,
Sept. 15th, 1888.

PREFACE.

THE object of this book is to draw the attention of Freemasons, who may not have previously examined the subject with care, to the circumstance that the original religious principles of Freemasonry were based on Christian Catholicity. It is believed that, in a well-meant but mistaken effort to let Freemasonry be all things to all men, this principle has been overlooked. Already we find that some Masons deny it altogether, asserting that all distinct profession of Christianity was abandoned in 1717, when the Grand Lodge was founded.

In the earliest known MS. Constitutions, and even in the printed ones of 1722, which, while unauthorized, have yet a claim to respect, the Christian Church was directly acknowledged, and honour demanded for it.

In the earliest authorized Constitutions, those of 1723, the religion of Freemasonry is stated to be Catholic, and although an advantage has been taken of this to claim that this term meant " all embracing," the context makes it clear that something more than this was intended. The Charge (No. 6) goes on to say "This Charge has been always strictly enjoin'd and observ'd; but especially ever since the Reformation in Britain, or the Dissent and Secession of these Nations from the Communion of Rome," implying to any un-prejudiced mind that the Catholicity of the Masonic Religion was a Christian Catholicity.

B

The 1738 Constitutions lead us to think that there was an intention on the part of the author to more distinctly premise Christian principles. The 1756 Constitutions, of the original Grand Lodge, show an alteration in this respect, and, to a certain extent, a disavowal of the 1738 issue.

In the same year that the Grand Lodge published these Constitutions—*i.e.*, 1756—a separate body which had sprung into existence and described itself as representing " Ancient Masonry " published Constitutions which reproduced the 1738 text, and otherwise showed distinct expressions of Christianity. The two bodies combined in 1813, and from thence onwards we have what is a mere theistic confession of belief.

Improving on this, we now have writers who are esteemed authorities, claiming that Masonry has *no connection whatever* with religion.

Full advantage of the errors which have, we believe, crept into the system, has been taken in India, and, as a consequence, what is the Great Light of the English part of the Masonic system has already to some extent been overshadowed.

An indifference to that which Freemasonry admits is its Great Light, must sooner or later have an injurious effect on the institution. The object of this book is not to loosen any ties between the Christian Mason and his Parsee, his Mahommedan, or his Hindoo brother, but to try to make each deal more seriously with the question of personal belief, which we understand is an avowed object of Masonry. We wish to show the professing Christian Mason that Freemasonry cannot in its principles countenance a worldly attempt to gain

universality for the system, and to show to others that the conception of the Masonic system is not that which would place all sacred volumes in a Pantheistic library.

The conception of Freemasonry on the English basis was to make men earnest livers, to live a life with a distinct religious purpose. This end cannot be attained by placing under one Constitution, or on one dead level, any and all books variously esteemed sacred. Yet this is what is now actually being done in part of India, and as yet there has been no protest, owing to assertive Masons stating that the procedure is in conformity with the universality of Masonry.

The writer, or perhaps it is more correct here to describe him as compiler, has purposely quoted extensively from former Masonic writers; they have said, in better language than he could himself employ, much of what he himself would wish to represent; some weight may be gained by Masons seeing that the contentions of the compiler have been previously urged by others.

It should be mentioned that the original collection of matter for this work included many more opinions than are now quoted. Acting under the advice, that not all opinions should be given, but a mere selection only, such as would not weary the ordinary Masonic reader, much has been omitted which it was at first intended to include. It must not, therefore, be imagined that any comprehensive collection is now published or that all has been said that can be said on the subject; although the present book may weary some who are indifferent to what Masonic principles really are, it must yet only be received as a mere fraction of the vast mass of evidence which can be given in support of the contentions advanced.

The book has been written for Freemasons only, and will not be fully intelligible to the non-Mason, no attempt whatever has been made to render it so.

H. J. WHYMPER, P. Dep. Dis. G.M. Punjab.

———

NOTE BY THE EDITOR.—It is but fair to Bro. Whymper to state that, owing to his return to India, he was compelled to place his MS. in a very incomplete and inchoate condition in my hands, to prepare for the press. That the book has consequently suffered in some respects can scarcely be open to doubt, for it is manifestly impossible for one man to do perfect justice to another's argument unless in complete accord with him. While, however, agreeing with Bro. Whymper generally in his premises, I am not altogether at one with him in his deductions, or in the remedies he proposes: but I have conscientiously tried to carry out his design, so that whatever shortcomings may be found to exist, arise from no lack of diligence on my part, still less from any want of sympathy; neither in fairness should they be accounted the fault of the author. Had Bro. Whymper been able to supervise the completion of the edifice he began, the book would undoubtedly have been stronger in argument and fuller in proof.

CHAPTER I.

INTRODUCTORY.

IN the year 1878 Colonel J. J. Boswell raised a question in the *Masonic Record* (India) as to under what authority the Koran was used in Freemasons' Lodges working under the English Constitution, or under the United Grand Lodge of England.

The question created some stir in Indian Masonic circles, and shortly afterwards the Master of a Freemasons' Lodge in the Punjab addressed the following letter to the Grand Secretary of that District:—

Dear Sir and Wor. Bro.,

Allow me to invite your attention to a correspondence which very lately appeared in a Masonic Journal (the *Record of Western India*) regarding the alleged practice in some Lodges of obligating persons on other than the Sacred Scriptures of the Christian Dispensation.

From the correspondence you may observe that opinion on the subject is divided: one brother who signs himself "P.M. 1215" alleging that the practice is in accordance with the spirit of Masonic law, whilst another brother, a "W.M." on the contrary, considers that it is in direct violation of Masonic law: in letter, in spirit, and the practice of antiquity.

As it has hitherto been the practice in *Lodge Ravee*, 1215, E.C., to obligate Muhammadan and Hindu candidates respectively on the "Koran" and "Shastrs," and Christians on the "Bible," I beg to refer the question, and should feel greatly obliged if you would kindly obtain the opinion of the R. Wor. the District Grand Master, whether, or not, in this respect the conduct of *Lodge Ravee* is consistent with Masonic principles and Masonic law.

In inviting your attention to the subject, I would respectfully mention that in my opinion the meaning of the words, "Volume of the Sacred Law," is not confined to the Sacred Law of the Christian Dispensation; but have a bearing fuller and deeper: a meaning as broad as Masonry itself.

As Masonry is *universal*, and combines persons of every clime and

creed, the "Volume of the Sacred Law" should be adapted to the different nations, and be the law held sacred by them, subject to the ancient landmarks of the Order: a belief in the G.A.O.T.U.—otherwise the binding influence of the oath would appear to be *nil.*

I beg the favour of an early reply, as at our next meeting, on the 21st current, it is intended to raise a Muhammadan brother to the H. and S. deg. of M.M., and it is very desirable that the obligation be administered in proper order, on the volume sanctioned by Masonic law. I may add, that in the 1st and 2nd degrees, this Muhammadan brother was obligated on the Koran: the Sacred Scriptures of the Christian Dispensation lying open the whole time on the pedestal.

I am, Dear Sir and Wor. Brother,

Yours very fraternally,

J. J. DAVIES,

Wor. Master 1215 (E.C.).

The following was the reply of the District Grand Secretary:—

To the Wor. Master Lodge Ravee, 1215, Lahore.

Lahore, 9th October, 1878.

Dear Sir and Wor. Bro.,

I beg to acknowledge the receipt of your letter dated 7th instant, requesting a ruling from the R.W. District Grand Master on the following points:—

1st. Whether it is correct for a Wor. Master to obligate a Muhammadan candidate on the Christian Bible, or on the "Volume of the Sacred Law" as accepted by him, viz., the Koran.

2nd. In the case of a Hindu or other Theist, what should be considered the Sacred Law in their respective cases.

Your queries have been duly laid before the R.W. District Grand Master, and I am directed to reply as follows:—

(1.) Masonry being universal, men of every creed are eligible for membership, so long as they accept the Fatherhood of God and the Brotherhood of man.

(2.) As all candidates for Masonry are obligated, to render that engagement a solemn and binding one, the candidate should be obligated on the "Volume of the Sacred Law" which he accepts as such in the case of a Muhammadan gentleman, the Koran, in the case of a Hindu the Shastrs, a Parsee the Zoroastrian code; in other words, it is the duty of a Wor. Master to ascertain before obligating the candidate, which Revelation from God to Man he accepts as that most binding upon his conscience, and the obligation should be given accordingly.

In the case of lodges working under the English Constitution, and of which Europeans are members, the English Bible must remain open, and be used in the Lodge; the other books being used for the obligation of the candidates only.

To summarise the matter :—In the case of your Lodge, a Muhammadan gentleman being a candidate, your procedure should be as follows—

The English Bible will remain open, being removed for convenience sake to the Eastern part of the Lodge; the Koran will then be placed on the Altar and the candidate obligated, after which it will be removed and the Bible replaced.

As however the matter is of great importance, a reference on the subject will be made to England. Pending a reply the above must be accepted as the law on the subject.

With kind greetings,

I am, Wor. Sir and Brother,

Yours fraternally,

GEORGE DAVIES,
District Grand Secretary.

And the following was the opinion of the Grand Secretary at headquarters in London (the late Bro. John Hervey)—

Freemasons' Hall, London, W.C.,
20th December, 1878.

MY DEAR SIR AND R.W. BROTHER,

I am in receipt of your favour of the 9th October, with copies of correspondence with the Wor. Master of the *Lodge Ravee,* No. 1215, on the subject of obligating candidates not professing the Christian faith, and beg to say that I fully coincide in your answers, which I do not think could have been better expressed.

Yours fraternally,

JOHN HERVEY,
Grand Secretary.

To Major M. Ramsay, *District Grand Master Punjab.*

Soon after the date of Col. Boswell's letter, the following article, from the pen of Bro. William James Hughan, appeared in the pages of a well-known Masonic journal.* It was entitled—

" THE KORAN AND FREEMASONRY.

" A matter of considerable importance to the Fraternity in India has been raised by Bro. J. J. Boswell,

---

* " The Masonic Record," vol. xv., page 249.

W.M. 1279. His question, 'What authority is there for a copy of the Koran being admitted to the Lodge?' should be answered at once, and authoritatively, as we cannot expect Freemasonry to be accepted as universal, and unsectarian if only the Bible is admissible on neophytes taking the usual obligation. In India particularly we must either be prepared to permit of candidates for our mysteries being received and obligated according to their religious and conscientious opinions and scruples, or make the Craft Sectarian and exclusive, which at present it is not, *though once it was entirely Christian.* Now, however, it is for all free men of mature age, sound judgment and strict morals, on an approved ballot, without respect to their colour, country, or creed. Should a candidate be a 'Friend' (or 'Quaker'), his affirmation would be accepted in lieu of the ordinary O. B., and I have had the pleasure of seeing members of the Society of Friends initiated in this way. A member of the 'Hebrew faith' would of course be obligated on the 'Old Testament,' and in the form prescribed by their rules, and certainly the followers of Mahomet who desire to become 'members of the Mystic Tie' would be received by being obligated on their sacred book, the 'Koran.'

"I have never been present at the initiation of a Mahommedan, but many brethren have, and those interested in the subject will find an illustrious example described in the *Freemasons' Quarterly Review* for A.D. 1836 (p. 192). The ambassador from the King of Oude to England was initiated a member of the 'Lodge of Friendship,' No. 6, London, on Thursday, 14th April, A.D. 1836. He could not speak English, and so Brother and Professor Meeya Ibraham (a Persian) was sent for, by command of H.R.H. the Duke of Sussex, M.W.G.M., to act as interpreter, and the Grand Master sent on a valuable copy of the Koran to be used on the occasion; another member had also provided one in case of need,

both being written on vellum, the former being of course preferred. The candidate eventually placed his hand on the M.S., bent his head, and respectfully saluted it with his lips. The W.M. at the time was a clergyman. In the first of the 'Old Charges' which preface the Book of Constitutions of the Grand Lodge of England, we are told that 'Let a man's religion or mode of worship be what it may, he is not excluded from the Order, provided he believe in the Glorious Architect of heaven and earth, and practise the sacred duties of morality,' but unless candidates are permitted to be accepted as members according as their religious faiths dictate or require, it would be absurd to claim that our beloved Society rests on an unsectarian basis."

Here the matter dropped. From 1878 until now the opinion or ruling of the District Grand Master of the Punjab has been acted upon in Punjab lodges, and has caused the author very serious thought. From Lodges the custom created has spread to Chapters, we find that lately in the Royal Arch degree other volumes than the Bible have been used to obligate candidates on. In other parts of India, in the Lodges working under the Scottish Constitution, official bearers of the Koran— the Zendavesta, and of other books esteemed as sacred in various religions, have been appointed. In some Lodges now, several of such sacred volumes are exposed at one and the same time, all being considered to be Masonically of equal importance.

Although Scottish Masonry in India has this recognition of the Zendavesta, the Koran, the Shasters by appointing bearers of these volumes, it should be noted the Grand Lodge of Scotland has no corresponding appointments. It appears somewhat curious that where a Grand Lodge has no office for any but a Christian minister, in its Provincial government it provides for several religions being represented. At one time we imagined these appointments had been unofficially made,

but we recently had, on a voyage, the opportunity of questioning Brother Sir Henry Morland, Past Grand Master of all Scottish Masonry in India, on this subject. He informed us that he was certain the offices we allude to had been sanctioned by the Grand Lodge of Scotland, although at the time he was necessarily not in a position to prove this.*

As an almost consequent result, the Bible is losing, if it has not already lost, that place in the Masonic esteem of many Freemasons which it should hold. Brethren joining Punjab and other up country Lodges in India working under the English Constitution, very largely bring with them the views and opinions they have heard in the Bombay Presidency and in other parts of India, and it is certain that there are now many Brethren who do not esteem the Bible to be the Great Light of English Masonry. By their conduct they deny its fitness to govern their faith and they replace it mentally with some other volume which they esteem sacred. They argue that this is not in conflict with Masonic teaching and Masonic universality, and they will not admit inconsistency even in upholding the Koran or any other book esteemed sacred as the guide of their life in an English Royal Arch Chapter!

A sequel to this is that we find English Masons inclined to retire from the institution, believing it to be degenerating into a medley of absurdity, and others, to justify the present condition of affairs, declaring

---

* NOTE BY THE EDITOR.—The following copy of a letter addressed to me by the Grand Secretary of Scotland will place the matter beyond doubt :—

"Freemasons' Hall, Edinburgh, Dec. 21, 1887.

"My dear Sir and Brother,—The statement to which you refer is correct. I cannot say when the arrangement was originally authorized, but the by-laws of the District Grand Lodge of India, in which the duties of Bible Bearer, Zend Avesta Bearer, and Koran Bearer are given were sanctioned and confirmed by Grand Committee in August, 1885, as per Certificate of Grand Secretary of date. With Christmas greetings, I am, ever faithfully,

D. MURRAY LYON, G. Sec.

that which is now alluded to, Masonic. A confusion of ideas apparently enables some to think any anomalous ignoring of, or mixing of, religion in Freemasonry is part of the system.* We find others again who are content to let matters be, either from indifference, or, from absolutely not knowing what the principles of English Freemasonry are. Others yet again hold the views which will be put forward in the succeeding chapters of this book regarding this most lamentable commencement of the abandonment of principle.

These divergent opinions have not as yet caused open dissension, but, notwithstanding the barrier which exists to the discussion of religious subjects within a Lodge, it is not improbable that the further progress of what has commenced will eventually occasion very serious discord.

It is the object of this work to try to place the subject of the religious tendencies and the religion of Freemasonry in such a light that harmony may prevail. It will be necessary to untangle several of the twisted knots which have been tied by Brethren, doubtless whilst acting with the best intentions. It will be necessary to point out forcibly how Masonic tenets have

---

* It is regrettable to find Bro. Mackenzie supports those who would sever the connection between religion and Freemasonry. In his Cyclopædia he writes under the heading of "Light"—"A very great deal of obscure nonsense has been written on this subject. The light of the Freemason is moral, and not incumbered by the trammels of any particular faith. Craft Masonry brings him to the knowledge of himself, and allowing him as a Master Mason to weigh the comparative safety of goodness and common sense against that of moral and mental obliquity, leaves him free to pursue either course. This has been the endeavour of moralists in all ages, and in the Masonic Fraternity the attempt to enforce the maxim has been on the grandest scale. *Hence it is that religion forms no part of the scheme of Masonry.*"

Bro. Mackenzie is very severe, we have no desire to attack him, but it must be remembered he it is who thus attacks Christian Freemasons, his Cyclopædia contains so many other mistakes of fact that it is hoped too much importance will not be attached to the above quotation. As a specimen of NONSENSE the Indian Freemason should read Bro. Mackenzie's article on "India" where he states a Grand Lodge of Hindustan was formed in 1875!

been departed from, and how, from a mistaken notion of the universality of Freemasonry, landmarks have been uprooted and inconsistent anomalies introduced.

The rectification of mistakes committed must at all times tend to strengthen the institution and to render it a more consistent agency for the moral and religious welfare of mankind.

The advance of religious thought, and the release of the mind from the shackles of superstition and bigotry in its search after truth, which has so character-ised the current century, and the contemporary advance of the Masonic Order, do but prove that ours is a progressive institution, and that the highest forms of morality lead to the most intellectually advanced forms of religion. A curious instance of this can be found by any Mason, if he will read Dr. Reville's Hibbert Lecture. The Masonic reader will almost insensibly imagine that he is perusing an advanced Masonic work.

It is possible that some may think the idea of a close connection between Freemasonry and Christianity is a modern one. Such is very far from being the case, and as regards English Freemasonry we personally incline to the belief that it should be included among the published landmarks. A very remarkable book was published exactly 113 years ago by William Hutchinson, entitled " The Spirit of Masonry." It was issued with the recommendation and sanction of the then Grand Master of English Freemasonry, of the Deputy Grand Master, and both the Senior and Junior Grand Wardens. Its authority could therefore hardly be more complete. In this book there is a final chapter or lecture, entitled a " Corollary," from which are culled the following extracts :—

" Our antiquity is in our principles, maxims, language, learning, and religion :—these we derive from Eden, from the Patriarchs, and from the Sages of the East; all which are made perfect under the Christian dispensation. The light and doctrines which we possess, are derived from the beginning of time . . . . ; but our modes

and manners are deduced from the different eras of Paradise, the building of the Temple at Jerusalem, and the Christian revelation."*

"I have explained to you . . . . that the first entry of a Mason represents the first worship of a true God."†

"The BOOK OF TRUE KNOWLEDGE is in the Lodge."‡

"In this assembly of Christians it is in no wise requisite to attempt an argument on the necessity which there was upon earth for a Mediator and Saviour for man . . . . "§

"Then it was that the Divinity . . . . sent us a Preceptor and Mediator, who should teach us the doctrine of regeneration, and raise us from the sepulchre of sin, ... He made the sacrifice of expiation, and becoming the first-fruits of them that slept, manifested to mankind the resurrection of the body and the life everlasting. In the MASTER'S ORDER the whole doctrine is symbolised, and the Christian conduct is by types presented to us."||

"It doth not now seem material to us what our originals and predecessors were, if we occupy ourselves in the true SPIRIT OF MASONRY; . . . . if we are true servants to our King . . . . Christians in profession and in practice."¶

Neither is the contention that Freemasonry has progressed with time, and altered or advanced its position with regard to what have been by various ages esteemed Masonic landmarks in any way surprising. It is an acknowledged fact that "many erroneous deductions"** have been drawn from the written law. If *that* has been so misinterpreted, it cannot be difficult to appreciate the liability of the *un*-written law to similar change. The understanding or interpretation of freedom of belief would mean very different things in the same age in different minds. But how much more would the idea of freedom of belief, or the conception of the highest beliefs, change as the minds of men expand with knowledge. That which now appears mere superstitious bigotry was once esteemed what would now be termed advanced thought. When we remember that it is one of the first claims of Masonry that it is progressive, we cannot wonder to find that it now discountenances what it once sanctioned, any more than to find that its members receive the ideas and discoveries of modern science.

---

* p. 227.　† p. 228.　‡ p. 230.　§ p. 232.　|| p. 232.　¶ p. 233.

** Paton's "Jurisprudence."

It is not only in recent times that changes and innovations have occurred, for in the charter granted by
Masons to William St. Clair, of Roslin, about A.D. 1600,
it is stated that "manyfald corruptiones and jmperfec-
tiones" had been "genderit" from the want of "ane
patrone ptectour and oversear."*

We have it on record that at the commencement of
the 18th Century the landmarks were few and isolated,
that no great attention was paid to that "harmony of
parts which is so essential to the character of a scientific
institution." That there were no lectures even late on
in the 17th Century is known. Change, innovation,
and alteration was thus an easy matter, and the opinion
that "instead of a revival, a discontinuance of Ancient
Freemasonry" took place after 1717, becomes possibly
correct from these circumstances alone.†

Thus change, even in modern times, cannot always
surprise us, neither should we in every case deprecate
it. There are, however, some changes which we believe
can only be injurious to the Institution. The constant
contention of this work will be found to be that the
original spirit, which animated Freemasonry in the
earliest times of which we have record, is in danger of
entirely disappearing owing to innovators, who stop at
nothing when advancing their universal theories. This
is strongly evidenced in modern works, which we unhesitatingly assert mislead as to the purpose of Freemasonry.
Even in the Preface of such a book as Mackenzie's
"Royal Masonic Cyclopædia"—a book inscribed to the
late John Hervey (Grand Secretary)—we find this
passage regarding Freemasonry, "But, above all
things, let it be clearly seen as a purely social institution, *having no political or religious* tendency at all,
tending to make men friendly upon vastly different
grounds than those of agrarian and political rights."

---

* Lyon's "History of Freemasonry," p. 58.
† "Origin of the Royal Arch."

Whilst putting forward this view the same Preface quotes Hutchinson, a writer who persistently upheld the religious character of the Institution; inconsistency could hardly go further. We have no concern with politics, but we strenuously maintain that to assert that Freemasonry has no religious basis is to teach the rankest heresy.*

There can be no agreement between a brother who maintains that Freemasonry has no religious tendency, and one who holds our views. To our shame, we have for so long allowed these heretical views to remain uncontradicted, that many modern Masons will doubtless even at first believe, the heresy is on our side when we claim that our Order is as nothing if its religious tendency be ignored. We can have no concern, neither can we at all sympathise with a brother who can read or repeat our ritual and yet attach no religious meaning to it. We maintain that the upholders of the belief that no connection exists between Freemasonry and religion, depend entirely on their own individual assertions, all the weight of evidence being on our side.

Remembering a saying of Emerson's that most people can only recognise a principle when its light falls upon a fact, we propose to rely where possible on illustration, by quotation, from what are admittedly genuine Masonic teachings, in the Constitutions which have at one time or another been in force, in the Charges, in the symbols used and in the opinions of Masonic writers. We will give as little space as possible to our own opinions, except in the language of others, and where it is necessary for us to speak in our own words we will only express views which can be proved to be in harmony with those of others.

Dr. Oliver, one of the most eminent Freemasons of

---

* Under "Order" in "Kenning's Cyclopædia," Woodford says— ' Dr. Johnson defines an Order to be a society of dignified persons distinguished by marks of honour; *a religious fraternity!* With both these meanings Freemasonry agrees."

his day, says, in his "Discrepancies of Freemasonry," that the system "undoubtedly contains anomalies, difficulties, and inaccuracies which appear to be insurmountable; and some of the discrepancies have been repeated and dilated on with such pertinacity for a series of years, that great multitudes of the Fraternity believe them to be indubitable facts, and are ready to gird up their loins in their defence whenever they find a brother bold enough to question their integrity. Some of these antiquated senilities are absurd, and others are not only antagonistic to the truth, but absolutely irreconcilable with it."* Again, a little later on, he says: "We are continually hearing complaints of anomalies which no one endeavours to reconcile or explain, under the impression that they are absolutely inexplicable."† And, continuing the subject, he asks: "Shall we rectify or retain them? The old laws of Masonry are averse to any change. Alter not the ancient landmarks. This decisive sentence has been pronounced *ex cathedra* by our Grand Lodge on every revision of the Constitutions."‡ He concludes his remarks by frankly admitting "that many difficulties are opposed to the satisfactory arrangement of the various matters at issue in this important inquiry. But," says he, "I am decidedly of opinion that if a committee were appointed by the Grand Lodge, including delegates invited to act upon it from the sister Grand Lodges of Scotland and Ireland, with ample powers to inquire into all the anachronisms and discrepancies of Freemasonry, and report upon them *seriatim*, much benefit would ensue from their deliberations."§

These remarks we believe are peculiarly applicable to the existing state of affairs in India. At a discussion supposed to take place after dinner at the hospitable table of Dr. Oliver, when the wine and dessert were

---

* p. 9.   † p. 11.   ‡ p. 14.   § p. 23.

being discussed, that defender of Masonic faith says* : " It is true that, as a Society, we adopt the creed of no particular Church, although during the last century the Book of Common Prayer formed an indispensable appendage to the furniture of our Lodges ; yet no one who is acquainted with our forms and disquisitions can doubt our attachment to the great leading principles of Christianity. If, as a body, we professed a predilection for the creeds or tenets of the Greek or Latin Church, or the Churches of England or Geneva, or any particular class of dissenters from them all, we might, by a trifling stretch of credulity, be pronounced *sectarian*. Although even in this case the term would be misapplied, for the Church of Christ, being represented in different countries by different establishments suited to the genius and disposition of the people, can no more affect the universality of Christianity than the unity of our noble Order can be effected or neutralised by the number of independent Grand Lodges that are distributed throughout the world. Freemasonry, however, professes an adherence to the Church of the first-born, or the universal Christians, whose names are written in heaven as denizens of a better country."

At another of these pleasant (and perhaps not altogether imaginary) gatherings, Bro. P. W. Gilkes comes to the front, and makes these undoubtedly sensible remarks.† " It is clear to me," says he, " that the real principles of genuine Masonry must be sought for at the time of the revival in 1717. The amplifications which our Lectures have undergone since that period include many innovations which are alien to primitive Masonry, because they have swallowed up and destroyed some of our most ancient landmarks. Even the old Gothic Charges have not escaped, but at the union in 1813 sustained several verbal alterations which

---

* In his " Discrepancies of Freemasonry," p. 214-5.
† *Ibid*, p. 275.

C

have materially changed their character. The oldest
Constitutions we are acquainted with, which were
directed to be read to every candidate at his initiation,
announce that, at a certain period in the annals of
Masonry, '*God's Messiah, the Great Architect of the
Christian Church came into the world.*' Again, in the
same book it is recorded, that, '*the foot-stone of the new
temple was levelled just forty-six years before the first
passover of Christ's personal ministry.*' Again, '*At this
time there was a general peace all over the world, and so
continued for twelve years together, which was a very
proper prelude for ushering in His coming, who was the
Prince of Peace; for at this period, Jesus Christ,
Emmanuel, the Great Architect of the Christian Church,
was born at Bethlehem in Judea.*' Once more, '*The Lord
Jesus Christ was crucified under Tiberius, without the
walls of Jerusalem, by Pontius Pilate, the Roman Governor
of Judea, and rose again the third day, for the justifica-
tion of all those that believe in Him. Tiberius afterwards
banished Pilate for his injustice to Christ.*'" The
question being raised where these important passages
might be found, the answer was prompt: " In the 'Freemason's Pocket Companion (first) published in the year
1736, with new editions in 1754, 1764, and 1771."*

It is quite certain that the Christian Chaplains of
our Lodges, the Christian Archbishops and Bishops, and
the many other eminent divines we have had as enthusiastic brethren and warm supporters of Masonry, would
not have always pointed to the principles of the Institution as being in perfect harmony with Christianity, if it
were formerly what it is now represented to be. The
late Rev. Dr. Oliver, as already shown and as will
again hereafter appear, argued over a period of half-

---

* The quotations are taken from the edition of 1764, pp. 54, 56
and 57; they are not found in earlier editions. Bro. Oliver's enumera-
tion of the various editions is also incorrect. They are 1735, 1736-8,
1754, 1759, 1764 and 1771.

a-century that English Freemasonry was a Christian institution, but his views are not generally acceptable, and will be quoted but seldom in this work. If, indeed, it can be shown that English Freemasonry was once distinctly Christian, one of two alternatives must be adopted. Either it can only have become non-Christian by a general violation of principle, or it is in reality still Christian and certain members are contravening its tenets. It is for us to consider in the first instance, are there any grounds afforded us for believing it Christian in origin and in principle, in the published records of the Craft? We will quote from certain lectures and prayers, which have been repeatedly published over a series of years, and see whether these are reconcileable with any but a Christian universality. We will next deal with the Ritual and the most remarkable of all Masonic legends, and enquire whether it is in any way rationally connectable with any other than a Christian interpretation of the aim of Freemasonry? We will, with the Ritual, consider the discovery in the Royal Arch Degree, to which the three previous degrees are but stepping stones. As we go through the foregoing programme we will give the opinions of well-informed Masons, and finally emphasize those opinions by quoting many others in general support of orthodox Freemasonry. We will conclude by attempting to show wherein mistakes have been made, and how, in our opinion, they possibly may be avoided in the future.

If, in the opinion of the non-Christian "universalist," we have failed in our endeavours we shall certainly hear of our failure, and, as this can only be shown by a vindication of the, we believe, utterly untenable " universal" hypothesis, the universalist will have to thank us for the challenge thrown down, the modern universal theory having never yet been supported by anything except assertion oft repeated.

c 2

CHAPTER II.

THE OLD AND NEW CONSTITUTIONS.

BY "Old Constitutions" we understand those ancient records of Operative Freemasonry which are thus described by Bro. Gould*—"The Old Charges, or Manuscript Constitutions, are known by a variety of names, *e.g.*, the Masonic Constitutions, the Constitutions of the Craft, the History of Freemasonry, the Legend of the Guild, &c., &c. Ordinarily they are in roll or scroll form, and consist of three parts—firstly, the Introductory Prayer, Declaration, or Invocation; secondly, the History of the Order, or the Legend of the Guild, which, beginning before the Flood, alludes to Euclid, Solomon (many other biblical characters), and Charles Martel, and generally ends with King Athelstane, or about 926; and thirdly, the peculiar statutes and duties, the regulations and observances which the Craft in general—or Masons in particular—are bound carefully to uphold and inviolably to maintain."

Of these ancient records some 50 or more are known, and date from 1390 (*circa*) to the nineteenth century. From them we learn the tenets and doctrine of our Fraternity before the era of Grand Lodges in 1717.

By "New Constitutions" we understand the various issues of the Book of Constitutions published by the Grand Lodge of 1717 at various dates, commencing 1723; or by its rival Grand Lodge of 1751 in London; or by other and sister Grand Lodges which have since arisen in different parts.

---

* Transactions of the Lodge Quatuor Coronati, vol. i., p. 69.

In this and the following chapter we propose to examine the evidence of these Constitutions and deduce therefrom—firstly, that Ancient Freemasonry was distinctly and undeniably Christian up to 1717 ; secondly, that at the formation of the Grand Lodge of 1717, there was no solution of continuity, no break in spirit or form intended, no deliberate rejection of the Christian dogma underlying the teaching of the Craft; that only one passage somewhat darkly expressed may, by wrenching it from its context, be perhaps held to imply a rejection of Christian doctrine; that in 1738 the Christian belief was emphasized by a remarkable alteration of this very passage; and that in 1756 although the earlier form of this passage was finally re-instated, an aggressive rival body of Freemasons adhered to the version of 1738, as did also the Craft in Ireland ; and thirdly, that although there are not wanting signs that, in order to conciliate and admit men of various creeds, owing to the spread of Grand Lodge Freemasonry, the distinctly Christian injunctions contained in the Charges of the Book of Constitutions were toned down, yet the Craft was so permeated with Christianity that this fundamental principle continued to be incorporated in these very same Constitutions, notably in the Historical Introductions, which only ceased to be issued after the Union of the rival Grand Lodges in 1813. And in a few concluding words we shall show that many foreign Grand Lodges still adhere firmly to the Christian interpretation of Masonry ; whilst in the course of our research it will become apparent that no resolution was ever actually taken, even in England, to avowedly break with the Christianity of Ancient Freemasonry, although by degrees the idea has been disseminated that the Craft is not specifically Christian. But no systematic effort having been made to de-Christianise the Craft, it can and will be proved to be Christian in its teachings and references to this very day.

In quoting from Masonic records we incur the danger of objections being raised to some of our extracts, as coming from rather doubtful sources of authority. We must admit this objection, whilst yet we give the quotation. If we do not quote from the earliest records we run the risk of a sneer being passed on our pusillanimity in not going back to them. That we have every right to quote from sources which are often referred to on very trivial matters can hardly be disputed. The reader can reject, on the ground of want of authority, whatsoever he pleases, and yet we venture to state there will remain sufficient to convince any unprejudiced person that we have a strong case.

The objection we allude to may be applied to our very first extracts, which are from what claims to be one of the earliest Masonic Constitutions.

When the Masonic world was agitated early in the last century by the formation of a Grand Lodge in London in 1717, and the subsequent decision of one of its Grand Masters to collect and publish the genuine Ancient Charges of Freemasonry, which had not then been printed, a volume appeared in 1722 with the following title, "The Old Constitutions belonging to the Ancient and Honourable Society of Free and Accepted Masons. (Taken from a Manuscript wrote above Five Hundred Years since)."

Only one copy of this work is known to exist. It was reprinted in 1871 by Richard Spencer with other Constitutions, which were edited by the Rev. J. E. Cox, and are now known as "the Cox Reprints." The history of the original is given as follows by Mr. Spencer :—"It came into my possession about a quarter of a century ago, bound up at the end of the scarce 1723 edition of the Constitutions, and from that time I have been searching for another unsuccessfully."

Bro. W. J. Hughan states, in his "Origin of the English Rite of Freemasonry," this book "was offered

for sale with others in July, 1875, when a number of the volumes in Bro. Spencer's library were sold ; was purchased for the late Bro. R. F. Bower, of Keokuk, Iowa, for £8 10s. (original cost sixpence), and is now one of the gems of the Library of the Grand Lodge of Iowa." Bro. Hughan adds it is really mainly a reproduction of the Harleian MS. No. 1942. Whatever may be the truth regarding the five hundred year old MS. there is no doubt about the existence of the book, which is the earliest known printed work devoted exclusively to Freemasonry.* From it we make the following extracts—after a Preface, which is clearly of the date of the publication of the book, the history of Free Masons is given, it commences—" The Almighty Father of Heaven, with the Wisdom of the Glorious Son, thro' the Goodness of the Holy Ghost, Three Persons in one Godhead, be with our Beginning, and give us his Grace so to govern our Lives, that we may come to his Bliss, that never shall have end. Amen."

The so-called history is then proceeded with and we are brought down to "the Reign of King *Athelston,* which some write *Adleston,*" he is said to have given Masons certain Charges. The History concludes " From that time unto this Day *Masonry* hath been much respected and preserved, and divers new Articles have been added to the said Charge, by good Advice and Consent of the Masters and Fellows." The Charge follows and runs—" I,—I am to admonish you to honour God in his holy Church ; that you use no Heresy, Schism, and Error in your Understandings, or discredit Men's Teachings." The entire Charge consists of twenty-six clauses, the twentieth is curious, being " You shall not (except in *Christmas* time) use any lawless Games, as Dice, Cards, or such like."

The second part of the book gives the Apprentice

---

* Hughan's " Old Charges," p. 18.

charge, commencing — "*Imprimis.* You shall truly honour God, and his holy Church, the King, your Master, and Dame," &c.

The whole concludes with a solemn oath, or, as we should now term it, an obligation, the final words of which are "So help me God, and the true and holy Contents of this Book."

We carefully refrain from expressing any opinion on the amount of value which should be attached to the foregoing, as we also do from claiming that the Operative Freemasonry to which it related had any close connection with the present Institution. The extracts are only given, as these so-called 1722 Constitutions describe their origin as in or before 1222. It is perfectly evident, however, that nothing at all approaching this high antiquity can be substantiated for the text of the document. We have placed it first because it *claims* to be the oldest yet discovered, a position which rightfully belongs to the record with which we shall next deal.

This is known in Masonic literature as the Halliwell MS., from Mr. J. O. Halliwell (now Mr. Halliwell-Phillips) having first drawn attention to it. Small editions of a transcript of this MS. were published in 1840 and in 1844. The manuscript is undoubtedly genuine and was written in the fourteenth century. Some place it as belonging to the early part of the fifteenth, but the majority favour its being of the late fourteenth ; Hughan dates it 1390. It is a poem written apparently for the more easy remembrance of Masonic teaching and laws. The extracts which here follow bear on the subject of our argument.

Plures Constituciones.

At thys semblé were poyntes y-ordeynt mo,
Of grete lordys and mastrys also,
Th^t whose wol conne thys craft and com to astate,
He most love wel God, and holy churche algate.

Ars quatuor coronatorum.

Pray we now to God almyght,
And to hys swete mod' Mary bryght,
That we nowe kepe these artyculus here.

* * * * * *

The emp'o' hade to hem gret luste ;
He wylned of hem a ymage to make,
Th' mowgh be worscheped for hys sake ;
Suche mawmetys he hade yn hys dawe,
To turne the pepul from Cryst's [Christ's] lawe.
But they were stedefast yn C'stes [Christ's] lay.

* * * * * *

The emp'o' let take hem sone anonn,
And putte hem ynto a dep presonn ;
The sarre he penest hem yn th' plase,
The more yoye wes to hem of C'st's [Christ's] grace.

* * * * * *

Later on these Constitutions state that Euclid—

Throgh hye grace of Crist yn heven,
He commensed yn the syens seven.

Still further on we read—

For Crist hymself, he techet ous
Th' holy churche ys Goddes hous.

It is also shown in quaint language that every drop of holy water used at the church door quenches a venial sin ; that Christ should be supplicated so that the laws of holy Church may be kept, and so on. " Jhesu Lord " is twice mentioned, and the poem concludes with these words—

Cryst then of hys hye grace,
Geve yow bothe wytte and space,
Wel thys boke to conne and rede,
Heven to have for yowre mede.
Amen ! amen ! so mot hyt be !
Say we so alle p' charyté.

The Harleian MS., in the British Museum, No. 1942, *circa* 1670, professes to explain the ancient history and principles of Freemasonry. It commences as follows— " The Almighty Father of Heaven, with the Wisdome of the glorious Sonne, through the goodnes of the Holy

Ghost, three persons in one Godhead, bee with our beginning, and give us grace soe to governe our lives that we may come to his blisse that never shall have end. Amen. Good Brethren and Fellows, our purpose is to toll you how and in what manner this Craft of Masonry was first began," &c.

Another genuine record of ancient Freemasonry is the Manuscript No. 23,198 in the additional manuscripts at the British Museum. This is attributed to the latter part of the fifteenth century. It was copied and published by Matthew Cooke in 1861. Hughan dates it 1490.* We extract the following from the reading given by Cooke—lines 831 to 838—" Who that coveteth for to come to the state of the foresaid art it behoveth them first, principally to God and Holy Church, and all-halows." Lines 602 to 609, and 359 to 364 will be found of some import, frequent references are made to the Bible, which, it is stated, supports Masonic history.

The manuscript,† known as the Wilson MS. (on vellum), 1650, *circa*, is apparently copied from a very much older one. It is in the possession of the Rev. J. E. A. Fenwick, Cheltenham. It commences with these words—" THE might of the ffather of heaven, and the wisdome of the glorious sone, through the grace and goodnes of the holy ghost, that beene three psons and one God, bee wᵗʰ us at our begininge, & geve us grace soe to govern us heerein our livinge that wee may come to his blisse that never shall have endinge. AMEN."‡

" THE first charge is this : that yee shall bee true men to god and holy church."

---

* Mr. E. A. Bond is of opinion that both the Halliwell Poem and the Cooke MS. are of approximately the same date, the first half of the fifteenth century. (Mas. Mag. II., pp. 77-78.)

† Printed in " Kenning's Masonic Archæological Library," vol. i., 1878.

‡ This prayer, modernised, is found in many Masonic records, Ahiman Rezons &c.

It concludes—"THEIS CHARGES THAT WEE have now rehearsed unto you and all other that belonge to masons yee shall keepe. Soe helpe you god and your Hallidome."

Let us leave this record and take up the Sloane MS., No. 3323, Brit. Museum, of 1659. This commences—"The might of the father of Heaven wth ye wisdom of the glorious son through the goodness of the Holy Ghost y^t be three in one God, &c. Be with us att our beginning and give us grace so to govern us in our living y^t we may come to his bliss that neer shall have ending."

Further on we have what is termed in the MS. "The worthy oath of Masonry." It begins—"The charge is you shall be a true man to God and the holy Church and that you use no heresie by your understanding or by teaching discreet men."

The Edinburgh-Kilwinning MS.,* ascribed to 1670, commences with a similar reference to the Christian Trinity, and it terminates thus—"These Charges that wee have now rehearsed unto yow, and all others that belongeth to Massons, yow shall keep; so help you GOD and your Halydoome."

The next Constitutions we shall quote from are those printed from a copperplate in 1729 and 1731 by Benjamin Cole, and dedicated to the Grand Master of the day, to his Deputy, Wardens, and the Masters and Wardens of all regular lodges. It is therefore to be presumed that they were consistent with the authorised teaching of that period. The extracts speak for themselves—

"**The** Beginning and first Foundation of the most worthy Craft of **Masonry**, with the Charges thereunto belonging.

"**The** might of the Father of Heaven, and the

---

* D. Murray Lyon's "History of the Lodge of Edinburgh," p. 108.

wisdom of the Glorious Son, through the Grace and goodness of the Holy Ghost; they being three persons in one God, be with us at our Beginning, & give us Grace so to govern us here in our Living, that we may come to his Bliss that never shall have an end.   **Amen.**

"**Good Brethren** & Fellows; our purpose is to tell you how, and in what manner this worthy Craft of **Masonry**," etc.

There are allusions to Christ at the Building of the Temple of Jerusalem—"finished nine years before the Birth of our Saviour, Anno Mundi 3956.

"**After** the Birth of our Saviour, **Aururiagus** being King of England, **Claudius** the Emperour came over with an Army," etc.

The terms *Anno Christi* and *Anno Domini* (the contraction *Dom* being generally used) occur frequently in these Constitutions.

It concludes—"**These** Charges that we have now rehearsed unto you and all others that belong to **Masons** ye shall keep; so help you God and your Hallidon. **Amen.**" These Constitutions, although evidently modernised from an old original, were first published after the erection of the Grand Lodge of England.

It is a positive fact that every single one of the Old Constitutions contains irrefragible proof that the basis of Ancient Freemasonry was Christianity. Culling quite promiscuously here and there, we call attention to the following extracts—

" He most loue wel God and holy Churche algate, And hys mayst{r} also th{t} he is wythe."* The Apprentice " shall be true to God and the holy Church, the prince, his Mr and dame whom he shall serve."† " We do swear, so God us helpe, and holy dome, and by the contents of this book."‡ " O Lord God Father of Heaven with the wisdom of the glorious Sonn through the grace

---

* Halliwell Poem (1390) 1st article.
† York MS. No. 4 (1693).   ‡ Melrose MS. (1581 and 1674).

and goodness of the Holy Ghost three persons in one Godhead." . . . . " These Charges that you have received you shall well and truly keepe, not discloseing the secresy of our Lodge to man, woman, nor child : Sticke nor stone : thing moveable nor immoveable, soe God you helpe and his holy Doome."* It will hardly be disputed that the " Booke" so often referred to was the Bible, and not merely the Old Testament.

We fear to tire the reader, but cannot refrain from giving the conclusion of the York MS. No. 6†, A.D. 1680, it runs—" Doe all as you would be done unto, and I beseech you at every meeting and assembly you pray heartily for all Christians.—Farewell."

It is unnecessary to give more excerpts from the old Masonic Charges ; every student of Masonic literature is well aware that wherever search is made amongst the old records there is always found clear and distinct injunction to the brother to respect the Church and to accept the doctrine of the Christian Trinity.

That Freemasons formerly acted up to this teaching could be amply illustrated, and we must admit it becomes the more strange how the universal theory now current sprang into life. In 1652 the Presbytery of Kelso held that Freemasonry was known to be compatible with the principles of the Church. Beyond this we have an actual record that money was subscribed in a Scotch Lodge last century for the defence of the King and the Protestant Faith.

In using arguments to refute the notion, or idea, that there were Lodges in America in the seventeenth century, Brother Hughan wrote‡ that the evidence which had been adduced was unreliable from the circumstance that the names given of the supposed members were Jewish, and that the Craft in the seventeenth century " was Christian in character." Accepting this as a fact, as

---

* Buchanan MS. (*circa* 1680).   † Hughan's " Old Charges," p. 13.
‡ " Origin of the English Rite," p. 13.

also that it is not in the power of any one to make innovation in Masonry, how has it now become Masonic
to insist that English Freemasonry is not distinctly
Christian? When was it announced that this radical
and all important change was to be made? Who
possessed the authority to make it? For ourselves,
we unhesitatingly maintain that no change ever has
been legally made.   The assertions alone, of pretenders
ignorant of the real principles of the Order, have given
currency to what is nothing more than a chimerical
idea, that some alteration has taken place by which the
Institution may now be considered to have abandoned
its old Christian principles. They cannot deny its
original Christian character, but very sweepingly aver
that it has not been Christian since 1717. They place
great reliance on their incomprehension of the attitude
the Grand Master of English Masonry once assumed
regarding Jewish Masons in Germany — an attitude
which was, and always must be a correct one, but
which affords no support whatever for any theory that
English Freemasonry thereby abandoned its old religious belief.

If this all be as we have stated, is it idle to enquire
how Freemasonry lost its distinctive Christian character,
or how it happens that such appears to be the case?
Our contention is that it never has in reality altered,
although from an improper interpretation of the
Christian catholicity which was first inculcated, the
system certainly appears to have become one with no
religious belief at all. To nominally comply with the
universality which was taught, a backboneless Deism has
of necessity been introduced and the institution has
taken a step towards abandoning that principle which
should be the basis of the system.

The reader has a right to expect us to give reasons
in support of our belief and, as he has doubtless had
enough of the old Constitutions, we will pass on to the

more modern ones, where will be found evidence which cannot but convince the unprejudiced that there has been a change such as we have referred to.

The earliest Constitutions of Freemasonry since the formation of a Grand Lodge in 1717, are those of 1723. How they came into existence is best shown by quoting from later Constitutions, for very oddly the edition of 1723 is silent as to their origin. Not having a copy of the 1738 Constitutions to refer to, we quote from the 1756 edition. We should perhaps state that the various editions of the Constitutions prior to the Union in 1813, issued by authority of the Grand Lodge of England are dated 1723, 1738, 1756, 1767, and 1784. These, with some issues having merely a re-dated title or supplement, represent all that appeared up to 1813, so far as the Grand Lodge established in 1717 is concerned.

In the 1756 Constitutions we read that at the Assembly held on June 24th, 1718, George Payne, Esqr., being Grand Master, it was desired that the brethren should " bring to the Grand Lodge any old writings and records concerning Masons and Masonry, in order to shew the usages of antient Times : And this Year several old Copies of the Gothic Constitutions were produced and collated."

We next read that in 1720 " at some private lodges several very valuable Manuscripts (for they had nothing yet in print) concerning the Fraternity, their Lodges, Regulations, Charges, Secrets, and Usages (particularly one writ by Mr. Nicholas Stone, the Grand Warden of Inigo Jones) were too hastily burnt by some scrupulous Brothers, that those papers might not fall into strange Hands."*

At Grand Lodge on Lady Day, 1721, John Duke of Montagu being present, was saluted as Grand Master elect. On the following 29th September we read " His

---

* page 191.

Grace's Worship and the Lodge finding Fault with all the Copies of the old Gothic Constitutions order'd Brother James Anderson, A.M., to digest the same in a new and better method."*

On the 27th December, 1721, " Montagu, Grand Master, at the desire of the Lodge, appointed fourteen learned brothers to examine Brother Anderson's Manuscript of the Constitution Book, and to make report."†

On the 25th March, 1722, " The said Committee of fourteen reported that they had perused Brother Anderson's Manuscript, viz., the History, Charges, Regulations, and Master's Song, and after some amendments, had approv'd of the Same." The Book eventually appeared, and was presented to the Grand Lodge on 17th January, 1723, when it " was again approv'd."‡

Dr. Anderson's name is always associated with that of Dr. Desaguliers in connection with the 1723 Constitutions, but what the latter exactly did, beyond writing a dedication, in which he refers to Dr. Anderson as " our learned author " is not clear. It appears to us certain that either the amendments above alluded to cancelled some of Anderson's views, and that he afterwards (in 1738) tried to put himself straight, or that as the result of subsequent study, he saw cause to disagree with what had been published as from himself. We are compelled to think that the difference between the Constitutions of 1723 and those of 1738, followed up as they are by, on the one side, the reversion of the Grand Lodge Constitutions back to the 1723 position, and on the other, by the publication, by those who claimed to be *ancient* Masons, of Constitutions (called Ahiman Rezon) following on the lines of the 1738 Constitutions, was in reality at the base of the dissensions of the last century—and marks the first departure from the old Christian Masonic principles.

* page 194.　　　　　　page 194.　　　　‡ page 195.

The History of Masonry (as the opening absurdity in the Constitutions is termed) contains, in all the editions of the last century, frequent references to Christ, but it is only in the 1738 issue that we find in the actual Constitutions (or Charges) an avowal of any connection with Christianity. But this is not so with the Histories; in spite of the emasculation to which the Old Charges were subjected, the Histories remained distinctively Christian until they finally ceased to appear from 1815 onwards.

The 1723 History first admits a connection. On pages 24-25 and 29 there are statements to the effect that Roman Masonry was Christian and arose from Christianity. "ROME which thus became the CENTER of LEARNING, as well as of imperial Power, until they advanc'd to their ZENITH of Glory, under AUGUSTUS CÆSAR, (in whose Reign was born GOD's MESSIAH, the great Architect of the Church), who having laid the World quiet, by proclaiming universal peace, highly encourag'd those dexterous Artists," &c., is a case in point. In other editions this is omitted, but other equally pertinent passages can be quoted from them or their history. Christ is repeatedly referred to, and that the Universal theory had not as yet made much way is shown by extracts such as these. "A great number of Masons were continued at work for the carrying on the outbuildings all the time of our Saviour's being here on earth—" "In the 26th Year of his Empire, after the conquest of Egypt, the WORD was made FLESH, or the Lord Jesus Christ Immanuel was born, the great Architect or Grand Master of the Christian Church." (Edition of 1756.)

Further on in the same edition, writing of Tiberius, we find "Under him the Lord Jesus Christ was cruci-fied—" "and rose again the third day for the justifica-tion of all that believe in Him." These quotations will also be found in the 1767 and 1784 Constitutions, and

D

afford complete evidence that, whether the Masonic authorities of the day did, or did not, wish Freemasonry to have a continuous and close connection with religion, they never entertained the least idea of an English Freemason denying Christ. The assertion is clear and as precise as we could wish, that Christ rose for the justification of those who believed in Him. If a more distinct Masonic expression of faith is desired, if a wavering Royal Arch Mason requires some assurance as to the meaning of his Degree, what more is necessary than the plain and unmistakeable Masonic declaration that the Word was the Lord Jesus Christ? The Divine incarnation by which the Word was made Flesh is stated in our Histories, each of which was issued under authority, to have been the birth of Jesus Christ.

As Histories these compilations are admittedly worthless, and as such we do not attach one atom of weight to them, but we do attach the highest importance to them as disclosing what the Masonic religious belief of the last century was. In them we find precisely what we should have expected from the known early tendency of the system.

We have sufficiently established that prior to 1717, when the Grand Lodge was formed, the Charges positively championed the Christian faith, and directly enjoined the brethren to attend Holy Church. The collecting of ancient documents with a view to discover the old principles of the Craft is reasonable proof that there was a wish to continue them. Had no such proof existed we should still feel assured that there was never any intention of altering principles, whether civil or religious, in 1717. We know that the old Institution was supposed to be suffering from a want of organisation, and that it was proposed to restore the system by a properly constituted Corporation. The movement was not to *destroy* but to *preserve*. The most carefully conducted search will fail to establish anything save that it was

proposed, in establishing a Grand Lodge, to more effectually carry out the original intentions of that quaint symbolism which was once the special property of a society of Operative Masons, but which had attracted others than workmen to join it, as old institutions always will do. A City Company of the present day is no inappropriate illustration of our meaning.

It is now the fashion to assert that by the establishment of a Grand Lodge in 1717 some change occurred, that the old principles ceased to govern Freemasonry, and that a Deistic, as opposed to a Christian, Faith was adopted.

The claim to great age, which Masons have never been slack in advancing on behalf of our Order, can only be based on the supposition that it inherits the principles which distinguished the institution or associations with which it claims relationship. If our Order has really altered its constitution and, being now nothing beyond a mere social, convivial, or deistically moral society, nevertheless still claims to directly descend from that society which we know was purely, simply, and wholly Christian, it must be condemned as a pretentious sham. It either has a title to the succession by inculcating those tenets held and taught prior to 1717, or it is pretending to perpetuate an institution, which it is impossible to deny was purely a Christian one, without really continuing it. In the latter case all assumption of antiquity should be abandoned, but if the Mason clings to his assertion that he represents an organisation which was Christian, he must be himself a Christian. It cannot be said that any society which is merely Theistic would comply with the required conditions. The Mason who maintains that the only Masonic condition required in a candidate is that he shall believe in a God—for it is this which is so often insisted upon—is only of necessity a Deist. That the conditions to which even the Universalists have reduced

D 2

Freemasonry, are those that only a Theist can comply with, can and will be readily demonstrated.

Our contention then is, firstly that there is no intimation that in 1717 any alteration in the fundamental principles of the Order was announced or contemplated ; secondly that those principles were then and had been from all time Christian ; thirdly that all records show that the principles of ancient Masonry were to be *preserved* by the formation of the Grand Lodge of 1717 ; and fourthly that if the present Masonic system is declared not to be Christian then it has no authority whatever as an ancient society. In such case it is an innovation, posing as a venerable institution of which the history and tenets are public property, and thereby attracting members, whilst it in reality not only neglects, but positively denies, the very basis by which it has acquired their adhesion.

But is it this ? Is Freemasonry only what some of its representatives say it is ? Our belief is, and can only be, that it is not yet what the Universalist would make it out to be. Masonry is said to be a progressive science ; the theory of its history, as similarly given by so many writers in the past, was that the final glories of civilisation were, and still are, only attained by Christianity, and that Freemasonry itself only culminated under the Christian dispensation. It is unnecessary to illustrate this, the most casual glance through the histories attached to the Constitutions of the last century will suffice to demonstrate the absolute truth of this assertion.

The student of the present day cannot attach importance to these histories *as* histories, yet no unbiassed person can refuse to recognise that they had an aim, or aims. One object sought was, without doubt, that of showing that the Craft was, or that its principles were, of great antiquity ; another perhaps arose from a vain wish to connect the Society with great personages ; but a third was to record how Freemasonry

grew with the spread of Chistianity. We may fairly go even beyond this; the Constitutions asserting that, so far as England is concerned, the sciences by which Freemasons carried out their works were preserved by the early Christians. We refer the reader to Chapter II. of the History of Masonry in Britain in the 1756 Constitutions.

If our arguments or assertions thus far be admitted correct, it logically follows that, it being a misuse of terms to treat progression and retrogression as identical, Freemasonry cannot be said to advance by harking back to that slough from which all old writers agree that it had escaped.

Their theory is—Freemasonry advanced up to the time of Christianity; the status in which it is placed if it reoccupies the ground which it held prior to the Christian era can therefore be only one of relapse, there is certainly no progression.

Until now we have dealt only with the so-called histories, published under the authority of the Grand Lodge which was established in 1717. These *histories* continued to reproduce the Christian allusions we have referred to throughout the century, but a very remarkable change took place with regard to the profession of religious principles in the *charges :* histories and charges in all cases forming consecutive parts of the same book.

The Charges of 1717 do not give any distinct profession of a Christian belief; they may be, and are, variously read by those who would advocate a *Christian* catholicity for the system, or by those who would treat the religion of Freemasonry as a mere *Deism*, of a more than usually vague type. It is perhaps advisable that we should state what we ourselves understand by Deism ; if our definition fail to satisfy our reader, that is of no material consequence if only he comprehend what we mean by the expression. We imply therefore by the term Deism a belief in one God, unaccompanied by any reception of Revelation, and consequently

without an acquiescence in any knowledge of God's attributes. This is in accord with the majority of published definitions. We understand by Theism a belief in one God *with* a reception of Revelation, and consequently a possible or even actual knowledge of the attributes of God. In Hook's Church Dictionary Deists are divided into four classes, one being represented to have "right apprehensions concerning the natural attributes of God, and His all governing providence, and some notion of His moral perfections also, yet deny the immortality of the human soul, and believe that men perish entirely at death." Hook's Dictionary has no exposition of Theism, under that head, so it will be more convenient to deal with these two forms of belief on our first definition.

The following table will justify our use of the terms—

DEISM.

DEIST.—One who believes in the existence of a God but denies revealed religion; one who professes no form of religion but follows the light of nature and reason as his only guides in doctrine and practise. — Ogilvie's Imperial Dictionary.

DEIST. — The words Deist and Theist are strictly speaking perhaps synonymous, but yet it is generally to be observed that the former is used in a bad, and the latter in a good, sense. Custom has appropriated the term Deist to the enemies of revelation, and of Christianity in particular; while the word Theist is considered applicable to all who believe in one God.—Irons.

DEISM.—Is the belief in natural religion only, or those truths, in doctrine and practise, which man is to discover by the light of reason, independent and exclusive of any revelations from God. Hence *deism* implies *infidelity,* or a disbelief in the divine origin of the Scriptures. — Webster's Dictionary, 1883, unabridged edition.

THEISM.

THEISM.—The belief or acknowledgment of the existence of a God as opposed to Atheism. Theism differs from Deism, for although Deism implies a belief in the existence of a God, yet it signifies in modern usage a denial of revelation which Theism does not. —Ogilvie's Imperial Dictionary.

THEISM.—Averse as I am to the cause of Theism or name of Deist, when taken in a sense exclusive of revelation, I consider still that, in strictness, the root of all is theism; and that to be a settled Christian it is necessary to be a good theist.—Shaftesbury.

In Roget's Thesaurus, under the heading "RELIGIOUS SENTIMENTS," (Piety) "A believer, convert, theist," are placed together, and under the heading "IRRELIGION" are grouped "Deism, infidelity, freethinking, unchristianness."

Feurbach, Essence of Christianity, p. 204, argues that a belief in the existence of God, necessitates theism.

If nothing beyond a belief in one God were required from a candidate for Freemasonry, which is often asserted to be the case, any Deist could become a member of our Society, but as it is a condition that he should express his conviction that God will hear and answer prayer, it will at once be perceived that a mere Deistic profession of faith is not sufficient; to this we shall allude in a later chapter. It will be sufficient to note for the present that a belief in one God is not the only pre-requisite in a Masonic candidate, to prove which we refer the reader to the second question asked of the aspirant in lodge.

That Anderson was not satisfied with the 1717 Charges is evidenced by the Constitutions which he published in 1738. That the Grand Lodge was on this dissatisfied with Anderson's revision may be deduced from the issue of the 1756 Constitutions, and that there was a Masonic party in sympathy with Anderson's later views is proved by the adoption of his 1738 revisions by the Irish and Scotch Grand Lodges, and by the publication of a counter set of Constitutions, under the authority of a dissentient body which had sprung into existence in England claiming to represent ancient Masonic principles. In the year 1756 the English Grand Lodge Constitutions reproduced the extraordinary statements in the Charges concerning the Religion of Masonry which had been abandoned in 1738. In the same year the book known as Ahiman Rezon was published, this in reality formed the Constitutions of a body which termed itself "Ancient Masons." The asserted point of difference between this society and the older institution was that the dissentients claimed that they practised Ancient Masonry and that the older corporation had introduced innovations. The Ancients maintained in the second edition of their book that there were material differences in the tenets of the two bodies, that the elder began its departure from

genuine principles in the reign of King George the First, and that the system of the Grand Lodge of England was thereby rendered incomplete. They asserted that members of the older society, whom they now disrespectfully dubbed " Moderns," were not qualified to appear in a Master Masons' Lodge.*

We will now pass on to the Charges in the Constitutions of both these classes in the last century, and see what evidence there is of a difference such as we refer to.

For ready reference, and to illustrate our assertions as to the alterations made in the definition of the religious principles of the English system, we give a tabular statement; we feel sure this should enable any brother to see how the original Charges recognised the Christianity of the system—how, in 1717, there was an evasion of any declaration of principles; and how in 1738 Dr. Anderson corrected this. We then see that two parties were formed, the Grand Lodge, which was established in 1717, taking the Deistic, and the Masons who claimed to be the representatives of Ancient Masonry taking the Christian side. In the same year, 1756, the two rival Grand Lodges published counter Constitutions, each specifying its own religious views.

The alterations or variations in the Charge " concerning God and Religion " cannot be treated as unimportant.

The wording of the earliest Charges which appeared under the authority of the Grand Lodge, in 1723, is

---

* Edward Spratt, Grand Secretary of Ireland, issued the Irish Book of Constitutions in 1751, copying from Anderson 1738. Dermott's Ahiman Rezon of 1756 is proved by internal evidence to be a copy from Spratt. We are unable, therefore, to argue that the Ahiman Rezon was a direct protest against the "Modern" Constitutions of 1756, but we maintain that it was clearly a continuance of those principles of 1738 from which the original Grand Lodge had departed, and is thus evidence that a certain proportion of English Masons sympathised with the 1738 views concerning the religion of Freemasonry.

Extract from the History and the Charges in the Old [Operative] Constitutions.
1722.

The Almighty Father of Heaven, with the Wisdom of the Glorious Son, thro' the Goodness of the Holy Ghost, Three Persons in one Godhead, be with our Beginning, and give us his Grace so to govern our Lives, that we may come to his Bliss, that never shall have end.

THIS CHARGE BELONGETH TO APPRENTICES.

Imprimis. YOU shall truly honour God *and his holy Church*, the King, your Master, and Dame; you shall not absent yourself but with the Licence of one or both of them, from their Service, by Day or Night.

The following is printed at the end of the 1722 Old Constitutions as "Additional Orders and Constitutions agreed to at a General Assembly held on 8th December, 1663."

I *A. B.* do here in the Presence of God Almighty, and of my Fellows and Brethren here present, promise and declare, That I will not at any Time hereafter by any Act or Circumstance whatsoever, directly or indirectly, publish, discover, reveal or make known any of these Secrets, Privities or Councils of the Fraternity or Fellowship of Free Masons, which at this time, or at any time hereafter shall be made known unto me. So help me God, and the true and holy Contents of this Book.

The Charges of a Free Mason.
1723.
(Anderson's Constitutions.)

I. *Concerning* GOD *and* RELIGION.

A MASON is oblig'd, by his Tenure, to obey the moral Law; and if he rightly understands the Art, he will never be a stupid **Atheist,** nor an irreligious **Libertine.** But though in ancient Times Masons were charg'd in every Country to be of the Religion of that Country or Nation, whatever it was, yet 'tis now thought more expedient only to oblige them to that Religion in which all Men agree, leaving their particular Opinions to themselves; that is to be GOOD MEN AND TRUE, or Men of Honour and Honesty, by whatever Denominations or Persuasions they may be distinguish'd; whereby Masonry becomes the CENTER of UNION, and the means of conciliating true Friendship among Persons that must have remain'd at a perpetual Distance.

2. **Behaviour** *after the* LODGE *is over and the* **Brethren** *not gone.*

You may enjoy yourselves with innocent Mirth, treating one another according to Ability, but avoiding all Excess, or forcing any Brother to eat or drink beyound his Inclination, or hindering him from going when his Occasions call him, or doing or saying anything offensive, or that may forbid an EASY and FREE Conversation; for that would blast our Harmony, and defeat our laudable Purposes. Therefore no private Piques or Quarrels must be brought within the Door of the LODGE, far less any Quarrels about RELIGION, or NATIONS, or STATE POLICY, we being only, as MASONS, of the CATHOLICK RELIGION above-mention'd; we are also of all NATIONS, TONGUES, KINDREDS, and LANGUAGES, and are resolv'd against **all Politicks,** as what never yet conduc'd to the Welfare of the LODGE, nor ever will. This CHARGE has been always strictly enjoin'd and observ'd; *but especially ever since the* REFORMATION *in* BRITAIN, *or the Dissent and Secession of these Nations from the Communion of* ROME.

NOTE.—The italics at the end of the last clause are ours, and if the two Charges given are construed by their light, it will become apparent that "the Religion in which all men agree" was simply Christianity, or as mentioned in the second Charge, the "Catholick Religion."

The Charges of a Free Mason extracted from their ancient records.
1730.
(Dublin.)

I. *Concerning* GOD *and* RELIGION.

A *Mason* is oblig'd, by his Tenure, to obey the moral Law, and not to be a stupid *Atheist*, nor an irreligious Libertine; that is *Masons* are to be good Men and true, or Men of Honour and Honesty, by whatever Denominations or Persuasions they may be distinguish'd; whereby *Masonry* becomes the Center of Union, and the means of conciliating true Friendship among Persons that must otherwise have remain'd at a perpetual Distance.

2. BEHAVIOUR *after the* LODGE *is over, and the* BRETHREN *not gone.*

You may enjoy yourselves with innocent Mirth, treating one another according to Ability; but avoiding all Excess, or forcing any *Brother* to eat or drink beyond his Inclination, or hindering him from going when his Occasions call him, or doing, saying any thing offensive, or that may hinder an easy and free Conversation; for that would blast our Harmony, and defeat our laudable Purposes. Therefore no private Piques or Quarrels must be brought within the Door of the *Lodge*, far less any Quarrels about Religion, or Nations, or State Policy we being only as *Masons*, of the Catholick Religion above-mentioned, we are also of all Nations, Tongues, Kindred, and Languages, and are resolv'd against all Politicks, as what never yet conduc'd to the Welfare of any *Lodge*, nor ever will.

Anderson's Charges of 1738.
(London.)
Reprinted, after adoption, by the Irish Constitution.

I. CHARGE.

Concerning God and Religion.

A Mason is obliged by his Tenure to observe the Moral Law, as a true *Noachida*; and if he rightly understands the Craft, he will never be a stupid Atheist, nor an irreligious Libertine, nor act against conscience.

In ancient Times the Christian Masons were charged to comply with the Christian Usuages of each Country where they travell'd: or work'd. But Masonry being found in all Nations even of divers Religions, they are now generally charged to adhere to that Religion in which all men agree (leaving each Brother to his own particular Opinion) that is, to be good Men and true, Men of Honour and Honesty, by whatever Names, Religions, or Perswasions, (*sic*) they may be distinguished: For they all agree in the three great Articles of *Noah*, enough to preserve the Cement of the Lodge. Thus Masonry is the Centre of their Union, and the happy Means of consiliating Persons that otherwise must have remain'd at a perpetual Distance.

VI. CHARGE.

Concerning Masons Behaviour.

1. Behaviour in the Lodge before closing.

You must not hold private Committees, or separate Conversation, without Leave from the Master; nor talk of any thing impertinent; nor interrupt the Master or Wardens, or any Brother speaking to the Chair; nor act ludicrously while the Lodge is engaged in what is serious and solemn: But you are to pay due Reverence to the Master, Wardens and Fellows, and put them to Worship,

Every Brother found guilty of a Fault, shall stand to the Award of the Lodge, unless he appeals to the Grand Lodge, or unless a Lord's Work is retarded; for then a particular Reference may be made.

No private Piques, no Quarrels about Nations, Families, Religions or Politics, must be brought within the Doors of the Lodge: For, as Masons, we are of the oldest Catholick Religion above hinted, and of all Nations upon the Square, Level, and Plumb; and, like our Predecessors in all Ages, we are resolv'd against political Disputes, as contrary to the Peace and Welfare of the Lodge.

The Old Charges of the Free and Accepted Masons, collected from their Old Records at the Command of the Grand Master, approved by the Grand Lodge, and ordered to be printed in the first Edition of the Book of Constitution, on March 25, 1722.

FROM CONSTITUTIONS.
By JAMES ANDERSON D. D.
REVISED BY JOHN ENTICK M. A., LONDON, 1767.

CHARGE I.
Concerning GOD and RELIGION.

A MASON is obliged, by his Tenure, to obey the moral Law; and if he rightly understands the Art, he will never be a stupid ATHEIST, nor an irreligious LIBERTINE. But though in ancient Times Masons were charged in every Country to be of the Religion of that Country or Nation, whatever it was, yet it is now thought more expedient only to oblige them to that Religion in which all Men agree, leaving their particular Opinions to themselves; that is, to be good Men and true, or Men of Honour and Honesty, by whatever Denominations or Persuasions they may be distinguished; whereby Masonry becomes the Center of Union, and the means of conciliating true Friendship among Persons, that must have remained at a perpetual Distance.

CHARGE VI.
2. BEHAVIOUR AFTER THE LODGE IS OVER, AND THE BRETHREN NOT GONE.

You may enjoy yourselves with innocent Mirth, treating one another according to Ability; but avoiding all Excess, or forcing any Brother to eat or drink beyond his Inclination, or hindering him from going when his Occasions call him, or doing or saying any thing offensive, or that may forbid an easy and free Conversation; for that would blast our Harmany, (sic) and defeat our laudable Purposes. Therefore no private Piques or Quarrels must be brought within the Door of the Lodge, far less any Quarrels about Religion, or Nations, or State-Policy, we being only, as Masons, of the Catholic Religion above-mentioned; we are also of all Nations, Tongues, Kindreds, and Languages, and are resolved against all POLITICKS, as what never yet conduced to the Welfare of the Lodge, nor ever will. This Charge has been always strictly enjoined and observed; but especially ever since the Reformation in BRITAIN, or the Dissent and Secession of these Nations from the Communion of ROME.

The Old Charges of the Free and Accepted Masons printed in Ahiman Rezon, London, 1756.

CHARGE I.
Concerning GOD and RELIGION.

A Mason is obliged by his Tenure to observe the moral Law as a true NOACHIDA; and if he rightly understands the Craft, he will never be a stupid Atheist, nor an irreligious Libertine, nor act against Conscience.

In antient Times, the Christian Masons were charged to comply with the Christian Usages of each Country where they travelled or worked; being found in all Nations, even of divers Religions.

They are generally charged to adhere to that Religion in which all Men agree (leaving each Brother to his own particular Opinion); that is, to be good Men and true, Men of Honour and Honesty, by whatever Names, Religions, or Persuasions they may be distinguished; for they all agree in the three great Articles of Noah, enough to preserve the Cement of the Lodge.

Thus Masonry is the Center of their Union, and the happy Means of conciliating Persons that otherwise must have remained at a perpetual Distance.

CHARGE VI.
Concerning Masons Behaviour.
1. Behaviour in the Lodge before closing.

You must not hold private Committees, or separate Conversation, without Leave from the Master; nor talk of any Thing impertinent, nor interrupt the Master or Warden, or any other Brother speaking to the Chair; nor act ludicrously while the Lodge is engaged in what is serious and solemn; but you are to pay due reverence to the Master, Wardens, and Fellows, and put them to Worship.

Every Brother found guilty of a Fault, shall stand to the Award of the Lodge, unless he appeals to the Grand Lodge, or unless a Lord's Work is retarded; for then a particular Reference may be made.

No private Piques, no Quarrels, about Nations, Families, Religions, or Politics, must be brought within the Doors of the Lodge; for as Masons, we are of the oldest Catholick religion, before hinted; and of all Nations upon the Square, Level, and Plumb; and like our Predecessors in all Ages, we are resolved against political Disputes, as contrary to the Peace and Welfare of the Lodge.

Antient Charges from Constitutions. London, 1884.

I.—Concerning GOD and RELIGION.

A MASON is obliged, by his tenure, to obey the moral law; and if he rightly understand the art he will never be a stupid atheist nor an irreligious libertine. He, of all men, should best understand that GOD seeth not as man seeth; for man looketh at the outward appearance, but GOD looketh to the heart. A mason is, therefore, particularly bound never to act against the dictates of his conscience. Let a man's religion or mode of worship be what it may, he is not excluded from the order, provided he believe in the glorious architect of heaven and earth, and practise the sacred duties of morality. Masons unite with the virtuous of every persuasion in the firm and pleasing bond of fraternal love; they are taught to view the errors of mankind with compassion, and to strive, by the purity of their own conduct, to demonstrate the superior excellence of the faith they may profess. Thus masonry is the centre of union between good men and true, and the happy means of conciliating friendship amongst those who must otherwise have remained at a perpetual distance.

CHARGE VI.
2. Behaviour after the Lodge is over, and the Brethren not gone.

You may enjoy yourselves with innocent mirth, treating one another according to ability, but avoiding all excess, or forcing any brother to eat or drink beyond his inclination, or hindering him from going when his occasions call him, or doing or saying any thing offensive, or that may forbid an easy and free conversation; for that would blast our harmony, and defeat our laudable purposes. Therefore no private piques or quarrels must be brought within the door of the Lodge, far less any quarrels about religion, or nations, or state policy, we being only, as Masons, of the universal religion above-mentioned; we are also of all nations, tongues, kindreds, and languages, and are resolved against all politics, as what never yet conduced to the welfare of the Lodge, nor ever will.

738.
h Constitution.

ligion.

ure to observe
ida; and if he
e will never be
ious Libertine,

Masons were
istian Usages
ll'd: or work'd.
l Nations even
now generally
on in which all
er to his own
be good Men
l Honesty, by
r Perswasions,
: For they all
cles of Noah,
: of the Lodge.
f their Union,
iating Persons
in'd at a per-

not applicable to all religions. Had any belief been current regarding the adaptability of the newly organised Society to all religions, we might expect that some mention of it would have been made. The Charges state "We are also of all nations, tongues, kindreds, and languages," but they do not say, of all religions. They do indeed mention "Denominations and Persuasions;" but when they go on to speak of a "Catholick religion," and to state that "this Charge has always been strictly enjoined since the Reformation and the secession of these nations from Rome," it is apparent that the words "Denominations and Persuasions" refer only to the various branches of Christianity.

In the 1738 Constitutions we read "In ancient times, the Christian Masons were charged to comply with the Christian usages of each country where they travelled or worked." This is of some importance, as showing how the Christian influence was treated in 1738. The 1723 Constitutions having stated "In ancient Times Masons were charg'd in every Country to be of the Religion of that Country or Nation, whatever it was," the alteration was clearly called for if Freemasonry was to pose as even only a moral institution. It may here be noted that the Irish Constitutions of 1730 did not print this monstrous injunction, although the work was a nominal reproduction of the 1723 English edition.

Why the English Constitutions of 1756 harked back to this assertion of 1723 we shall probably never know, but the fact remains that in this and subsequent editions of the Constitutions we find the statement repeated, that in ancient times Masons were enjoined to be of the religion of any country in which they chanced to reside. We refer to the editions of 1756, of 1767 by John Entick, of 1769 and of 1784 by John Noorthouck.

In 1739 the Grand Lodge of Ireland adopted the

English statement (1738) that Masons were only enjoined to comply with Christian customs in foreign lands.

Whether the Grand Lodge disagreed with Dr. Anderson in reference to this particular matter we do not know, but we do know there was some disagreement, and we see by the 1738 Constitutions that Dr. Anderson virtually disavowed the 1723 statement.

With this solitary exception we are not aware that any Constitutions have been openly disavowed by any member of the Order either on account of their containing Christian references, or because such were omitted. Towards the middle of the last century there was a great dissent or a party arose which disclaimed all connection with the older society. The dissenters asserted that those from whom they separated, or with whom they would not associate, were not practising ancient or genuine Freemasonry, and they, the members of the new body, adopted the title of " Ancient Masons "— dubbing the older society " Modern Masons." It is no less strange than true that the older Grand Lodge, whilst it continually railed against the schism and treated the newer one with contempt, never as a matter of fact particularly protested at the titles which arose out of the schism. It seems to have suffered the names with some kind of assent that they did not incorrectly describe the two Masonic parties. It is not foreign to our purpose to see whether there is evidence in the Records that these assertions by the Ancients had any foundation.

The new seceding body in due course published what are in reality Constitutions, and these so completely went back to a recognition of Christian principles that it becomes almost certain what were some of the points, wherein they differed with the older body. Under the first clause of Charges headed " Concerning God and Religion, " as is still customary in our Charges, we read—

" A Mason is obliged by his tenure to observe the moral law as a true Noachida,* and if he rightly understands the Craft, he will never be a stupid Atheist, nor an irreligious Libertine, nor act against Conscience.

" In antient Times, the Christian Masons were charged to comply with the Christian Usages of each Country where they travelled or worked, being found in all Nations, even of divers Religions.

" They are generally charged to adhere to that Religion in which all Men agree, leaving each Brother to his own particular Opinion ; that is, to be good Men and true, Men of Honour and Honesty, by whatever Names, Religions, or Persuasions, they may be distinguished ; for they all agree in the three great Articles of Noah, enough to preserve the Cement of the Lodge."

These Constitutions were called by the curious name of " Ahiman Rezon," the first edition was published in 1756, and seven other editions were published before the Union of the two bodies in 1813. The following is an extract from this work, as late as 1801 :—

A Prayer to be said at the Opening of a Lodge or making of a Brother.

Most holy and glorious Lord God, thou Great Architect of Heaven and Earth, who art the Giver of all good Gifts and Graces ; and hast promised, that where two or three are gathered together in thy Name, Thou wilt be in the Midst of them ; in thy Name we assemble and meet together, most humbly beseeching thee to bless us in all our Undertakings, that we may know and serve thee aright, that all our Doings may tend to thy Glory, and the Salvation of our Souls.

And we beseech thee, O Lord God, to bless this our present Undertaking ; and grant that this our new Brother may dedicate his Life to thy Service, and be a true and faithful Brother among us : Endue him with a Competency of thy Divine Wisdom, that he may, with the Secrets of Free-Masonry, be able to unfold the Mysteries of Godliness and Christianity.

This we most humbly beg in the Name, and for the Sake, of Jesus Christ our Lord and Saviour. *Amen.*

---

* The term Noachidæ or Noachites is applied to Freemasons, they claiming that their belief descended from Noah, who amidst the general impiety and depravity before the Flood, alone preserved a true knowledge and worship of God.—See Krause (York) MS., also Mackey and Peck's Lexicon, articles " Noachidæ " and " Noah, Precepts of."

We ourselves, therefore, cannot fail to believe that whatever other points existed between the two bodies, the Christian principles of the Order was one of the issues. If an inspection of the Charges does not satisfy the reader, perhaps the following will make the point clearer :—" A Mason is obliged by his Tenure to believe firmly in the true Worship of the eternal God, as well as in all those sacred Records *which the Dignitaries and Fathers of the Church have compiled* and published for the Use of all good Men : so that no one who rightly understands the Art, can possibly tread in the irreligious Paths of the unhappy Libertine, or be induced to follow the arrogant Professors of Atheism or Deism."*

We shall show further on, in our Chapters on the Rituals, that the Ancient Masons used prayers which were distinctively Christian, and that they drew a definite line between Jewish and Christian Lodges.

Before we leave the Constitutions let us point out one more piece of evidence indicative of a seeming intention in the middle of the last century to eliminate Christian allusions. The 1723 Book of Constitutions contains a collection of Masonic songs, as do all editions up to 1784. The 1723 copy contains the following lines, that of 1756 omits them, whilst giving a portion of the song " The Master's " to which they belonged.

> But when the conqu'ring Goths were brought
> *T" embrace the Christian Faith*, they found
> The Folly that their Fathers wrought,
> In loss of Architecture sound.
> At length their Zeal for stately Fanes,
> And wealthy Grandeur, when at Peace,
> Made them exert their utmost Pains,
> Their Gothic Buildings to upraise.
>
> *Thus* many a sumptuous lofty Pile
> Was raised *in every Christian Land* . . .
> . . . .
> The Craftsmen highly are esteem'd,
> By Kings, as Masters of the Lodge,
> By many a wealthy noble Peer,
> By Lord and Laird, *by Priest* and Judge.

---

* "Ahiman Rezon," 1st Edition, 1756, page 14.

When we remember that one of the differences between the Ancient and Modern Masons was to all appearances a point of doctrine, the omission of the above is perhaps more than a coincidence.

One of the Charges appears to have escaped destructive attention, yet it perhaps as prominently denotes the Christianity of Freemasonry as anything else ; we refer to the fifth Charge, which commences " All Masons shall work honestly on Working Days, that they may live creditably on Holy Days." We are not aware that " Holy Day " in 1723 bore any other signification than " Festival of the Church."

In 1782 the Grand Lodge ordered the Constitutions to be revised, and a new edition to be published. The Preface of this book bears date 1784, and its publication took place in the same year. The Frontispiece is a well-known print by Cipriani and Sandby, engraved by Bartolozzi and Fitler, and published " By the Society of Free-Masons at their Hall in Great Queen Street, Lincoln's Inn Fields, 1786." We do not know how the discrepancy in the date arose, the plate appears to have been inserted after the book was bound up. There is no doubt whatever that the print was published under authority, for in the body of the book it is correctly described, as follows : " Truth is attended by the Three Theological virtues—Faith, Hope, and Charity : under these the Genius of Masonry is descending into the Hall." A reference to the engraving shows Faith as a female figure, with an open book resting on her left knee, and with her right hand raised she grasps the stem of a cup, from which rises a Latin or Christian Cross.

Bartolozzi was a Freemason,* he was also a Roman

* It is in evidence that Bartolozzi was a Freemason, as on the large plate, " Charity exerted on proper Objects," the names of painter and engraver appear as follows :—" Painted by Brother Stothard, R.A. ; engraved by Brother Bartolozzi, R.A., Engraver to His Majesty." Bartolozzi and his Works, by Andrew W. Tuer. 2 vols. London, 1881.

The print above referred to is a procession of Charity Children in a Masonic Lodge.

Catholic, and an acknowledged master of Christian symbolism, and it is incredible that this symbol was introduced by accident. However this may be, the Grand Lodge in 1786 committed itself to an emblem which bears but one interpretation, and that a Christian one.

It is rather remarkable that this symbol should have been published in 1784 or 1786. In 1773 Dissenters petitioned against the Test and Corporation Acts, by which they were excluded from holding any public office if the applicant refused to take the Sacrament at the Established Church. In 1779 an Act was passed* "whereby the benefits of the Toleration Act were granted to Protestant Dissenting ministers and school-masters, upon condition of their taking the oaths of Allegiance and Supremacy, making the declaration against Popery, and declaring their belief of the Holy Scriptures as containing a Divine revelation." Previous to this, any Dissenters who kept public schools were liable to a fine of £40, and three months imprisonment. As late as 1811 Lord Sidmouth tried to replace Dissenters in this position, but failed. It must therefore have been treading on dangerous ground about that time to engrave pictorial allusions to the Sacrament.

The symbol may be read as one of the Catholic Church opposed to the Romish Church which denies the cup to the laity. It may have had the lower meaning of Charity only.

This Chapter was written without any knowledge of the Articles and letters which appeared on the subject in the *Freemason* for 1871.

---

* History of all Religions, p. 319.

CHAPTER III.

ENGLISH AND FOREIGN CONSTITUTIONS AND OTHER
RECORDS.

THE previous Chapter will have shown that, in what it is no misuse of terms to call *Ancient* Masonry, there was a very full recognition that a Freemason was bound to be an earnest Christian. Whatever Freemasonry *was* that it should still be. The introduction of members who were not actually working masons was never intended to alter the quaint symbolism, of which we have historical proof that Freemasons applied it to their profession in the earliest times.

We agree with Bro. Hughan where he says " It is of no avail to argue that the gentlemen who became Freemasons in early days worked a different rite." " They were either members of this same operative body, actually or by succession, or they were nothing." . . . . " We have no other means of judging what Masonry was than by studying what is left of its aged documents." To this we would add that what Freemasonry was, that it must continue to be, and is, whatever may be said to the contrary.

We have by no means exhausted the evidence in old documents in favour of our contention. The oldest known Lodge warrant is dated " in the year of our Lord God 1731,"* is this an ignoring of Christ ? Again, let us quote from the copy of the New York Certificate of 1767, published in the *Freemason* of November 19th,

---

* No. 7, Irish Constitution.

1887, by Bro. W. J. Hughan. It concludes "Given under our hands and seal in our Lodge at New York this Ninth day of July in the year of Masonry 5767 and of Salvation 1767."

In this and in many similar ways it can be completely established that in former (and even in recent) times Masonry not only recognised Christianity, but positively laid down in its symbolism that the entire Institution was dedicated to Christ.

In examining old lists of Lodges, one cannot but be struck with the Christian names adopted by Lodges in early times.

The first Lodge to assume a distinctive title was apparently the " University Lodge," in 1730, meeting at the " Bear and Harrow," in Butcher Row, London. Previously, and in the majority of cases for many years subsequently, Lodges were known by the sign of the house at which they met. A reference to that monument of industry and classification, Bro. Lane's " Masonic Records," a register of all the English Lodges that ever existed, reveals a curious fact. We append a list of every Lodge which previously to 1760 had acquired or assumed a name of its own, but have omitted such as obviously owed their appellation to their place of meeting, such as " The Rock," Gibraltar ; or to the peculiarity of their membership, such as the " French Lodge," London ; the " Steward's Lodge," &c. :—

Date*.	Name of Lodge.	Place of Meeting.
1730	University	London.
1735	*St. John's, No. 1*	Boston, Mass.
1740	*St. Michael's*	Barbadoes.
1740	Perfect Union of Strangers	Lausanne.
1742	Union	Frankfort.
1743	*St. George*	Hamburg.
1743	Prince George	Charleston, Sth. Carolina.
1744	The Great Lodge	Antigua.
1745	Absalom	Hamburg.
1745	Zerubabel	Copenhagen.

* Not of Constitution, but at which the name was assumed.

1749	-	*St. John's, No. 2* -	- -	Boston, Mass.
1749	-	L. of Orange	- -	Rotterdam.
1749	-	*St. Martin's*	- -	Copenhagen.
1750	-	Hiram - -	- -	New Haven, Conn.
1752	-	*St. John's* -	- -	Barbadoes.
1752	-	*St. Peter's* -	- -	Barbadoes.
1753	-	*Evangelists'*	- -	Antigua.
1753	-	La bien aimée	- -	Amsterdam.
1754	-	*St. Paul's* -	- -	Barbadoes.
1754	-	*St. Michael's*	- -	Schwerin, Mecklenburgh.
1755	-	Unanimity -	- -	Dukinfield.
1755	-	Union	- -	Charleston, Sth. Carolina.
1755	-	Charity	- -	Amsterdam.
1755	-	Frederick -	- -	Hanover.
1756	-	Peace	- -	Amsterdam.
1756	-	*St. David's* -	- -	London.
1757	-	*St. John's* -	- -	Providence, R.I.
1757	-	*St. John's, No. 2* -	- -	New York.
1758	-	*St. James's* -	- -	Barbadoes.

It will be observed that out of 29 Lodges, whose names may be supposed to be a matter of choice and not of circumstance, no less than 14 are distinctly and unmistakeably Christian. It is not probable that this should be accidental, neither can it be credited that a purely cosmopolitan non-religious body would have adopted names whose very enunciation must have been tantamount to a declaration of the religious belief of the Lodge. Had the present Universal theory been then current, we should certainly have found some allusion to it in the nomenclature of these Lodges, more especially as the majority of them were established abroad in places where, if universality had been a part of the Masonic scheme, it would necessarily be more assertive than in England. If *any* belief in the universality of the system was entertained by our brethren abroad it could only have been in a Christian sense, or assuredly it would not have been the prevailing custom to name Lodges after Christian Saints. The adoption of these titles tends strongly to subvert the assertion in the 1723 Constitutions that brethren were enjoined to be of the Religion of any and every country.

E

It can be very satisfactorily proved that in recent times Lodges under the English Constitution, working in Mahommedan countries, have distinctly held that they should *not* be of the Religion of the country.*

Amongst other evidences in our records is that which is afforded by what is termed the year of Masonry, and the use by our early brethren of the Christian era. Had this era been the result of an oversight or accident, it would be childishly unfair to attach any importance to it; but we know that it was adopted with deliberation and we are therefore fully entitled to draw attention to it.

All Masons are probably aware that the different Masonic rites date from various special epochs. We have no concern with any rites outside of Craft Masonry consisting of the first three and the Royal Arch Degrees. We may nevertheless point out, *en passant,* that the Ancient and Accepted Scottish Rite uses the Jewish chronology. The Degrees known as the Royal and Select Masters count, or should count, from what is termed the year of deposit, which would make the year 1887 read as 2887. Craft Masonry, however, has two chronologies, the one actually Christian and the other *based* on Christian chronology.

That this matter received full consideration in the last century is proved by a reference to the foot-note of Noorthouck's Constitutions (p. 5), and it is noticeable that this Brother after discussing eras adopted the Christian chronology on his title page.

Deliberately then, Masonic events were described as belonging to various years in the time of our Lord. There was no kind of necessity to have written " Anno Domini." The term " Anno Mundi " was not uncommonly used in the last century. If this did not suit, " Anno Hebraico " might have served the purpose, there

---

* Minutes of the D.G. Lodge of Turkey, No. 4783c British Museum.

could hardly have been any objection to choosing an occurrence such as Hebrew chronology dates from, which has always afforded a Masonic illustration, as a starting point. But if this was open to objection then a "year of the Order," as in the Templar Degree, might have been adopted. With all this, and much more choice, our brethren adopted the Christian era as being most appropriate to Freemasonry. They, in fact, declared their principles—Christ was their Lord.

Had they stopped here it would have been sufficiently remarkable, but they went further, and believing, Masonically, that when God first placed man on the earth, He gave a revelation of Himself, they adopted a system to mark this belief. The use of the letters A.L. is known to all Masons as denoting "Anno Lucis," which is dated 4000 years before Christ, thus accepting Biblical chronology as fixed by Archbishop Usher.*

It is needless to enlarge on this circumstance— everyone who has lived in Asia is aware how even a man of business has to attend to chronologies which show that one, which is very far from universal, was considered by Masonic authority appropriate in the last century.

The persistent manner in which the letters denoting "Anno Domini" were used is a somewhat remarkable fact. At the laying of the foundation-stone of Freemasons' Hall the published accounts were dated A.D. 1775. The engraved plate deposited in the foundation-stone is stated to have been dated A.D. MDCCLXXV. Ray makes this statement, although

---

* Noorthouck drew attention to the error of four years, *i.e.*, the difference should be 4004 years, but he treated it as an unnecessary degree of accuracy for a Mason. In the present century we find the year of Masonry given as 4000 and also as 4004 years before Christ, with utter impartiality. Thus the Scottish Constitutions of 1836 are dated A.D. 1836, A.L. 5836. In 1848 the date reads A.D. 1848, A.L. 5852. The last edition simply gives 1886, without any prefix on the title page, but in the "authorization" we have "year of light 5890."

E 2

Preston does not. As, however, Ray cannot be held to favour any Christian theories, and as, being in America, he only copied the programme he publishes, his state-statement is probably correct. Many other instances can be adduced of the complete adoption of the Christian, as the Masonic, era.

We find A.D. and Craft dates of Masonic occurr-rences very constantly conjoined. Preston quotes a case where at the laying of a foundation-stone by the Provincial Grand Master for Banfshire, two inscriptions were placed in the stone—one was engraved with the words "In the year of our Lord 1801, and of the æra of Masonry 5801," and the other ran "Anno Christi MDCCCI. Aræque Architectonicæ, VMDCCCI."

Edward Spratt, Grand Secretary of Ireland, drew attention to the fact that the Freemasons' chronology was the vulgar Christian computation, some 150 years ago. Possibly we cannot give a better explanation of the era adopted by Masons than was offered by Dr. Oliver in 1853. He says, quoting from Dr. Kitto, the birth of Christ is usually referred to the autumn of the year 5 before Christ, which is an apparent anomaly requiring explanation. The Christian era was not commonly used until about A.D. 532 in the time of Justinian, when it was introduced by Dionysius Exiguus, a Scythian by birth and a Roman abbot; it only began to prevail in the West about A.D. 730. Chronologists agree that Dionysius placed the birth of Christ too late; the error has been variously estimated from two to eight years. The general conclusion, which is adopted in the English Bible is that Christ was born some four years before the zero of the Christian era. Dr. Oliver adds that the zero of the Masonic era is frequently placed 4004 years before that of the Chris-tian era.

The date of the first Constitutions of the Grand Lodge formed in 1717, is given as "in the year of

Masonry 5723, Anno Domini 1723," and this appears to have been the usual standard adopted in Europe and America. It may indeed be said to have acquired universal acceptance, but it can hardly be rationally upheld.

Another fact which may be fairly dealt with in this section is the motto on the Grand Lodge seal used in the last century, or at all events for some part of the century. We again quote Bro. Hughan,* "My attention was first drawn to the motto on the Grand Lodge seal—'In the beginning was the word' *in Greek*, by examining a photo of the warrant [*i.e.*, of the Lodge of Relief, No. 42, Bury], but since then, as previously indicated, I have traced similar mottoes in connection with the G.L. arms on other old warrants. When it was first used, and when dropt, are interesting enquiries, but far from being easy of solution, but the fact of such a motto designating the Grand Lodge of England in the fourth decade of the last century is curious and remarkable to say the least."

It has been maintained by some writers of distinction and authority, that the Continental Guilds of stone masons were, equally with our own, imbued with the spirit of speculative Masonry. This claim has been more especially set up for the Steinmetzen of Germany. It may therefore be pertinent to enquire briefly into their tenets as disclosed in their records. The Masonic students of a more recent school who, like Bros. Gould and Speth, question or deny this resemblance, will naturally consider our remarks superfluous and irrelevant. We ourselves do not presume to decide the matter one way or the other; we merely suggest that *if* the analogy did exist, some slight reference to Continental views may be acceptable.

The Steinmetz Constitutions of 1459 begin thus:

---

* *Freemason*, 12th November, 1887, " Old Warrants."

"In the name of the Father and the Son and the Holy Ghost and the Blessed Mother Mary, and also their saintly servants the Holy Four Crowned Martyrs." One clause reads: "And no workman or Master shall be received into the guild who does not go yearly to the Holy Sacrament, or keep Christian doctrine; or loses his substance at gaming"; and again "No fellow or Master shall employ a workman who lives with a woman in adultery, or openly lives a dishonest life with women, or fails to go to confession regularly, and to attend the Holy Sacrament as befits a Christian," &c.*

The Constitutions of the same body (revision of 1563) omit the invocation altogether. It will be observed that it was somewhat more than Christian, it was Roman Catholic, and the Reformation may account for its suppression. But the code is still Christian, as witness Clause XVII., "No Craftsman or Master shall be received into the guild who goes not yearly to Holy Sacrament, or keeps not Christian discipline, and squanders his substance in play."†

Or if we refer to Constitutions supplementary to the first quoted, drawn up at Torgau in 1462,‡ we find once more as follows: "In the name of the Father, and of the Son, and of the Holy Ghost, in the name of the blessed Virgin Mary, and in honour of the Four crowned Martyrs." "After the birth of our dear Lord Christ." "And every Master shall on all acknowledged Fasts cause four Masses to be said." "And the first Mass of the Trinity, the other of our dear Lady, the third of the four crowned Martyrs. . . . ." "And no Master shall employ any fellow who . . . . . goeth not to confession. . . . ."

In the Craft Guilds of France, in the Early and Middle Ages it was compulsory for the Apprentice to be

---

* Heldmann, p. 203, *et seq.*

† Gould's "History of Freemasonry," p. 124.   ‡ *Ibid*, p. 134, *et seq.*

a Catholic. The following is from a code preserved at Amiens, and dated June 15th, 1407. It is styled the "Statutes regulating the Fraternity."*

"It is ordained that all those of the said Craft who do earn money here, living in the City of Amiens, shall be required to belong to the said "candle" (*i.e.,* "Fraternity"), to enter into it. . . . ." This candle or Fraternity to which every Ancient Mason was constrained to belong was a Society instituted for the support of a special altar in the church.

"The Statutes of the Masons of Rheims," 26 July, 1625, contain the following clause xvi. :†—"The Masters of the said Craft shall be required every year, at the procession of the Holy Sacrament of the altar, according to their invariable custom, to carry four torches of the weight of ten pounds each one, which torches shall be borne by the four junior masters of the craft." The Masons of Paris in 1260 had to pay their fines to the Chapel of St. Blaise.‡

In other and even older codes we read that Masons were not allowed to work on Saturdays in Lent after Vespers were chanted. In fine, search where you will in the genuine records of Ancient Freemasonry, and you will always find it inseparably connected with Christianity. That Freemasons, soon after the Reformation, should have embraced the reformed religion is not strange, for it is certain that although the Church of Rome had Operative Masonry under its wing for a long time, there was no great sympathy between the priest and the workman. On many of their monumental buildings there are intimations that Masons were opposed to the prevailing corruption in the morals

---

* In full " Statutes regulating the Fraternity (cierge, candle) of the Masons' trade (du mestier de Machonnerie) of Amiens." Gould's " History of Freemasonry," vol. I., p. 195.

† *Ibid,* p. 196.   ‡ *Ibid,* p. 197.

of the clergy, and even to the dogmas of the Romish Church.*

It was only about 1723, when Dr. Anderson, originally authorised by the Duke of Montagu, Grand Master, published the General Regulations and Charges of a Freemason, that we find the Charges omitting all direct reference to Christianity. For a complete criticism of the labours of Dr. Anderson and the value which should now be attached to them, the reader is recommended to study the pages of Gould's " History of Freemasonry." By reading the first volume of that work carefully he must come to the conclusion that Christianity was always recognised, in the most complete manner, as *the* only religion, prior to the time when Dr. Anderson came upon the scene. That Freemasons on the Continent of Europe recognised Christianity long after it had disappeared from England does not admit of the shadow of a doubt.

As regards the Craft in France, it is true that until the 10th August, 1849, the authorised Constitutions of the Grand Orient make no precise reference to religion at all. But who can doubt that it was distinctively Christian ? And, note well, its Christianity was derived from England, because Freemasonry was only introduced into France in 1725. However much some writers may strive to prove the existence of Freemasonry among the old operative Masons of the Continent, none pretend that there is any direct connection between the two societies. In France, as in Germany, a distinct break occurs, and Freemasonry starts fresh on the scene as an importation from England, confined solely to gentlemen, to the complete exclusion of the artisan. The first prominent exponent of French Freemasonry was the Chevalier Ramsay. The following extracts from his Oration of the 21st March, 1737, speak for themselves :

---

* Findel's " History of Freemasonry."

" Our Ancestors, the Crusaders, ... desired to unite into one sole Fraternity the individuals of all nations." Not all *religions.* " The Order of Freemasons [was established] to make men . . . . the faithful adorers of the God of Love." The God of Love is undeniably the Christian's God. "To the last [masters] are explained the Christian Virtues."*

Bro. Speth, in the London *Freemason*, of 27th June, 1885, published the Statutes of the Grand Lodge of France, 1755. We gather from these that the Universal idea had already taken root, because all reference to Christianity is studiously omitted. The invocation is, " In the name of the Supreme Architect." Art. I., " God being our Head." But the underlying Christianity peeps out where least expected, and probably quite overlooked. " Article 15. You shall meet regularly once a month on a holiday or a Sunday after the conclusion of Divine Service, because on working days you should attend to the duties of your profession." We attach no importance to the word Sunday, it might be looked upon as the *civil* holiday in France for all religions ; but why only AFTER Divine Service ? Does not this show that the supposition was the Brethren would wish to attend worship, and service on Sunday must be Christian Service.

It is certain that French Lodges formerly did not see anything incongruous in the fullest recognition of the truths of the New Testament. There is a description of the banqueting hall of the lodge in Marseilles in Calcott's Candid Disquisitions, 1769. By this we learn the Masonic virtues were illustrated by various paintings of Scriptural scenes, of which *six were taken from the New Testament.*

In spite of the known creed, or rather want of creed, of the Grand Orient of France, even in that country

---

* Gould's History, Vol. III., p. 84, *et seq.*

there have been efforts made to revive the connection between Freemasonry and Christianity. Thus in a work published early in this century, the " Histoire de la Fondation du Grand Orient de France," 1812, there is an account of " L'Ordre du Christ," started by a Portuguese, who claimed that the Templars of France had been abolished. It seems to have had a short life in Paris, but to have lasted longer in the Provinces. It was attached to some of the regular lodges.

The absence of a definite creed in French Freemasonry—the allusions in the 1755 code, already cited, were not incorporated with the later Regulations of the Grand Orient—produced the effect which might have been anticipated. The French Craft immediately before and after the Revolution became contaminated with infidelity. On the 10th August, 1849, it was sought to apply a much needed corrective, and the first clause of the new Constitutions then voted, reads—" The basis of Freemasonry is a belief in God and in the immortality of the soul and the solidarity of humanity." We are here a long way off the original Christian doctrines, yet so permeated with infidelity had the Craft become that even this broad view evoked protest. In La Rousse's " Grand Dictionnaire Universel du XIXe Siecle," 1865 (a work more than equivalent to our " Encyclopædia Britannica "), speaking of the new Constitution of the Grand Orient of France, we find this ominous commentary, " It distinctly affirms a belief in the existence of God and the immortality of the soul." The writer of the article continues: Here is "a double affirmation which threatens to bring into the breasts of French Masons interminable discussions. It is difficult to harmonise with the respect due to absolute liberty of conscience, the formal recognition . . . . of two dogmas to-day relegated to the domain of critical and scientific philosophy." But all efforts of the wiser brethren have failed. Christianity had long given place

to Theism, then to Deism, for a time Indifferentism
ruled, for a brief space a cold and formal Deism was
re-asserted, and even this has finally been displaced.
On the 10th September, 1877, the Grand Orient once
more altered its first clause, and Freemasonry is thus
defined—" Its basis is absolute liberty of conscience and
the solidarity of humanity."*

The Grand Lodge of England has replied to all this
by a refusal to recognise the Grand Orient, in consequence of its non-religious character having culminated
in a waiving of all belief in the Grand Architect of the
Universe. If English Freemasonry has really advanced
as is now asserted,† it would appear that the Grand
Lodge of England will shortly have to efface *itself* or
put a check on doubtful Masonic progression.

In Germany, where Masonry has been a serious
occupation from its first introduction, and never the mere
relaxation of an idle moment, the religious question has
been ever prominent, and is to this day unsettled. In
the last century the eminently Christian Rite of the Strict
Observance almost extinguished Craft Freemasonry for
a long series of years, and it is but very recently that
Jewish members have been admitted anywhere. In the
Grand Lodge of Hamburg their reception dates from
the beginning of this century, and until 1811 this Grand
Lodge was a Provincial Grand Lodge under England.
In the Grand Lodge of Frankfort (Eclectic Union)
also an English Provincial Grand Lodge till 1823, the
Jewish question was a bone of contention for many
years. In 1840 Jewish Brothers were at last admitted
as visitors, and in 1848 the ritual was altered so as to
permit their initiation. And within these last 25 years

---

* Gould's History, vol. iii., pp. 191, 192.

† " But above all things, let it be clearly seen as a purely social
institution, having no political or religious tendency at all."—" The
Royal Masonic Cyclopædia " (p. 7), by Kenneth R. H. Mackenzie,
London, 1877.

a Frankfort Lodge has been subordinate to a foreign jurisdiction (England) because its members were Jews. The Jewish question was the cause of several of the Frankfort Lodges seceding in 1845 to form the Darmstadt Grand Lodge on a rigidly Christian basis. This latter system has, however, since then also adopted the Universal theory. In Berlin there are three Grand Lodges. A mutual ordinance of 1842 rendered the exclusion of Jews, even as visitors, incumbent upon all three. For disobedience a Cologne Lodge was erased in 1848. The Grand Lodge of the Three Globes (Berlin) in 1868 resolved to admit Jewish Brethren as "permanent visitors" (if made elsewhere), but they are still excluded from initiation. This is the most powerful jurisdiction in Germany. The next most important is the National Grand Lodge, which follows the Swedish system (of which more hereafter), and consequently rigidly excludes all but Christians. The Grand Lodge of Saxony was founded upon the Universal theory, but did not come into existence till 1811. To this day, in the great majority of German Lodges, a *non*-Christian candidate is ineligible. And be it noted that England, in spite of the Universal theory, has never protested, has never had the courage of her convictions, and avoided intercourse with intolerant Masonic bodies; it has merely declined fellowship with France because of too great tolerance. England has protested against her certificate not being recognised as valid, and has laid down the law that no body of Masons is justified in going behind the record; that an English Mason of whatever religion must be acknowledged and received as a Mason by those who wish to remain on friendly terms with the Grand Lodge of England; but it has never insisted that the Freemasonry which sprung from her loins is, and must be, in all cases and everywhere, undenominational. The following extract from Gould*

---

* History of Freemasonry, Vol. III., p. 18.

will show that such is the case. "On December 3, 1845, the Grand Master announced that certain English Masons 'who professed the Jewish Faith, had been refused admittance as visitors into a Lodge at Berlin, holding under the Grand Lodge Royal York of Friendship, on the ground that the laws of that Grand Lodge excluded, even as visitors, Brethren who were not Christians.' In the following June the subject was again referred to by Lord Zetland, who stated that the Grand Lodge Royal York at Berlin, declining to receive and acknowledge all certificates from the Grand Lodge of England without regard to the religion of those presenting them, the two bodies would no longer continue to exchange representatives. This estrangement lasted untill 1847, when the principle stipulated for was gracefully conceded ; and in 1872 the Grand Lodge Royal York 'resolved to initiate Jews and men of all religions.' The subject was again brought forward in 1877, on the refusal of the former [the Grand Lodge of the Three Globes] to receive as Candidates for admission or joining any persons who were not Christians, when it was decided by the Grand Lodge of England to refrain from any interference with the system of Freemasonry adopted by the Three Globes Lodge in 1740."

The natural result of eliminating Christianity from the Craft has been very well remarked and commented on in the last edition of the " Encyclopædia Britannica," but it is certain that the passage does not apply to Lodges under the " Three Globes " or the " Grand National Lodge of Germany." " Masonry in each country of course takes its colouring from the state of thought and feeling by which it is surrounded. But it cannot be disputed that the German, Dutch, Belgian, and French magazines of the Craft occasionally exhibit a tone which is not favourable to Christianity, regarded as a special revelation. The tendency of political opinion in such an Association is also necessarily

democratic; and while it would be absurd to make the Brotherhood answerable for the opinions of Mazzini or the outrages of the Commune, and while the majority of brethren are loyal subjects, and probably also orthodox Christians (in the theological sense) the institution itself undoubtedly 'makes for' liberty in matters both civil and spiritual."

A French work published in 1865, "La Franc-Maçonnerie en dix demandes et réponses," says that "In regard to religious exclusiveness, it must be said that the Grand Lodges of Sweden, Denmark, Prussia, Hanover, and Darmstadt do not admit non-Christians into their Order." As we have shown, Prussia is divided on this matter, and Darmstadt has since adopted the universal theory. The Grand Lodge of Hanover has ceased to exist since the incorporation of that kingdom with Prussia.

Bro. Gould in his recently published great work says: "Owing to the *Christian* colour of Freemasonry in Sweden, Solomon throughout is but a type of Christ, and his Vicar* consequently becomes Christ's Vicar, a species of Protestant Pope. That the office is now always held by the king of the country is therefore only natural." "They still work the same ceremonies that originally riveted their attention about 1760."† This is somewhat important.

In one of the most popular American Masonic works we read that the "Swedish Rite is adopted not only in *Sweden* and *Norway*, but also in *Denmark*, and by the Grand Lodge of *Prussia*. Additional interest has been manifested with regard to the Swedish system since the initiation, at Stockholm, of our present Royal Grand Master, H.R.H. the Prince of Wales. There are 12 degrees of which the

---

* The title is Grand Master and Vicarius Salomonis.
† "History of Freemasonry," vol. III., 1886.

1st. Apprentice, entitled ' laborious.'

2nd. Fellow-Craft or Companion, called ' zealous.'

3rd. Master Mason, entitled ' worshipful.'

4th and 5th. These form, in fact, but one degree, the members being called 'Elected and Right Worshipful Apprentices and Companions of St. Andrew's Lodge.' "*

From the above it will be seen that in Sweden and elsewhere the same Christian colour which Freemasonry had in 1760 still distinguishes it.

In a letter, which will be found in several editions of Preston's "Illustrations," from Charles, Duke of Sudermania, dated from the Grand Lodge of Sweden, 24th January, 1798, to the Grand Master of the Grand Lodge of England, we read : " This uniformity of situation as well as the fundamental principles of the Craft which we equally profess, authorises us to draw closer a confidence," &c. This surely goes to prove that the principles of the two systems were then in unison, whereas the same cannot be said now. The letter from the National Grand Master of Sweden concludes : " We remain always, most illustrious and most enlightened Brother, *by the Sacred Numbers*, your devoted brother, Charles Duke of Sudermania."

In replying the Prince of Wales wrote, let our labours " be characterised by our adoration of the Almighty," and he concluded, " I salute you by the Sacred Numbers." We leave the Universalist to digest this at his leisure—it will hardly assimilate with a belief that Christian principles were not recognised at the close of last century.

It is scarcely beside the issue to mark what many of our Continental brethren believed and subscribed to at so recent a date as 1865. In a little brochure published at St. Gall, Switzerland, and entitled " La

---

* Mackey and Peck's Lexicon.

Franc-Maçonnerie en Dix Demandes et Réponses," we find the third question and answer read as follows :

(*Question*).—" How does the Union behave in regard to the State and the Church ? "

After a preamble, which says that " It is the relations of man with God which give birth to religion and those with the world from which result politics. The idea of religion embraces those connections of man which are purely divine; those with politics include all his exclusively temporal interests," the answer is made in the following terms—

" The Masonic union does not prescribe any creed to its members; it leaves them to obey their own convictions. Admission into Freemasonry is, for that matter, open to the followers of the most diverse religions and creeds, and true Freemasons will not repulse any free man of good reputation, on account of his religious convictions, or the worship to which he is attached, if he asks to be admitted to their body. The Masonic alliance itself desires that its members should have religion—each of the solemn conclaves of the brethren commences and concludes with prayer—it expressly approves its members remaining faithful to the faith in which they find the most truth; but it wishes also that they should not forget the principles of humanity; that neither Catholicism nor Protestantism should make them forget Christianity; that Christianity, Judaism, and so forth should not make them lose sight of man; that they approve, I do not say indifferentism, but very much a genuine tolerance.

" There are some dissidents in the union of Free-Masons, who think that only Christians should be admitted into the Masonic Alliance. But this view of the case is in opposition to the spirit of Freemasonry, and is born of a confusion of pure Christianity with its confessional forms.

" But one may be Christian in spirit without ranging

oneself on the side of any of the numerous dogmatic creeds which form Christianity in its positive sense. On the contrary, the true Mason, whether baptised or not, is always Christian in spirit, and that for the reason that the principles of Freemasonry are nowhere better formulated than in the Gospels ; promising that they do not interpret it by a preconceived faith."

We are also of opinion that Freemasonry does not exclude any man on account of his religion (within certain limits, of course). Our argument is simply that any Jew, Mahomedan, Parsee, or other Theist is eligible for initiation ; whether his religious convictions will allow him to proceed further is a matter for his consideration, not for ours. The principles and Faith inculcated by our ritual are to this day, in spite of past emasculation, Christian, and none but a Christian can accept them as taught by us : he can only proceed by placing his own interpretation on our symbolism and exhortations. We may well allow a Jew to confer the remaining degrees, according to his light, in a Jewish Lodge, or the Parsee in a Zoroastrian Lodge ; but are we not recreants to our Masonic Faith if we permit our symbols to be perverted in a Lodge which regards the Christian Bible as the Great Light ?

And, taking a still wider range, we find, in a work of instruction, &c., published at Philadelphia (U.S.) in 5809 (*i.e.*, 1809), in the French language, the following question :—

Que signifient les trois coups de l'expert ? " (" What is the signification of the expert's three knocks ? ") The answer being, " Three words of the Holy Scriptures : Knock ; they will open to you : Seek ; you shall find : Ask ; you shall receive." (It shall be given unto you).

Further on in the same work, in the " Catéchisme du Grade de Maître," the question arises—

" Are there any precious (articles of) furnitures in the Master's lodge ?"

F

(*Answer*).—"Yes, Most Venerable ; to the number of three, which are the Gospels, the Compasses, and the Mallet.

(*Question*).—"What is their signification ?"

(*Answer*).—"The Gospel demonstrates Truth, the Compasses Justice, and the Mallet, which serves to maintain order, makes us remember that we ought to be amenable to the lessons of Wisdom."

Here again the contention is plain and definite— "The Gospel demonstrates Truth;" not the Gospel is the accidentally English symbol for the Truth, but it is the truth. And so says our W.M. in other words to this day, and when he shall cease to say so, then will Freemasonry have finally severed its connection with the past. But as long as he makes any similar assertion, so long is the Craft Christian.

Let it not be supposed that we are the first to discover that the spread of Freemasonry into non-Christian lands and amongst people of other religions would demand a re-modelling of some of our arrangements. Others have foreseen that candidates might and probably would be legitimately admitted who would be unable conscientiously to proceed to the subsequent degrees, because unable to "maintain and uphold the principles inculcated in the first degree," that is, Christianity. We claim the discovery in a sense, because it was self-evolved in us before reading Preston; Preston had previously perceived the same truth.

In Preston's well-known "Illustrations" we find the emphatic statement that those Freemasons who are not Christians must nevertheless take it with all its Christian types. Further on he says : "Any person of irreproachable morals, who will publicly acknowledge and subscribe to the Being of a God, may claim initiation into its mysteries, whether he be a Jew, a Christian, a Mahometan, an Hindoo, or a North-American Indian. The laws of Masonry are not exclusive, and its portal

is wide enough to admit any worthy man who is willing to accept its conditions. *Any Brother professing an adverse religion has the power of absenting himself from the Meetings.*" Here we see that Preston foresaw that men might become Masons who yet would disagree with its teaching—or that their religion would—and that the system could not be universal throughout. "To exclude a Brother from a Lodge on account of his religion is un-Masonic . . . . The Grand Lodge of Prussia, however, under an absurd belief that Freemasonry is exclusively a Christian society, directed its subordinate Lodges to close their doors against the admission of persons professing any other religion . . . . The Grand Lodges all over the world repudiated the action of the Prussian Grand Lodge," *

Further on, in the same work, Preston says :† "Indeed the possibility of any genuine Mason seceding to any open profession of infidelity may reasonably be doubted ; and it would require some extraordinary pressure to induce a well-instructed Brother to subscribe to the insidious hypothesis which would persuade him that Masonry repudiates the Redeemer of mankind, or ignores and banishes from the Order those ameliorating doctrines and influences which are derived from his moral teaching." Preston says that the sacred truths of Christianity run like a vein through the Masonic lectures.

We consider this is a very remarkable utterance of Preston's. Here he states as plainly as it is possible to state anything, that he believed the Craft would obtain, by reason of its universal character, to which it is entitled by its catholic reception of all, certain members to whom its religious tendencies, or even belief, would not be acceptable. He does not allude to the teaching being unacceptable to an *outsider* or one who is not a

---

* Preston's "Illustrations," pp. 435-6.   † *Ibid,* p. 450.

F 2

Mason, he distinctly states "any brother." He contemplates Freemasonry acquiring members who, whilst fulfilling all initial requirements for membership would necessarily disagree with the religious doctrines which would in due course be disclosed to them.

The high aim of a Freemason is to walk uprightly before heaven and before men, "neither inclining to the right or to the left;" "neither becoming an enthusiast nor a persecutor in religion, nor bending towards innovation or infidelity." "In private life he should yield up every selfish propensity, inclining neither to avarice, malice, or revenge, envy or contempt." "As the builder raises his column by the plane and perpendicular, so should the Mason carry himself towards the world." These are high aims, indeed, and, carried out, embody the spirit of true Christianity.

While Freemasonry remained in the operative stage, there can indeed be no doubt of its Christian connection. That pious brotherhood, to whom we owe those grand temples devoted to the worship of the One God and of His Son, our Saviour, which adorn every civilised capital, great city, or even large town of Europe, were not mere Theists, or those grand monuments of pious art would never have been erected.

In the preceding chapter we stated that the Irish Book of Constitutions followed, or led, the Ancients in the recognition of Christian principles as opposed to the Universal principle in Freemasonry. Many instances can be adduced of the Irish Constitution having acknowledged these principles, and as a matter of fact the Grand Lodge of Ireland is still Christian. We shall content ourselves with calling attention to extracts from a Lecture published with the "Constitution and By-Laws of the Grand Master's Lodge of Free and Accepted Masons in Ireland." Dublin, 1852.

"Whoso discovereth secrets loseth his credit and shall never find a friend to his mind."—*Eccles.*, 27, 16.

"A new Commandment I give unto you, that you love one another as I have loved you."—*John*, 13, 3.

"By this shall all men know that you are my disciples, if ye have love for another."—*John*, 13, 35.

"He that loveth not, knoweth not God."...*John*, 4, 8.

"For God is love, and he that dwelleth in love dwelleth in God, and God in him."—*John*, 4, 16.

"And this Commandment we have from him, that he who loveth God loveth his brother also."—*John*, 4, 21.

"And be ye kind to one another, tender hearted, forbearing and forgiving one another, even as God, for Christ's sake, hath forgiven you."—*Ephes.*, 4, 32.

Some few of our preceding remarks have perhaps departed from the strict object of this book, but it is returned to when we quote, for the benefit of the Anglo-Indian Freemason, a verse from a Masonic song published in the *Oriental Masonic Muse*, Calcutta, in 1791* which enjoins us as Freemasons to—

> "Proclaim aloud, with grateful theme,
> The great Redeemer's blessed name;
> The Eastern Star now shows us light,
> Let us not go astray."

It is very little that there should be an Institution in which one God is recognised, but it is much that anyone should think this alone will reconcile religious prejudices or beliefs. Divergencies in religions arise not so much from any question about the existence of one God—it requires no system to recognise this—but from the *attributes* of that one God. We have already cited quotations stating that in ancient times Freemasons were charged to be of the religion common in the country they might happen to be residing in. If this really was so, Freemasonry did away, or tried to do away, with all conscientious religion whatever.

---

* No. 4785 b.b. 28. British Museum. This book contains several Christian references—one especially, to St. Peter passing Masons into Heaven. It also has Dunckerley's "Hymn for the R.A. Degree, in which occurs—

> "The sacred place where three in one
> Comprise Thy comprehensive name."

How religious prejudices or beliefs were likely to be reconciled by a system which enjoined a Buddhist to practise Presbyterianism for a while, or a Mahommedan to worship a few score idols for the nonce, I leave to others to explain. Such a system must have tended to disgust, not to reconcile, brethren. Yet if we are to accept the views of those who dissent from us, this in our very earliest authorised Charges is actually termed a " Catholic religion ;" the second clause of the VI. Charge running " we being only, as Masons, of the Catholic religion above mentioned." It continues " we are also of all nations, tongues, kindreds and languages, and are resolved against all Politicks, as what never yet conduced to the welfare of the Lodge, nor ever will. This Charge has always been strictly enjoined and observed, but especially ever *since the Reformation* in Britain, or the dissent and secession of these nations from the Communion of Rome."

If words means anything this is a clear admission that Freemasonry was not universal to any but those of a Catholic belief who had severed themselves from the Communion of Rome. There was no known belief in 1723 which could have been described as Catholic, save some form of Christianity.

It is not claimed that the seventeenth century originators of Speculative Masonry ever intended to found a new religion; the evidence is complete that they accepted as part of their system some existing Catholic belief without regard to " denominations and persuasions." The words " denominations" and " persuasions " are used in the 1738 Constitutions, and cannot be read as covering " all religions." The whole phraseology of the earliest Charges tends to show that Christian sectarian differences should be dropped by Masons when within the doors of the Lodge, but there is nothing in them to indicate that anything beyond this was ever aimed at.

Whilst we must deplore the changes which have been made, we must not further be blind to the results which have accrued from them in India. By the elimination of Christianity a very different Institution now exists there to that which prevailed in Britain prior to 1717, and into which it is tolerably certain neither Mahomedan nor Parsee could, or would have entered. The Institution has now so changed its character that there is no bar to any of these peoples, or to their beliefs. The political good which must result, even if no other arises, cannot of course, be ignored, and we use the word " political" in its widest sense, and as apart from national or party politics. Neither do we wish to deprive the Craft of the mission of Charity which it is thus enabled to perform. None can value more highly than we do our Jewish and Parsee Brothers; they fulfil most scrupulously the glorious and sublime injunction first enunciated by our Grand Master and Redeemer, and since sedulously preached by our Fraternity, " Love one another." But we maintain that their co-operation has been obtained on a wrong footing: the arrangements gradually introduced to conciliate them have caused us to violate our principles and veil our faith, and must in the long run entail the contempt of these very Brethren themselves. THEY never for one moment sink their professions or belief; on the contrary, they have secured for a visible symbol of their faiths a place of honour in our Indian Lodges. It is not required of us as Masons to acknowledge any religion as being equally true with our own. We owe due respect to the cherished faith of a Brother who is dear to us, but we are not called upon to raise it to a place of honour beside our own. In doing so we are recreants to our own Faith, and therefore bad Masons. Our Indian Brothers assert their Faith, whilst respecting ours, and are therefore good Masons. The only legitimate, honest, and manly way is to be

true to one's self and to one's creed. In the First Degree every God-fearing man may be admitted, and obligated naturally on that book which he holds most dear and sacred, but in an English Lodge the Bible must not be displaced, it is our Great Light, not the symbol thereof. This fact impressed upon our Indian Brother naturally meets with his dissent. Shall we, then, retract our words, and say, " Oh no, we mistake; the Zendavesta is the Great Light, at least, whilst we are addressing you !" Let us be honest, and say, " Brother, this is *our* Great Light, it is not yours; remain our dearly loved Brother ; on this point we differ; come and see us as a visitor and be always heartily welcomed; but if you cannot accept our Light, betake you to a Lodge which shall reverence YOUR Great Light. Form there a Lodge composed entirely of your own faith, where you may confer the 2nd and 3rd degrees according to your conscience; but do not profess for one moment to believe there can be a plurality of Great Lights, and do not attempt to constrain us to any such profession. It would be a mere mockery : we *cannot* accord your Great Light a place in our hearts equal to our own, neither can you do the same by ours ; we should neither of us really believe our own professions. But in your own Lodge we will visit you as a brother, and show that respect to YOUR Great Light which our consideration for your feelings demands, and you will, without violence to your religious sentiments, do likewise when visiting us."

Thus and thus only can we be consistent as Masons, as Christians, as Jews, as honest believers in any religion.

As a finish to this Chapter we draw attention to the woodcut at the commencement. This is an engraving of a rubbing of the ornament on the cover of the Bible used in the Grand Lodge of England. The combination of Triangles is peculiar and would hardly be intelligible

RUBBING FROM THE COVER OF THE BIBLE USED AT THE MEETINGS
OF THE UNITED GRAND LODGE OF ENGLAND.

(See p. 68.)

but for the letters which denote that the Masonic Trinity is composed of God the Father, God the Son, and God the Holy Ghost.

The Grand Lodge Bible is dated 1769. There is nothing to show when it became Grand Lodge property, or how it was acquired. There must have been two Bibles to choose from in 1813 at the Union. Was that of the Ancients with this sign of the Christian Trinity adopted? It would almost appear so.

CHAPTER IV.

THE LECTURES.

THE Lectures delivered before Masonic Lodges naturally embody the leading tenets of faith held by the Brethren of the day. Even if they should have undergone modification, amounting in some cases to entire change, the historian will, nevertheless, naturally, find in the Lectures material for this work. In many cases too, the Lectures are more outspoken and more unguarded than are the contemporary and formal Charges and Constitutions of the Order. To them then we may well turn for evidence of the religious ideas and beliefs held by the members of the Craft at any particular epoch.

It is an oft-repeated assertion that it is not in the power of anybody to make innovations in the body of Masonry. Mackenzie asserts that whatever modifications have been attempted or suggested have hopelessly collapsed; unfortunately we cannot agree with him, we only wish his statement were correct. He admits that the Lectures have been very greatly improved in " style and perspicuity." Mackey goes further, saying that they have undergone repeated modifications from the time of Anderson : he instances innovations, but excuses them under the plea that the prohibition of innovations in the body of Freemasonry merely indicated that the Landmarks should remain untouched. A change from Christianity towards Deism has thus gone on and has been treated as an improvement which has not interfered with the Landmarks.

We propose to show that such changes as have been made have largely removed Christian references and Christian emblems from the Lectures, and in some instances from the Tracing Board itself. In the " Freemason's Quarterly Magazine " for 1850 (p. 343), it will be seen that the London Lodges were accused of being farther removed from old Christian principles than the Country Lodges then were. It is not improbable that much evil has been worked by some Masons maintaining that their system was purely and only a moral one. It is described in the Ritual and Lectures as a *peculiar* system of Morality, and it is also treated and described as a system leading up to eternal salvation. If any such claim be genuine, Freemasonry certainly cannot be any mere ordinary system of Morality.

The first Lectures of which we know anything were prepared by Drs. Anderson and Desaguliers in 1720. Mackey says they were the production of the infantile age of lecture making. These Lectures did not give satisfaction for long, as, in 1732 the Rev. Martin Clare, F.R.S., who was afterwards Deputy Grand Master, was appointed by Grand Lodge to revise them. Clare's system of revision, " consisted but of additions to the old ones (*i.e.*, Lectures) in the shape of moral and scriptural admonitions, and retained a Christian character, recognising the Trinity and our Sunday."*

About 1763 other Lectures were prepared by William Hutchinson ; these also had a Christian character, as was to be expected from his belief that a Master Mason represents a man under the Christian doctrine, saved from the grave of iniquity, and raised to the faith of salvation.

The next reviser was Thomas Dunckerley who compiled his Lectures about 1770—he is said to have introduced many types of Christ and the two great Christian parallels. Very shortly after this William

* " Kingston Masonic Annual," 1871, p. 25.

Preston elaborated his version; it appears this was commonly used in the south of England for some time whilst Hutchinson's was used in the north. The Hut- chinson and Preston systems were eventually combined, and in this new form generally used in England until the Union in 1813.*

It was then decided the Lectures should be revised. Mackey says "this duty was entrusted to the Revd. Dr. Hemming, the Senior Grand Warden, and the result was the Union or Hemming Lectures, which are now the authoritative standard of English Masonry. In these Lectures many alterations of the Prestonian system were made, and *some of the most cherished symbols of the Fraternity were abandoned, as, for instance, the twelve grand points, the initiation of the free-born, and the lines parallel. Preston's lectures were rejected in consequence, it is said of their Christian references;* and Dr. Hemming, in attempting to avoid this error, fell into a greater one, of omitting in his new course some of the important ritualistic landmarks of the Order. Hence it is that many Lodges still prefer the Prestonian to the Hemming Lectures.†"

Mackey states,‡ with disapproval, that all the Lectures from 1717 to 1813 Christianised or entirely recognised the Christianity of the English Masonic System. It may not be altogether unreasonable to argue that, as the Masons of the last were nearer to the source of Speculative Masonry than those of this century, they had possibly a clearer knowledge of what constituted the genuine tenets of ancient Masonry than can now be gathered from oral tradition.

Mackey emphatically asserts that from the time of the Clare to the time of the Hemming Lectures, *i.e.,* for over 80 years, there was always *a disposition* in the

---

* Much of the foregoing is dependent on Dr. Oliver's testimony.
† "Encyclo. of Freemasonry," Philadelphia, 1884.   ‡ *Ibid.*

Grand Lodge of England to Christianise Masonry through the Lectures ; he adds, the system completed by Dr. Anderson in 1723 "was comparatively free from this defect."* Mackey wrote in 1874.

Mackenzie in his Cyclopædia dismisses the subject of the Lectures with a rather curt remark "that they have been frequently revised." The Emulation Lectures, as all Masons know, are now very generally used. They are based on the Lectures as they stood after the 1813 revision and omit the two parallels. There are still, however, Lectures in existence which contain the two parallels and which conclude with the Charge, "*The two grand parallels in Masonry, may we ever imitate their virtue and profit by their pious example.*" We would here note what may possibly have escaped attention. This "Charge" is designated in all the old Lectures with which we are conversant as the "OLD Charge." There are fourteen other Charges in the first three Degrees, all of which are merely described as "Charges," this one alone being designated the "Old" Charge.

Although both Mackey and Oliver agree that Dr. Hemming is primarily responsible for omitting the two Christian parallels from the Lectures, this is perhaps not quite certain. In a book entitled "The whole of Craft Masonry," it is stated by the author, with reference to the parallels that "the late Bro. Gilkes managed to have them left out while I was absent from London. The only reason assigned was because *he* considered them offensive to the ears of the Hebrew brother. I have repeatedly worked them in their presence and never heard an expression of the kind." We believe many changes have been introduced into Masonry in this way. A brother has only to be sufficiently assertive, and he will always find supporters for any proposed change.

* "Encyclo. of Freemasonry," Philadelphia, 1884.

Dr. Oliver writes with regard to the expurgation of this passage, "It is an innovation in the ancient Lectures; and as a Christian Mason, I most earnestly wish to see these two parallels restored."

The following are allusions to them from the "Entered Apprentice Lecture," 5th section—

Q.—King Solomon being an Hebrew and living long before the Christian era, to whom were they next dedicated?

A.—St. John the Baptist.

Q.—Why to St. John the Baptist.

A.—He being the fore-runner of our Saviour, preached repentance in the wilderness, and drew the first line of the Gospel.

Q.—Had St. John the Baptist an equal?

A.—He had.   St. John the Evangelist.

Q.—Wherein is the Evangelist equal to the Baptist?

A.—He, coming after the former, finished by his learning what the other had begun by his zeal, and thus drew a line parallel.

Many of the old Lectures give even a fuller explanation than this regarding the two grand Christian parallels. They state that St. John the Evangelist completed the work which St. John the Baptist "began by his zeal, and thus drew a line parallel, since which time *all Christian Freemasons' Lodges* have been as regularly dedicated to the Evangelist as to the Baptist."

The Emulation Lectures, now so commonly used, term the above an unorthodox supplement. This again is mere assertion, contrary to evidence, as we believe.

The following is from the *same section* (*i.e.*, the fifth, First Lecture) in the system of T. S. Webb, composed by him in America about 1797:

"In all regularly constituted Lodges there is represented a certain *point within a circle*, the point representing an individual brother; the Circle representing the boundary line of his duty to God and man; beyond

which he is never to suffer his passions, prejudices, or interests to betray him on any occasion. This circle is embordered by two perpendicular parallel lines, representing St. John the Baptist and St. John the Evangelist, who were perfect parallels in Christianity as well as Masonry; and upon the vertex rests the book of the Holy Scriptures, which points out the whole duty of man. In going round the circle we necessarily touch upon these two lines." To this Dr. Oliver adds " No Lodge can be esteemed perfect, which does not contain a visible and self interpreting emblem of the Christian religion." Writing generally regarding old Lectures (*i.e.*, prior to 1813) he says " all the general truths of religion as they are received *amongst Christians* are brought into a lucid point of view."

The following is from the 6th section of Hutchinson's Entered Apprentice Lecture with reference to the Star:

" We may apply this emblem to a still more religious import: it represents the star which led the wise men to Bethlehem; proclaimed to mankind the nativity of the Son of God; and *here* conducting our spiritual progress to the Author of our redemption."

Further on in the 7th section of the Master Masons' Lecture Hutchinson states—

" ' The Sprig of Acacia,' points to that state of moral obscurity to which the world was reduced previously to the appearance of Christ upon earth; when the reverence and adoration due to the Divinity were buried in the filth and rubbish of the world; when religion sat mourning in Israel in sackcloth and ashes, and morality was scattered to the four winds of heaven. In order that mankind might be preserved from this deplorable estate of darkness and destruction, and as the old law was dead and become rottenness, a new doctrine and new precepts were wanting to give the key to salvation, in the language of which we might touch the ear of an

offended Deity, and bring forth hope for eternity. True religion was fled; those who sought her through the wisdom of the ancients were not able to raise her; she eluded the grasp and their polluted hands were stretched forth in vain for her restoration. Those who sought her by the old law were frustrated, for death had stepped between, and corruption had defiled the embrace; sin had beset her steps, and the vices of the world had overwhelmed her. The Great Father of all commiserating the miseries of the world, sent his only Son, who was innocence itself, to teach the doctrine of salvation, by whom man was RAISED from the death of sin unto a life of righteousness; from the tomb of corruption unto the chambers of hope; from the darkness of despair to the celestial beams of faith; and not only working for us this redemption, but making with us the covenant of regeneration, whence we become the children of God and inheritors of the realms of heaven."

The Sprig of Acacia, or Cassia, which was formerly—even in our own time—represented by a piece of some evergreen shrub, is not now to be commonly seen in Lodges.

The very early Ritual, *said* to have been introduced by Sir Christopher Wren, recognised a connection with Christianity. We do not claim that Sir C. Wren was a Mason, or that he had any connection with the Ritual, which is a matter of no moment. One of the questions was—"In the name of the King and *Holy Church* are you a Mason?"; another allusion is "R.W. the M. and Fellows of the Holy Lodge of St. John from whence I come, greet you." Desaguliers' and Anderson's Ritual was worked about 1720,* it also alludes to the Holy Lodge of St. John. In the Fellow Craft's Degree the Grand Architect of the Universe is described as

---

* *Pace Dr. Oliver.*

"He that was taken up to the top of the pinnacle of the Holy Temple."*

In Martin Clare's Lectures the staves, or rungs, of the Masonic ladder by which the Mason is to ascend, are said to be immoveable, but that the three principal ones were indicative of *Faith in Christ, Hope in Salvation and Charity with all mankind.* The ladder is said to rest on the Holy Bible.†

In Dunckerley's Ritual " the three principal steps of the Masonic ladder were referred to the Christian doctrine of the three states of the soul."

Again here is a question—" What Lodge are you of?" The answer was—" The Lodge of St. John symbolised by the Triangle and Cross." *Question*— " How does it stand?" *Answer*—" Perfect E. and W. as all Churches and Chapels do."‡

The Rev. Moses Margoliouth, in the early part of the present century, was one of the most scholarly divines among the many clergymen and Fellows of colleges, who have believed in Freemasonry as a great religious, as well as social, power. In one of his lectures§ he speaks as follows regarding the lessons taught by the ceremonies and symbols of the Order :—

" The allegory and symbol of the third degree, are not only most solemn lessons in the history of our redemption, but are also august and sublime. The name H.A. introduced to our notice, is one which does not occur in the whole volume of the sacred law ; there is not the slightest allusion to his ' untimely death,' as related in the course of the lecture on the occasion. But if you bear in mind that ' Masonry is a system of morality (and religion) veiled in allegory and illustrated by symbols,' the difficulty vanishes, for you will observe

---

* Lecture on Rituals by Revd. G. Oliver delivered in Lincoln in 1863. † *Ibid.* ‡ *Ibid.*

§ " Genuine Freemasonry Indissolubly connected with Revelation," 1852.

G

that the narrative must be taken in an allegorical and not a literal sense. It is absurd to contend for the latter sense, since it is contrary to the definition of Freemasonry. The name given to Him who personifies our Grand Master, who is said to have met with an untimely death from the hands of three ruffians, is important; inasmuch as the appellation signifies, HE WAS EXALTED TO HIS FATHER.

"The tools by which his death was effected, viz., the Level, Plumb Rule, and Mallet, are also remarkable; as the two former, when placed one above the other, present the figure of a cross. The mallet is a necessary tool for fastening anything to the cross; and hence we have the whole of the instruments by which the death of H.A.—of Him who was exalted to His Father—was caused. The presence of the tools, however, is necessary for a double purpose: in the first place, as illustrations of the theory just propounded; in the second place, to inculcate, by their shape, &c., those lessons which are so impressively furnished by the W.M. to the newly-initiated brethren.

"I am pleased to say that I am not singular in my view on this point. The following is an extract from a letter which I received from Brother E. G. Willoughby, of Tranmere, a Mason whose fame is known in all good and worthy lodges: 'You are aware that my opinion is that every mark, character, and emblem depicted in a lodge has a reference to the Christian system. It is said in our lodge-lectures that "all squares, levels, and perpendiculars are true and proper signs to know a Mason by." The same may be said of Christians, externally; the cross is a figure which consists of all squares, &c., and at baptism the same symbol is applied to the forehead as an outward and visible sign, &c. . . . . But that part of our ceremonies to which I may have referred when speaking to you about the symbol of the cross, is in the third degree. You may

remember that the candidate is reminded that the instruments with which our Grand Master was slain were the plumb-rule, the level, and the setting-maul. These are generally thrown promiscuously, ... and are also depicted on the tracing-board. And if the level be placed in a regular position, and the plumb-rule placed immediately under it, they will form the cross, and evidently allude to the instrumentality by which Christ, the Grand Master of the Universe, or, as he is styled in the oldest book of Constitutions, the Grand Architect of the Christian Church was slain. . . . . However ancient Masonry may be, it is evident that the third degree has been introduced during the Christian era, though the allegory in which it is veiled is taken from an earlier period ; . . . and however humble the illustration, I do not know how so important a portion of Christian doctrine could be better illustrated by symbols.' Taking this view of the third degree, we have not only the picture of the manner of our Grand Master's death, but also a graphic portrait of the murderous conspiracy of Caiphas, Herod, and Pontius Pilate."

In the United States, where Freemasonry has long flourished and is highly esteemed, the Lectures hold a very important place, and are compiled and delivered by the ablest men in the Lodges. Here is a recent encyclopædic summary in regard to Masonry there* which could hardly be excelled for conciseness and absolute truth :—

"The traditions of Freemasonry have handed down to us the character of many of the fraternity, whose learning and talents were the charm of their own and all succeeding time. The brethren of the Mystic Order take pride in seeing inscribed on their rolls the names of so many philosophers, scholars and statesmen of

---

* From the article "Freemasonry," in the Encyclopædia Americana, 1886. This grand work is in no way intended to rival or clash with our Encyclopædia Britannica, but to *supplement* it, by bringing every subject (largely including American subjects, of course) to date.

glorious renown who have mastered their mysteries. Its emblems convey moral lessons, teaching the brethren to feed the hungry, to clothe the naked, to reclaim the wandering, to instruct the ignorant, and to relieve the distressed. The fraternity professes the highest veneration for King Solomon, ' the beloved of the Lord,' and it adopts as its peculiar pattern St. John the Baptist, the harbinger of Jesus Christ. Everyone received into the Masonic Order in Christendom is given the Holy Bible as ' the rule and guide of his faith and practice.' "

The following is a quotation from a well-known Lecture on the spirit and scope of Freemasonry published in 1860 by Bro. W. T. Wilkinson under due authority. It was originally delivered before a Lodge of Instructon, which of itself lends a certain weight to it. In this Lecture the candidate is addressed in the following words—

"Your very position is designed by Masonry to remind you that in a state of nature, you are—poor—and ignorant—and blind—and naked ; you are taught to look upon the HOLY BIBLE, as the only source of the true riches—wisdom—enlightenment—and happiness. The *Author* of this holy Work is Almighty God :—the *design* is, to be ' a light to your feet, and a lamp to your path,' —' to guide your feet into the way of peace :'—the *end* is, to make you ' wise unto salvation through faith which is in Christ Jesus,'— to teach you that true wisdom, which is, the fear of the Lord,—and that understanding, which is, to depart from evil. We present it to you as God gave it ; we ask you not what your particular views of abstract doctrines may be : particular creeds, and particular opinions must not be introduced here ; all we ask is, that you will make it your study, and that you will make your life and actions to conform to the Divine commands."

In alluding to the Apron belonging to the First Degree Bro. Wilkinson said—

" To provide you with this dress a lamb was slain that you might appear in his clothing. Let this remind you, that if you hope to ' sit down with Abraham, Isaac, and Jacob, in the kingdom of heaven,' —to join the innumerable company of the redeemed, who are arrayed in white before the throne of God, it must be through faith in the all-sufficient sacrifice of our Lord and Saviour Jesus Christ—' the Lamb of God, which taketh away the sin of the world ;' and that you are acceptable in God's sight, only when clothed in His righteousness, which is ' unto all, and upon all them that believe.' "

The above is no unfair statement of views held in Lodges under the English Constitution not long since ; now, all this is changed, or rapidly passing away.

An alteration which marks Masonic progress is the description of the Creation in the second section of the Second Lecture. In all old Lectures with which we are acquainted, the Almighty is described as creating the world in six days and as resting on the seventh. In modern Lectures " *days* " are altered to " *periods.*" We have no great objection to this, but when we see other emendations we are suspicious of the tendency of these changes. The alteration has not done away with the doctrine conveyed in the Lecture, which is that man is strictly commanded by the Creator to rest on the seventh day and return thanks in God's sanctuary for blessings received. In this Lecture the Fellow-Craft Mason is most strictly enjoined to treat the seventh day as sacred. In practice Freemasonry has always treated the seventh day as being the Christian Sunday. If some other seventh day should ever be substituted, as a concession to non-Christians, the fact can still not be done away with that for some hundreds of years Freemasonry undoubtedly recognised the Christian Holy day as its Holy day. It is very inconsistent nowadays. We ought to give up St. John's day and, instead of going to Church, we should perhaps try to conciliate by

dancing at the Mohurram, or paint ourselves during the Holy Festival!

But in spite of all alterations, all tinkering with our Rituals, in deference to the feelings of non-Christian members, Christianity is not yet eliminated from our Lectures. We are told that our Lodges stand on Holy Ground because of three Grand offerings. We would point out with reference to these three grand offerings that they could not enjoy universal acceptance. Most positively, holiness would not be attributed by many religious believers to Abraham's intended sacrifice of Isaac, nor to the burnt offerings of Solomon. Such instances as these would be treated at the present time, by half the world, as acts which must have been abhorrent to the Almighty. To the members of certain religions they convey an idea diametrically opposite to that intended. By many pious men in Asia they would be regarded as the most monstrous impiety. Granting that the Christian Mason will accept them as types of the greater sacrifice of Christ, who else will? The Jew may treat the sacrifices as in themselves acts of holiness; the Buddhist and most Hindoos would regard them as acts of the vilest wickedness.

But the Lectures assure us in various places that the " Sacred writings are to rule and govern our faith." "The Volume of the Sacred Law may be justly regarded as the spiritual Tracing Board of T.G.A. O.T.U." Now, not even our Hebrew Brother can accept this teaching, for no one will dispute that hereby are intended the Old and New Testaments combined. The Christian could not declare that the Sacred writings were to govern his faith, if he thereby alluded to the Old Testament only, for our faith, though founded on, is not governed by the Old Testament, but by the New; and the Jew cannot accept the dictum unless the New be excluded. But this point has been, and will be, so often adverted to, being the very pith and marrow of our

argument, that we only touch on it here, fearing to weary our readers with needless iteration. No Christian can in his heart believe that any writings, however good, however moral, however philosophic, are really SACRED, except the Holy Bible: why then pretend to believe so? This is not toleration, but self-degradation. No right feeling Brother would wish to speak disrespectfully of the Book or Books held sacred by his fellow Craftsman, any more than he would defile the floor of a mosque. Nevertheless, it would require very extraordinary considerations to induce a Christian to call the mosque a holy place.

The Lectures on Freemasonry are divided into two classes; one on the whole ritual of Freemasonry, and the other on what are termed the tracing boards, which, as all Masons are aware, have depicted upon them emblems which are deemed appropriate to the Degree of Masonry under elucidation. By means of these emblems the lecturer illustrates the various truths or statements he utters. These tracing boards, again, have furnished most of the Masonic emblems which have been printed on a variety of charts for general information.

In dealing, therefore, with the subject of the Lectures in Masonic use either now or in the past we may rightly consider the emblems which are, and which have been, employed in English Masonry.

We have already shown that Freemasonry has had one symbol (the parallel lines) removed, as it clashed with Universality. It can be equally demonstrated that this process of abandoning Christian references and principles, by giving up Christian emblems or symbols, has gone further still, and that what has already taken place justifies our fear that this pernicious emasculation may be extended until the great Masonic Light itself— the Bible—shall be extinguished.

Allusion has been made to the Masonic ladder which, as depicted on one of the tracing boards, and as

described in old Lectures, rests on the Bible. By this ladder the Freemason is supposed to ascend to the Grand Lodge above. The rungs of this ladder now commonly bear the initials F. H. C., as indications of the virtues, Faith, Hope, and Charity, necessary to the true Brother. It will surprise some to learn that these letters are an innovation, the older marks on the rungs of the ladder being a Latin cross, an anchor, and a heart. To eliminate the objectionable Christian cross it was apparently necessary to remove the anchor and the heart, replacing the three emblems by the letters noted above.

"Emulation" working, *i.e.*, the practice of the famous Lodge of Instruction bearing that name, which cannot be accused of undue Christian proclivities, does, we are glad to admit, give on its tracing board the cross instead of the letter F. If further evidence is required by the Christian Freemason that a belief in Christ once was recognised by the Order in its Lectures, it will be found in Deputy Grand Master Martin Clare's Lectures,* which, it is said, were ordered by Grand Lodge in 1732 to be used by all Lodges.

We would seriously ask the Universalist whether, in substituting the letter F for a cross, he has made the symbolism of Freemasonry more or less universally comprehensible? The letter F, in most countries in the world, must require explanation before it can be understood. Admitting the statements of certain brethren that Freemasonry has no connection, or an exceedingly slight one, with religion, and that it should be viewed as being strictly a moral system, this F will require a great deal of explaining. The Masonic ladder is supposed to reach to heaven. The Mason ascends it by the aid of certain rungs, staves, or steps. His first step used to be in Faith, signified by the Christian cross.

---

* Clare was a Grand Warden in 1735, and Deputy Grand Master in 1741.

"Faith is the foundation of justice, the bond of amity, and the chief support of society; we live by faith, we walk by faith, by faith we have a continual hope in the acknowledgment of a Supreme Being; by faith we are justified, accepted, and finally received. A true Christian faith is the substance of things hoped for, the evidence of things not seen; this well maintained in answering our Masonic profession, will turn faith into a vision, and brings us to those blessed mansions, where we shall be eternally happy with God the Grand Architect of the Universe, whose Son died for us, and rose again, that we might be justified through faith in His blood."*

The letter F still signifies, we presume, that the first step is to be taken in Faith. If religion be eliminated as no part of Freemasonry, what is this Faith? Will anyone venture to assert that Freemasonry ever taught that Faith could exist without religion? Bro. Kenneth Mackenzie says Freemasonry must be viewed as a "purely social institution." It may be that this is all it will be before long, but Faith in such an institution, as a means of ascending to heaven and attaining salvation, partakes of the ridiculous. Freemasons have very generally been accused of believing more than is good for them, will they further justify the accusation in this instance. The position occupied by the innovator who rejects religion and yet retains faith is too absurd to require further exemplification.

In some plates of Masonic emblems the Master's column will be found to carry a three-branched candlestick; the candles on either side are lighted, the centre one is covered with the pentalpha, which is irradiated. We possess one which has this emblem; at the foot of the engraving there is the Christian cross. The pentalpha is of course an exceedingly common sign in many

* "Illustrations of Masonry," by J. Cole (dedicated to His Royal Highness, George Prince of Wales), London, 1801.

countries, and was used as an emblem ages before the birth of Christ. In Christian countries, however, its significance has long been exclusively Christian. The points of the star refer to the five wounds of Christ. The pentalpha combined with the circle is the emblem of the God-Man. Such a symbol placed over the light which represents one of the persons in a Masonic trinity can only bear a Christian interpretation.

It may be consistent with Masonic progress that this symbol should disappear, we would, however, point out that to be thorough the Universalist must thereafter remove one of the sides of our principal triangle, he must erase the figure 3, and otherwise play havoc with triads. Is he prepared to do all this?

The removal of the Cross from our symbols need occasion no surprise when it is remembered that one of our Grand Masters similarly gave up using the figure of a fish which, it was feared, being an emblem of Christ, would prevent Jews from joining English Lodges.* Margoliouth says " In former days the Grand Master of our Order used to wear a silver fish on his person ; but it is to be regretted that, among the many innovations which have of late been introduced into the Society to conciliate the prejudices of some who cannot consistently be members of it, this beautiful emblem has disappeared."† Margoliouth clearly saw that there was a certain inconsistency in non-Christians belonging to a Christian system.

---

* The writer is unable to state *where* he saw it, but he did once see on a Masonic chart the two bisecting segments of circles, known in symbolism as the "vesica piscis," with two parallel lines, one on either side. He neglected to make a note at the time, and would be obliged if anyone who knows of this symbol having been used, would send him information regarding it.

† "Vestige of General Freemasonry." The following paragraph from Dr. Hook's Church Dictionary throws more light on the subject of the above:—"Piscis, Pisculi, and Vesica Piscis.—The fish is an hieroglyphic of Jesus Christ, very common in the remains of Christian art, both primitive and mediæval. The origin of it is as follows : From the name and title of our Blessed Lord, ' Jesus Christ, the Son of God,

Whether brethren will be convinced of the attempted elimination of Christianity from Freemasonry by the foregoing, we do not know—the current reading of a symbol they know very well should carry conviction. The English Cyclopædist states that the Blazing Star is an emblem of Divine Providence, the American says that the Blazing Star constitutes one of the ornaments of the Lodge. Formerly it was said to be " commemorative of the star which appeared to guide the wise men of the East to the place of our Saviour's nativity. But as this allusion, however beautiful, interferes with the universal character of Masonry, it is now generally omitted, and the Blazing Star is said to be an emblem of Divine Providence. In the English Ritual it is emblematical of Prudence."*

In the Lecture on the Tracing Board the rungs of Jacob's ladder, already alluded to, are described as " Faith . . . . Hope in salvation . . . ., &c." Now salvation must be FORCED to convey a very different meaning from that usually attributed to it, if it be not the Christian's salvation. This is one of those unnoticed relics of early Freemasonry which has up to the present escaped the reformer's hands. And once more——

---

the Saviour,' the early Christians, taking the first letter of each word (in Greek) formed the name ΙΧΘΥΣ *Piscis*, a fish. From this name of our Blessed Lord, Christians also came to be called *Pisiculi*, fishes, with reference to their regeneration in the water of baptism. . . . Thus Tertullian, speaking of Christians, says, ' For ever after our Lord and Saviour, our ΙΧΘΥΣ, are also fishes, and born in the water, nor are we otherwise saved than by remaining in the water.' The *Vesica Piscis*, which is in the figure of an oval, generally pointed at either end, and which is much used as the form of the seals of religious houses, and to inclose figures of Jesus Christ, or of the saints also, has its rise from this name of our Blessed Lord. Clement, of Alexandria, in writing of the ornaments which a Christian may consistently wear, mentions the fish as a proper device for a ring, and says that it may serve to remind the Christian of the origin of his spiritual life. Fishes are found very commonly amongst Saints' emblems. Husenbeth, in his celebrated work, gives many instances. Its more general application, however, was as a symbol of the second person in the Christian Trinity. See ' Twining's Symbols,' &c."

* " Mackey's Lexicon of Freemasonry."

" This ladder rests on the Volume of the Sacred Law, because by the doctrines contained in that Holy Book, we are taught to believe in the wise dispensations of Divine Providence, which belief strengthens our Faith, and enables us to ascend the first step, this Faith naturally creates in us a Hope of becoming partakers of some of the blessed promises therein contained." Will this apply to all sacred books of all religions; will it even apply to the Old Testament? We repeat, there is much to be done yet before Freemasonry is de-Christianised. Or again we quote, "The Volume of the Sacred Law is derived from God to man in general, because the Almighty has been pleased to reveal more of his Divine will in that Holy Book than he has by any other means." Imagine, for one moment, the hideous mockery of a Christian instructor or W.M. addressing these words to a Mahommedan initiate, alluding all the time to the Koran. If, indeed, he directly alluded to the Bible he would know that the candidate could not fail to mentally dissent from him; while if the remarks were ostensibly applied to the Koran, the initiate would at once recognise that the W.M. was a disbeliever in his own solemn assertion.

But it is not alone in the English Lectures that we find an avowal of the intimate connection that was intended to exist between Freemasonry and Christianity. In a series of Lectures and Charges translated from the French by Bro. John Yarker, we see what was formerly taught even in France before Atheism was there considered to be Masonic.

These Lectures attribute to Masonry an early theoretical history which would not be popularly received in England now; we attach no importance to it, our only concern is to show *what* was taught with reference to religion. We read " Christianity came and enlarged the circle of initiation, it extended to all men the benefits and the moral parts of the Mysteries." The Lecture

then goes on to show how the Mysteries alluded to developed into Freemasonry under Christian influence.

In a Lecture on Masonic principles we have as follows—"Masonry, then, was the system which our Sovereign Master chose as the means to preserve benevolence and learning upon earth, and though we may see some fail in their duty and defame our noble institution by their wickedness and folly, do we not know that on earth nothing is perfect, and that virtue even is subject to abuse? Let us remark, however, that when these abuses multiplied, and everything seemed a prey to evil, God drew from the treasure of his inexhaustible love, his most priceless gift. Jesus appeared—that sublime Regenerator, that supreme and incomprehensible Being, that glorious Light shining between the past and future. Masonry not only buckled on the sword and shield for the defence of society and religion, but furnished with the square and compasses," &c., &c.

Over and over again do these Lectures show us that Masonic teaching in France was once entirely Christian. They state that it is owing to Christian progress we are able to partially raise the veil of Masonry without tearing it away entirely. Towards the conclusion of one Lecture there is stronger language addressed to the Masonic detractor than we should ourselves care to use—we quote it as showing that French Masonic Lecturers of old had no fear in expressing their belief in the scope of Freemasonry. "So much may be permitted in answer to rash people, who, scarcely upon the threshold of the Masonic Temple, are persuaded that everything is in the exterior symbols that strike the eye, and exclaim in disdain—'We have looked into the depths of Masonic science, and have found it a void.' Oh! rash fools, you have only lifted the first veil of the Temple of Isis. To you the oracle of the Temple of Apollo remains silent. Go! blaspheme not that of which you are ignorant."

CHAPTER V.

The Ritual.

SOME objection may be taken to our separating the Ritual from the Lectures, and placing these first, when considering Masonic principles as displayed in Lodge teaching. The division is of no serious importance, the Lectures are a species of commentary, more or less authoritative, on the Ritual—and their precise wording has never been considered so rigidly necessary as verbal exactitude in delivering the Ritual of the Degrees. Our former Grand Master, the Duke of Sussex, himself gave expression to this view. We have a right then in dealing with the Ritual, which we have not when considering the Lectures, to attach the highest significance to the precise language employed. We should not hold ourselves justified in deeming of supreme importance a mere word in the Lectures, whereas we maintain that it is justifiable to weigh every word of the Ritual in the nicest balance attainable. We are aware of the doubts and questions which may be raised from the existence of several Rituals, and will accordingly attempt to confine our arguments to points regarding which dispute can hardly arise.

Holding the belief that there has been a wanton disregard of propriety, if not a criminal contempt for truth and honesty, in the publication of alleged Rituals by individual brethren, we are ourselves compelled to speak somewhat enigmatically in this chapter, as we are barred from stating, with anything approaching distinctness, what are the exact words of our Rituals.

We trust, nevertheless, that our quotations will be intelligible to brethren without our resorting to such compromising precision. In passing, we may remark that we are of the number who believe, with all respect, that the Grand Lodge might, at the present time, well consider the advisability of issuing some form of ritual, or appoint somebody to carry out this duty. The want of such a guide has given an opening for misconduct on the part of unscrupulous brethren.

The Ritual of Freemasonry comprises the details of the ceremony of reception in the various Degrees, together with the primary exoteric display and the primary esoteric explanation, of the symbolism of the Order. In these explanations sufficient information is supposed to be afforded the Brother to enable him to continue the esoteric teaching on the lines thus laid down. The definition of Freemasonry itself, as given in the ritual is, that it is a *peculiar system* of morality which is veiled in allegory and illustrated by symbols. The early manner in which working Masons emblemised the tools of their handicraft is preserved in the Ritual. There can be little doubt that it was this peculiar symbolism which first induced non-Operative Brethren to join the Society, and it is easily comprehensible that a body of artisans would be flattered by their quaint conceits being deemed worthy of attention, and be quite willing to throw open their doors, wherever it was possible to do so without violating any principle.

A similar symbolism is familiar to any person who has resided long in the East, and who has made himself acquainted with the habits of the people. We have no intention of raising fanciful theories regarding the Oriental origin of any of our ceremonies, but we cannot but express surprise that Eastern customs have not received more Masonic attention. We believe they explain to some extent the avidity with which natives of India grasp the symbolism based on the working tools

of Freemasonry; they are probably perfectly unconscious why the symbology appeals to them—it is the counterpart of their daily life. An exceedingly common sight is to see a native groom touch the hoof of the horse in his charge before commencing his daily work. Similarly, a carpenter will, as a first duty, touch and salute his tools, or some one of them, with an evident respect (his salute is in the ordinary Eastern manner) before he begins his work. Western culture is perhaps unable to enter into the spirit of symbolism which induces the Eastern mind to thus deal with material things. Not far removed from this custom is that of the Mahommedan when undertaking any new enterprise. Even an ordinary tailor will say "Bismillah" before he puts a stitch into a garment. There are so many brethren in India who are more fitted to deal with this subject than ourselves, that we merely note it in passing; but that much of our emblemogy was usual amongst the Chinese at least as long ago as the time of Confucius, the following extract will show—

"What a man dislikes in his superiors, let him not display in the treatment of his inferiors; what he dislikes in inferiors, let him not display in the service of his superiors; what he dislikes in those who are before him, let him not therewith precede those who are behind him; what he dislikes in those who are behind him, let him not therewith follow those who are before him; what he dislikes to receive on the right let him not bestow on the left; what he dislikes to receive on the left, let him not bestow on the right. This is what is called the principle with which, *as with a measuring square,* to regulate one's conduct."*

The tools, with which an ordinary mason would prepare stones for a material building, are in Freemasonry used to illustrate that high morality which should be exercised by the speculative Mason in preparing his

---

* The Great Learning, p. 34. Legge's Chinese Classics, Vol. i.

mind as a temple fitted for the reception of divine truth. Whilst one tool is to be considered as denoting the incisive force of education, another represents conscience, and so on. There can be little doubt this symbolism is exceedingly ancient. The early adoption of the Bible as a guide in a system which is steeped in allegory, would point to the source whence the early Freemasons derived their metaphors, even if we had no other means of forming an opinion. We have however in so many emblems direct references to the Bible, that it is not possible to deny that ours is a purely biblical symbology. The temple the Mason is to erect should be built as was Solomon's, viz., to the glory of God. And to illustrate the duty enjoined on us to allow none but men of pure morals to share our labours, we are reminded that the Almighty refused to allow David to commence the work (afterwards undertaken by Solomon), for well known reasons. As David was not allowed to build the Temple so should we refuse to allow any men, whose conduct must of necessity be displeasing to God, to join in the work of Masonry.

At what period the Bible was adopted in English Masonry as the Great Light we do not know, but we do know that it was considered a necessary part of Lodge furniture prior to the erection of the Grand Lodge. The formation of the Grand Lodge did not in any way cancel any principle on which we insist. This Body did not indeed stipulate for attendance at Holy Church as a necessary act of obedience, but in the first Constitutions which it issued, the Christian catholicity of Freemasonry was expressed.

There is less reason to suppose that the Ritual has been much changed than there is regarding the Lectures, although the latter always seem to point to very much the same details, however much the interpretation of these details varies. Evidence dating prior

H

to the middle of the last century indicates that in many important particulars our ceremonies, which are based on Ritual, are at this day in remarkable accord with old Lodge working. The student cannot but be struck with the identity of ceremony, showing that the changes which have taken place are only in the esoteric part of Masonry, the exoteric part being unaltered in all essentials. It is with this fact before us that we attach great importance to the teaching of the last century. Finding, therefore, that nearly every writer of that time insisted that Freemasonry and Christianity were almost identical we can but apply an esoteric Christian meaning to the allegory of the Ritual. We are unable to see that any modern succession ever repudiated ancient principles; on the contrary, all unite in asserting that ancient Masonry, whatever it was, was preserved. Of the Christianity of Masonry prior to 1717 there has never been any doubt. The views which writers of the last century took of the Ritual will be found in another chapter, our own are admittedly of the same complexion.

The Masonic Ritual is consistent with what we have already stated. At the first introduction of the candidate we find that his morality has been a primary Masonic qualification, but this alone has not been deemed a sufficient voucher. Before an atom of Masonic information is vouchsafed to him, assurance has to be given that his religious conceptions are of such a nature as will enable him to appreciate Masonic teaching. It has been well said that a Christian must first be a Theist, so says Masonry regarding its candidates. A Deist believes in a God, it is true, but he does not believe we possess any knowledge of God's attributes, whereas the first declaration required from a Masonic candidate is that he believes in the efficacy of prayer to God. This primary condition is worthy of notice, for in it lies the essence of Theism. The Masonic requirement is emphatically that the candidate shall believe that God

will hear and answer prayer, which necessarily involves some conception of God, or of his attributes. A Freemason is thus, perforce, in the first instance a Theist.

This is the chief condition, should it appear that the candidate is unable to comply with it, he cannot advance; in such case provision has been made that he shall leave the Lodge without in any way becoming acquainted with even the method of conducting Lodge proceedings.

We next come to a supposition, on which much hangs. It is part of our symbolism to assume that the candidate is in a state of mental darkness, but desirous of receiving light, especially Masonic light. The first part of the First Degree is an allegory of this. We care not whether he be a Christian, a Mahommedan, or a Hindoo; it is nothing to us. We have a candidate seeking for light, we believe we possess it, and it is part of the Masonic system that we should impart it to all such as we deem worthy to receive it. No matter how gross his conception of the Deity may be, if there exist, in the candidate, a trust in God such as we have described, we are bound to proceed with our instruction and attempt at enlightenment. The initiate having expressed a wish for Masonic light it is then for the first time intimated to him that the Light of English Masonry is the English Bible. It is described as the Volume of the Sacred Law.

We now draw attention to some expressions which have never been varied to any extent in English Ritual. It is taught that the Sacred Writings are to rule and govern our faith. There is no ambiguity in the exact words of the Ritual, with which every brother must be familiar. The faith of an English Freemason should be ruled by the Bible. That is why the Sacred Volume is in his Lodge, it is to him God's law. It contains the code which is to govern his faith and action.

The Ritual states, in some brief words, which are not to be mistaken however wilfully the dissentient might

H 2

wish to misconstrue them, that it (the Bible) is the unerring standard of truth and justice, and that a Mason should regulate his actions by the divine precepts contained therein. There is no use made of the indefinite article in the Ritual—we are not left to believe that the Bible is *an* unerring standard, although that would be pretty plain ; we are told it is *the* unerring standard.

This is not all. The Ritual proceeds to give reasons *why* the Mason is to accept it as his authority through life, by stating that the Almighty has been pleased to reveal *more of his Divine word and will in that Holy Book than by any other means.* Now the height of absurdity would be reached if it were insisted on that this Ritual was ever meant to apply where *several* sacred volumes were under consideration. If it is Masonic, as we ourselves believe it to be, to try to make men earnest by living up to their religious belief, no matter what that belief may be, how could such an end be attained by the misuse of this Ritual, or by interpreting it in any sense save in that conveyed by the strict words we have employed ?

It is not an altogether insignificant circumstance that the Mark Degree which now flourishes as a side or independent Degree, was once, or some portion of it was once, part of the original Fellow Craft Degree. It is not now recognised by the Craft proper in England, but it is the Fourth Degree in American Freemasonry, coming between the Third and the Royal Arch. There is some doubt as to what portion of the Mark Degree was used in the Second, but it is tolerably certain that the Christian allusion to "the stone rejected by the builders becoming the head-stone of the corner," was used in Craft Masonry.*

---

* We are aware that our contention of the former connection between the Mark and Second Degrees is not admitted by all Masonic Students. This argument is therefore one of those to which we have already alluded, as subject to rejection without materially diminishing the mass of evidence on which we rely.

Another noticeable circumstance is that the Grand Lodge of All England, held at York, recognised five Degrees in 1779. These were

1st. The Apprentice Degree.
2nd. The Fellow Craft Degree.
3rd. The Master Mason's Degree.
4th. The Royal Arch.
5th. The Knight Templar Degree.*

The full significance of this arrangement of the Degrees will be evident to every Christian Freemason.

We would now draw the attention of those brethren who hold that Freemasonry has no religious import, to certain references in the Ritual. The first working tool with which the Entered Apprentice is presented is, amongst other uses, to mark that portion of time which should be passed in prayer to Almighty God; we fear that the lapse of time has made some Masons forget this, or they could hardly argue or assert that Freemasonry has no religious significance. The second working tool, in a similar manner, is so to be used that our words and actions may ascend unpolluted to the Throne of Grace. Has not this been forgotten? Passing to the Second Degree, the tools there presented to the brother are to be so applied, symbolically, that the candidate may hope to ascend to those immortal mansions whence all goodness emanates.

In the Third Degree we are reminded of the straight and undeviating line of conduct laid down for our pursuit in the Volume of the Sacred Law. Is any Mason satisfactorily assured that in every volume in this world, esteemed as sacred by some section or other of the community, there is a straight and undeviating line of conduct laid down? We do not ask, has some one or other asserted that this is the case? but we ask the

---

* See quotation from Minute Book, Hughan's "Origin of the English Rite," p. 68.

brethren who use this formula, do they possess any
knowledge which carries with it the required conviction?
The two tools, the last, which are next presented to the
brother are to remind us of God's unerring and impartial
justice. We here admit that as He has defined in the
Bible certain limits of good and evil, we shall be rightly
punished if we disregard His divine commands. What
we have stated must be familiar to every Mason, and
it is impossible to apply this teaching to all sacred
volumes, or to all that are so esteemed ; the application
can only be to the Bible.

There is one circumstance to which we think sufficient attention has not been paid, and which supports
our arguments used in other places. This is the great
difference in the obligations of performance expected
from the Fellow-Craft as compared with the Apprentice
Freemason. We find Preston and Emulation working
agree regarding this.

After his initiation the neophyte is *recommended* to
seriously contemplate the Volume of the Sacred Law, he
is *charged* to consider it the unerring standard of truth
and justice, and to regulate his actions by the divine
precepts it contains. This point is of the highest
importance in considering what are the duties of a
brother, who is not a Christian at the time of his
initiation. The Ritual makes it perfectly clear that
neither at, nor after, his initiation is the brother obliged
to support principles of which he was, previously thereto,
ignorant. He is, in effect merely charged, recommended
to be a Christian, for the words used can only refer to
the Christian's Bible.

It is obvious that after their disclosure he might dis-
approve of those principles and decline to conform to
them without prejudice to his status as an Apprentice,
but the position is changed when the Second Degree
is taken. In taking this Degree a distinct approval of
the principles of the First is given. To make sure of

this a preliminary and solemn engagement is exacted that the principles inculcated in the First Degree, which, as we have shown include Christianity, will be maintained. In the Charge after Passing the Craftsman is told that he is bound to perform certain duties, and that in his *new* character it is expected that he will conform to the principles of the Order. The language used by Preston in his book a hundred years ago and that used in the Ritual at the present day are alike.* He is no longer *recommended* or *enjoined* (charged) to be a Christian, but in future, it is, in conformity with his solemn obligation, *expected* of him. It is thus emphasized that a knowledge of principles is all that an *Apprentice* is expected to preserve, *but that a Fellow Craft is bound to maintain those principles.*

Our contention therefore is, that no matter what the position of the brother was before he took the Second Degree, however little he agreed to Masonic teaching whilst he remained only an Entered Apprentice, when he has once given his formal assent to the principles of the First Degree before taking the Second, he is no longer free to accept or reject any one of the principles of the Order. One of these principles in English Masonry relates to the Bible, and we assert without the least fear of adverse authority, that no Fellow Craft Mason can reject the Bible and be true to his obligation. That he has not taken this into consideration is very probable, indeed it must be so when we find that after, as before initiation, some decline to accept the Bible as the guide of their life. Their requiring any other volume for the purpose of obligation is proof that they still retain their old faith in their former guide.

This should have been foreseen if Freemasonry was to have an Universal application; it certainly was not. A Ritual which is thus anomalously improper for

* See Preston's "Illustrations," p. 59; also Emulation working, Charge after Passing.

Universality continues to be used, and it must sooner or later work confusion.

The expression of belief, required in the First Degree, enables us to embrace as brethren, members of many of the principal religions of the world. To preserve our secrets we insist on a promise of secresy. We consider that, to be binding, this obligation should be on that book which the candidate believes to be divinely inspired. This is the only use for any book except the Bible in a Lodge of English Freemasons. A mistaken view of this has already led to error. We properly open our doors to any man who believes that there is a God who will hear and answer prayer, without reference to whatever other conceptions he may cherish. It is Masonic teaching that even a man with this initial belief is yet in a state of darkness. The glimmer of light he possesses is, according to Masonic teaching, of no avail, for long after he has acknowledged this initial belief he is presumed to be in darkness. He is supposed to enter Freemasonry with a desire to find light and, by a ceremony familiar to all Masons, light is given. This light is not represented as afforded by the Koran—the Grunth—or the Shasters, but by the Bible. We have nothing to do with the element of absurdity which surrounds this matter, by being treated in Lodge as *a secret* whilst it is published in every Lexicon of Freemasonry in England and America; we only insist that we have correctly described a Ritualistic ceremony. The Ritual does not offer any theory by which a brother, who is not a Christian, could at once apply a symbolical meaning to the Bible and thereafter consider it simply as an emblem of some other volume,—neither does any decision of Grand Lodge with which we are acquainted. It is unquestionably open to the brother to refuse to receive the Bible as his Great Light in Masonry, or in any other sense. He may have the utmost contempt for its teachings and yet there is no known way of entirely

cancelling his connection with Masonry. Neither do we desire to do so, if he be a just and God-fearing man : he remains our dear brother in Masonry. He may, in short, by choice remain in darkness, Masonry can only show him the light, it has no power to compel him to accept it. But it must be remembered that this is only in the primary stage. Before Freemasonry can be further disclosed an assent to principles is demanded. This is too often lost sight of. It is impossible for any man, no matter what his former belief may have been, to become a Fellow Craft Mason in English Masonry, and refuse to accept both the Old and the New Testaments. The great principle taught has to be accepted in the Second Degree. We do not assert that this entails the adoption of any specific form of Christian belief. We do not wander beyond the exact length we are entitled to go—which is, that a Fellow Craft Mason must accept the Bible as the guide of his life or he has not done that which he has solemnly promised to do.

The more the Rituals of the Four Degrees in Masonry are studied, the more will it be evident that if the end of Masonry were merely to proclaim the unity of the Godhead, three of the Degrees are superfluous. If the end were (what we unhesitatingly assert is only the beginning) merely to express a belief in one God— then nothing more than the First Degree is required. The succeeding Degrees do not in any way further exemplify unity *per se,*—this is overlooked by the Universalist. The Degrees after the First introduce matter which establishes that Masonic belief goes further. If we are not to proceed beyond mere unity, why is the Ritual so careful to display the doctrine of the Trinity ? We are not ignorant that Triad faiths are exceedingly common. We admit it might be possible to establish, that a belief in some kind of a Trinity is as widely spread as any conviction of the Unity of God. The Hindoo would at once oblige us in this

respect and satisfy enquiry by producing a Trinity, but no one can seriously argue that our system was founded with any such idea of Universality: if not, then what interpretation is bound up with our Triads, which are admittedly but mere symbols?

Have any of our readers ever thought out this matter of the ever recurring Triads in our Ritual? In the Library of the Quatuor Coronati Lodge, London, No. 2076, is a MS. book,—original and unique,—designed and compiled by Bro. C. E. Ferry, a member of the Correspondence Circle or Literary Masonic Society attached to that Lodge. It is called "The Triad," and presents us with no less than 78 Triads selected from our Ritual. The collection is still obviously incomplete, and the author states that motives of prudence caused him to omit some. Surely only the partial blindness of familiarity can prevent us seeing the significance of this pregnant fact!

We are not here raising any theory as to Hiram being a type of Christ. If any other than the English Constitution can receive Hiram as typifying some one else, well and good, it is nothing to us. If another Constitution can differently apply all the symbols which, when introduced into our system, were intended to have a Christian significance, so be it; but any applicability which may be discovered concerns us not. If it really be the case that, when our Society was formulated, by some happy chance, all its esoteric teaching regarding matters relating to religion was available by all religions, then Freemasonry must have a right to lay claim to higher consideration than any Mason, in his very wildest dreams, has ever as yet vaguely imagined. Nothing short of the inspiration of Omniscience could afore-thought produce such a miraculous result.

The manner in which the high Degrees in Masonry, which are admittedly Christian, came into existence, we think somewhat bears out our views. We believe that,

as the genuine principles of Masonry began to suffer by ideas of Universality, the system was seen to have no finality, or that it would have none with the removal of the Christian element. It could then only be unsatisfying and incomplete. There was immediately a reason for high Degrees—to complete the structure—which did not previously exist. The high Degrees are said to have "crept in" at a time of Masonic degeneracy. They could not have crept in unless there was some room for them. Now we are told that the reason why the Craft does not recognise the high Degrees is, because the latter are Christian. We are of opinion that this theory could be fully supported by argument, for the present we will merely draw attention to the strong grounds there are for surmising that the Royal Arch Degree was originally part of the Master Mason's Degree.

A reference to Bro. Hughan's "Origin of the English Rite of Freemasonry," p. 52, will be instructive. He there quotes from Bro. Whytehead (of York), Dr. Mackey, Dr. Oliver, and the late lamented Bro. Woodford, none of them mean authorities, and some of the very first rank, and all agree in the opinion, for which they give their reasons, that the Royal Arch Degree is a shred torn from the cloak of the Master Mason's. Then we have the fact that in a Ritual of 1730 the Third Degree contains an allusion to the word "which was once lost and is now found."* We are bound to confess that that excellent authority, Bro. Hughan, does not himself hold these views, although he goes some short way with us. He says† "We favour the theory that a *word* was placed in the 'Royal Arch' *prominently*, which was previously given in the *Sections* [*i.e.*, Lectures] of the Third Degree, and known 'as the ancient word of a Master Mason.' We understand it is still so communicated in some Master Masons' Lodges

---

* "Origin of the English Rite," p. 55.   † *Ibid*, p. 61.

on the Continent, and we know that it is to be found on old Tracing Boards of early last century." Bro. Hughan therefore admits that some part of the present Royal Arch Degree formed a part of the Master Mason's, and considering the importance attached by Masons to words under certain circumstances, our Brother's admission is of some consequence to us.

But whether the Royal Arch Degree ever was, or was not, identical with, it is in reality now part of, the Master Mason's Degree, the complement thereof, and can hardly possess Masonic significance apart from it. We will as briefly as possible enumerate the Christian references in it.

In the course of the ceremony a Redeemer is specially mentioned.* Portions of the Scriptures are read at various stages. The Lord God of Israel is referred to, thus excluding all but Jews, Mahommedans, or Christians. At one time allusion was made to the prediction that the sceptre should not depart from Judah, nor a law giver from beneath his feet until Shiloh come. This is now usually omitted.

In a Ritual before us of the first half of this century, occurs the opening verse of the gospel according to St. John—"In the beginning was the Word, and the Word was with God, and the Word was God." Whatever may be the present meaning attributed to the *Word*, there can be very little doubt, after this, what it used to be.

The Royal Arch Degree is the capestone of Craft Masonry. The discovery of the long lost word, or knowledge of God, is its subject, and its relation to its predecessors is briefly as follows—

Throughout the Ritual of the preceding Degrees one idea is ever brought prominently forward, which is, that by a course of study, by earnest and arduous search, by a pure and moral life, a fit temple can be prepared for

---

* Metropolitan Working R.A.

the reception of the knowledge, or word, of God. The ultimate discovery and acquirement of this word is the subject of the Royal Arch Degree and the crowning or completion of the ideal Masonic edifice.

The actual characters which are feigned to be discovered, and which are supposed to form an ineffable name, are, like all else in Masonry, symbolical. The characters and the name they form are in themselves of no value whatever, but symbolically they are of the greatest importance. The meaning of the name itself is of doubtful authenticity. One acknowledged authority writes—"The name of God must be taken in Freemasonry as symbolical of truth, and then the Search for it will be nothing else but the search after truth."*

The Ritual explains the allegory to a certain extent, stating that Father Lord, *Word* Lord and Spirit Lord are contained in it. To this explanation, none other than a Christian interpretation appears possible. But we know that a purely Jewish meaning has been attached to the discovered word. Whether, in a system which, it is generally admitted, leads up to a pure Christianity (if it does not typify Christian life itself?), there be not retrogression when a Jewish interpretation crowns the edifice, we leave others to decide. We are, however, justified in asserting that no system can be made *more universal*, than a Christian one, by adopting a Jewish interpretation. Christianity is at least more generally prevalent than its forerunner, Judaism, and possibly more acceptable to those who are at present of neither persuasion. Overlooking this very self-evident fact, Freemasons have been content to allow that to be variously expounded which should be carefully preserved as a Christian allegory. Accept a Jewish exposition and Universality must go to the winds. It is not our wish to say anything which could give the least offence to

---

* Mackey and Peck's Encyclo.

our Jewish Brethren, but, it is our duty to point out, that the most exclusive religion in the world is not likely to satisfy aspirations of Universality.

We trust it may not be imagined that we attach any serious importance to the particular word supposed to be discovered in the Royal Arch Degree. Our belief in the matter is, that for Masonic purposes it might just as well be any other word. It may, or may not be, capable of the interpretation attributed to the combinations formed from it; this is of no importance: its use is to convey an idea, and this idea is not solely and entirely the Unity of God.

An advance has been made in Masonic belief, and we now find Masonry teaching a more important doctrine than that which was required of the Candidate for the First Degree. Masonry here shows itself progressive. All Royal Arch Masons know that a certain explanation of the combinations which it is thought possible to form out of a single name, is given in this Degree, and that this explanation marks an advance on a mere doctrine of unity. The English words which are employed denote in the plainest manner that the primary Masonic belief has developed into something higher.

Admitting therefore, for argument, that the primary belief is universal, we have now to consider whether this supplementary doctrine is also capable of being universal?

It is conceivable, for instance, that there is nothing in the lower Degrees of Masonry which could not be, by the adoption of certain renderings, received by a Mahommedan, but we are unable to imagine how any doctrine which specifically advances beyond a precise recognition of the unity of the Godhead can be acceptable to him. Certainly he cannot acquiesce in any form of Trinitarian belief.

If the Royal Arch Degree taught a doctrine of divine duality, no one would care to assert that this

would obtain the concurrence, after clear explanation, of a Mahommedan. It requires no argument to show that the teaching could not be received, the ability to accept it would not exist. The Royal Arch Degree does not teach a doctrine of duality, but what it does teach is even more unacceptable to such a one than duality would be. Each Degree in Masonry is a part of the system, and if any Degree be liable to rejection, then the system is not Universally applicable.

The acquiescence of a Mahommedan in this Degree can only arise from not comprehending what is taught, for if every allusion to Christianity were ignored, there must yet remain in this Degree points which conflict with the Mahommedan faith.

It should be remembered, but it is sometimes forgotten, that there are several Degrees in Freemasonry, with peculiar secrets attached to each. Together they form one harmonious whole. These Degrees are only supposed to be conferred according— firstly, to merit, and, secondly, to ability. Every Mason is familiar with this old law, indicating that it was foreseen that some would not possess the ability to take successive Degrees. If there be in the religious belief of a brother, some main principle which conflicts with the teaching of a Degree, inability to proceed becomes self-evident. In order to advance in Masonry certain articles of faith are necessary, which are supplementary to those originally insisted on. If these are not possessed by the Brother he has not the requisite ability.

It therefore logically follows that it is an anomaly to confer a Degree in which the teaching is known to be contrary to the Candidate's religious belief. If he believes one thing, and the Degree teaches another, he does not possess the required Masonic ability to advance. The most complete admission of this logical principle distinguishes the First Degree in Masonry.

In the Royal Arch, as in the case of Craft Lodges, we think the name selected for the first chapter is not a little significant. It was " The Rock and Fountain Shiloh." We do not ourselves think that any but a Christian interpretation of this is possible.

The distinct manner in which the Triune character of the Deity is emphasised in the Royal Arch Degree is its most remarkable feature. Without any argument from us, most Masons will admit that the triple T is an emblem of salvation and eternal life. Brother Nash says with regard to the triangle, "the equilateral triangle viewed in the light of the doctrines of those who gave it currency as a divine symbol, represents the Great First Cause, the creator and container of all things, as one and indivisible, manifesting himself in an infinity of forms and attributes." * We thus have here a departure, or, more properly speaking, an advance, on the original belief in a purely monod God. We now have a recognition of a triune God. The Ritual of Metropolitan working recognises this as fully as do other Rituals. It is stated that the triple T denotes His triune essence. We have already shown that one of the persons, the second, in the Royal Arch Trinity is the Word—the Son.

In the Grand Lodge of England there is a roll of parchment dated " Anno Domini 1183." Brother Hughan says this " is evidently a mistake of the copyist, and most likely was intended to be A.D. 1583, as that is about the period when it was written." On the back is written, at some date later than that of the MS. itself—

> " In the beginning was the word
> And the word was with God
> And the word was God
> Whose sacred and universal law
> I will endeavour to observe
> > So help me God."

* Mackey.

" The opening of the Chapter is the business of the Three Principals, *who are severally three Masters, and conjointly only one;* and they, by a series of rites known to themselves alone, commenced this important duty at the original establishment of the Order by each repeating one of the three clauses in the first verse of the first Chapter of St. John, and then conjointly the whole verse. We ourselves who occupied all the offices in a Chapter before the Union, speak from experience when we affirm that such was the formula at that period (*i.e.* 1813), although the passage has been since expunged."*

Despite this exposition (which it never should have been necessary for us to give) we find teachers offering explanations that the word discovered was no more than the Ritual states, forgetting that the Ritual is admittedly merely allegorical wherever possible. The discovery thus resolves itself into the finding of a batch of seven letters forming a supposed name of God, which there is some reason to believe has no real significancy at all, beyond that, in its combinations, the Christianity of the Degree is evidenced. This mere word might for all illustrative purposes have just as well been any one of half a dozen other words. If no other teaching underlies the Degree than that a name to conjure with had been revealed, the Kabbala would furnish equally important words. The word " Temura," intimating that a transposition was desirable, would be more appropriate.

We have, in fact, with the Royal Arch Degree one of the greatest possible anomalies firmly established in the minds of some brethren, who, whilst perfectly ready to apply a symbolical meaning to everything else in Masonry, are prepared to treat the supposed recovery of the lost word as a veritable discovery of a name highly important in itself, but not symbolical in its nature. That this view is entertained in India we know.

---

* Oliver's " Masonic Jurisprudence," p. 380.

I

Neither do we see how, if no Christian interpretation is allowed to the word restored to mankind, any other than a Kabbalistic view can be entertained. With a Jewish exposition we have no concern—we have no desire to interfere with it; its operation can only be a Jewish one, and given a Royal Arch Chapter composed of Jews only, such a modification of our Ritual would be very appropriate.

Since writing the foregoing we have been kindly furnished, by a valued Parsee brother, with copies of the Rituals commonly used in Bombay, both in Lodges and Chapters.

In this Ritual of initiation, Christ is spoken of as " *our Saviour* " and the Christian parallels in the Fifth Section of the First Lecture are also referred to. This, whilst correct according to our views, is somewhat astonishing. That these references should be made in Lodges which place all sacred volumes on an equality is hardly consistent. With mixed feelings of pleasure and discontent we turned to the Ritual of the Royal Arch Degree, that which is the culmination of the previous Degrees. With a full recognition of Christianity in the lower Degrees, we could only expect to find that, in the complement, this principle would be enlarged upon. To our bewilderment, and positive dismay, we find a reversion to the earlier religion.

The Royal Arch Degree is thus described, in the Ritual before us, as being " in its strictest sense a Jewish Lodge, or at all events acceptable at all times to our Jewish brethren." This indeed is a pretty confusion. Here we have a Masonic system, or what purports to be some part of a system, recognising Jesus Christ as the Saviour of Mankind in its lower degrees, and, in its completion considering the " word," once again made manifest to mankind as some real or assumed Hebrew name of God ! Thus the perfection of a Christian system culminates in the adoption of Hebrew dogma

which rejects all the former belief! A long residence in India has certainly tended to make us think that a Mason is never properly consistent unless he indulges in a certain amount of inconsistency, but we admit being somewhat staggered with this last instance. We are aware that some brethren are sufficiently callous to pass over even such a confusion of thought, as that of which we have adduced evidence, without notice; but unless Freemasonry is to be classed as utter tomfoolery, it is time attention were drawn to Masonic principles.

In speaking of our ceremonies Hutchinson said, "Our lights are typical of the Holy Trinity."* This was at least Masonic teaching in 1775. Again in speaking of the columns at the entrance of a Lodge, and the promise that the house of David should be established for ever, Hutchinson said, "In commemoration of this great promise to the faithful, we ornament the entrance into our Lodges with these emblematical pillars; from our knowledge of the completion of that sacred sentence accomplished in the coming of our Redeemer."†

Referring to the Master Masons' Degree and Ritual, Hutchinson said "The great Father of all, commiserating the miseries of the world, sent his only Son, who was innocence itself, to teach the doctrine of salvation."‡ He goes on to say that "the devotees of the Jewish altar, had hid religion from those who sought her,"§ and that "Our Order is a positive contradistinction to the Judaic blindness and infidelity, and testifies our faith concerning the resurrection of the body.‖" Many more opinions could be given to the same purport from this old writer, who completely recognised the Ritual as a Christian one.

It is needless to state the obvious fact, already alluded to, that many writers have regarded H.A. as the

---

* Hutchinson's "Spirit of Masonry," 1st edition, 1775, p. 119.

† *Ibid*, p. 147.   ‡ *Ibid*, p. 159.   § *Ibid*, p. 160.   ‖ *Ibid*, p. 164.

I 2

type of Christ, but one Christian allusion still remains in our Ritual, closely connected with the Hiramic ceremony—we refer to the bright Star whose rising brings *peace* and *salvation* to the faithful and obedient of the Human Race.

It would be most interesting to hear our Preceptors and Univeralists attempt to expound this in any other than a purely Christian light. We commend the allusion to Ritual mongers and manglers as one urgently calling —from their point of view—for prompt excision.

Perhaps nothing more clearly shows the religious tenets of the Fraternity than the Prayers formerly and still in use.

As regards the earlier prayers, for such are in effect the invocations at the head of every one of the "old Charges" or MS. Constitutions, nothing can be plainer; they are Christian and Trinitarian. So many examples have been adduced in Chapter II. that we refrain from here quoting even one of them.

The authorised prayers of to-day in the various Degrees of the Craft are de-Christianised, for proof is extant that they were formerly Christian. But the mere fact of engaging in prayer at all, proves at least that the Craft is not, as maintained by some, a body totally unconnected with religion. Why, for instance, invoke " the continual dew of Thy blessing" "upon this convocation assembled in Thy Holy Name," unless the subsequent proceedings be of a religious import. To deny the religious nature of the consequent ceremony is to confess that God's Holy Name has been invoked for a trivial and worldly purpose, *i.e.*, " in vain"; a crime in the eye of Jew, Gentile, and Christian alike. In another prayer do we not thus address the Almighty ? " Vouchsafe thine aid, Almighty Father of the Universe, to this our present convention." If our purpose be not connected with religion, what right have we to appeal for *divine aid* in our undertakings.

That the " Ancients" retained the Christian character of their prayers is certain. The following is from the Ahiman Rezon, editions 1756 to 1801.* It is also to be found in many Masonic works of the last century, including the "Freemasons' Pocket Companion," Edinburgh, 1764 :—

PRAYER to be said at the opening of a *Lodge*, or making of a *Brother*.

Most Holy and Glorious LORD GOD, thou Great Architect of Heaven and Earth, who art the Giver of all good gifts and graces; and hast promised that when two or three are gathered together in thy Name, thou wilt be in the Midst of them; in thy Name we assemble and meet together. most humbly beseeching thee to bless us in all our Undertakings, to give us thy Holy Spirit, to enlighten our Minds with Wisdom and Understanding, that we may know, and serve thee aright, that all our Doings may tend to thy Glory, and the Salvation of our Souls.

And we beseech thee, O LORD GOD, to bless this our present Undertaking, and grant that this, OUR NEW BROTHER, may dedicate his Life to thy Service, and be a true and faithful BROTHER AMONG US; endue him with Divine Wisdom, that he may, with the Secrets of MASONRY, be able to unfold the Mysteries of Godliness and Christianity. } To be added when any Man is made.

This we humbly beg in the Name and for the sake of JESUS CHRIST our LORD and SAVIOUR.   AMEN.

We thus see that one of the two great branches of English Freemasonry preserved its Christianity up to the time of the Union and the proof is given in its authorised Constitutions. As regards the "Moderns" or original Grand Lodge, the proof is not so absolute, because the Constitutions contain no authorised prayers. The so-called exposures are full of Christian prayers, but our difficulty in this case is to estimate how much reliance may be placed on their trustworthiness. Take, for instance, the prayer at initiation, from Jachin and Boaz ". . . . . be with us, O Lord, as thou has promised, when two or three are gathered together in thy Name. . . . . Let Grace and Peace be multiplied unto him, through the knowledge of our Lord Jesus Christ . . . . . and grant that we may be

---

* And substantially the same to the last edition of 1813.

all united as one, through our Lord Jesus Christ, who liveth and reigneth for ever and ever.—Amen."

But publications only one degree removed from the official character of the Constitutions tell the same tale.

This is the conclusion of a Prayer in "The Pocket Companion and History of Free Masons," London, 1763

And we beseech thee, O Lord God, to bless this our present undertaking, and to grant that this our brother may dedicate his life to thy service, and be a true and faithful brother among us ; endue him with divine wisdom, that he may, with the secrets of Masonry, be able to unfold the mysteries of godliness and christianity.

This we humbly beg in the name, and for the sake of Jesus Christ, our Lord and Saviour.—Amen.

In London, perhaps, during the present generation, prayers have been purely Theistic ; not so in the provinces. Nay, not even without exceptions in London. The well-known Lodge of Israel, composed largely of Jews, offers up two graces before meals ; the first in Hebrew, and the second in English, "*for the Christian Brethren.*" In this Lodge, at least, neither of its component parts hides its light under a bushel.

In 1844 the Rev. Henry Grylls, A.M., Prov. Grand Chaplain for Cornwall, published "A Selection of Masonic Prayers for the use of the Craft." The introduction is very much in our favour. "The officiating Brethren having frequently experienced great inconvenience from not readily finding a prayer suited to the occasion for which they were met, the Editor has deemed expedient to issue from the Press for the convenience of the Craft, this little Volume, containing such a Selection of Prayers as are usually required at Masonic Meetings. This motive, we trust, will shield it from the severity of Criticism. He lays small claim to originality, *the Prayers being chiefly a Selection* from his Portfolio, which he had from time to time *collected from various sources,* since his Initiation into the Craft." We are therefore entitled to presume that these prayers were common to the Craft only 45 years ago, and thus arrive at the usage of the times, at least in some Lodges. Of the 33

prayers in the book, 22, or exactly two-thirds, are emphatically Christian. We will omit those before the Sermon at a Provincial Meeting, or on laying the foundation-stone of a new church,—although, on both these occasions, if a Jewish Brother happened to be a Lodge officer for the year, he would find it difficult to evade attendance,—and quote only from a prayer to be actually used in the Lodge room. Thus, on the consecration of a Lodge—"Shed abroad in them (the brethren) the effusion of *Thy Holy Spirit.*" The prayers at a Brother's funeral are all Christian, and it is not only conceivable that a non-Christian Mason might be present, but, possibly even, the service might be conducted over his mortal remains. The possibility of such a case never apparently presented itself to the Author.

The official Constitutions of the Grand Lodge of Ireland contain authorised prayers for various occasions. We quote from the latest edition, 1884. The prayers do not ALL absolutely mention the Redeemer's name, but many do. Thus, at the opening of a Lodge—". . . . . . unite us in the same unto our lives' end, through Jesus Christ our Lord.—Amen." At the initiation of a Candidate—" . . . . . and hast promised that when two or three are gathered together in thy Name." Now, inasmuch as this promise was made by Our Saviour, this prayer must be directly addressed to the Second Person of the Trinity. At passing—" . . . . . and that by the help of thy divine grace, we may one and all be guided into the way of everlasting life, through Jesus Christ our Lord.—Amen." At raising—" O Most High God . . . . . who hast built thy Church upon a sure foundation, Christ Jesus being the chief cornerstone, &c." The prayers which are not essentially Christian are identical with those under the English Jurisdiction. As these are undoubtedly the earlier, and can be traced back for a century or more with very slight variations, it would appear as if the Grand Lodge

of Ireland had gone out of its way to make a profession of Christianity.

The following prayers are culled from American usage of a very recent date—

"Let us, while in a state of existence, support with propriety the character of our profession, advert to the nature of our solemn ties, and pursue with assiduity the sacred tenets of our Order. Then, with becoming reverence, let us seek the favour of the Eternal God, through the merits of His Son our Saviour."*

"Though like our Brother, whose remains now lie before us, we shall soon be clothed in the habiliments of death, and deposited in the silent tomb, yet through the mediation of a divine and ascended Saviour, we may confidently hope that our souls will bloom in eternal spring."†

"May our souls, disengaged from their cumbrous dust, flourish and bloom in eternal day; and enjoy that rest which thou hast prepared for all good and faithful servants, in that spiritual house, not made with hands, eternal in the heavens, through the great Redeemer.—Amen."‡

We have lately examined a MS. book belonging to the Kelso Mason Lodge, dated 1818. It may be called an appendix to the Ritual, as it includes Forms to be observed at opening, at closing, at change of officers, and a list of toasts after the opening of the Lodge. These are divided into Masonic, General, Public, and Individual Toasts. At p. 15 we find the last of the Masonic Toasts, "As it is not the Masonry of Stones and Bricks that we profess, nor the Cement of Lime and Sand that we work with; May our Masonry always be the Moral Masonry of the Mind and our cement *Christian* love." The worthy old Lodge at Kelso evidently never contemplated the latest developments of Scottish Provincial Freemasonry in India.

---

* The Arcana, New York, 1854. Extract from "Funeral Service" for the use of Lodges. † *Idem.* ‡ *Idem.*

CHAPTER VI.

THE VOLUME OF THE SACRED LAW.*

AN institution which hides all its knowledge and method of conveying instruction under a somewhat complicated symbolism, is in some danger of undergoing change, from the different readings to which that symbolism may be subjected by the members of various religious tendencies who are received into it. The wonder is not perhaps so much that English Freemasonry has been greatly misunderstood in foreign lands, but rather that the misconceptions have not been greater. To introduce into India a symbol which has there always received a certain interpretation, with the intention that it shall in future receive another or Masonic signification, is playing with fire.

However correctly a Christian Mason may view such a symbol as the point within a circle, there is a distinct danger that it may suggest a very different meaning in India. This danger is intensified when Freemasonry claims that the fact of its symbols being found in many lands, furnishes distinct proof of the Universality of the system. For instance, any student of symbolism knows the various meanings which may be attached to the Hand. It may be, and possibly has been, an attraction to some of our Eastern brethren to find in Freemasonry emblems with which they are well acquainted, but it is not by any means certain that the brother, who has for perhaps thirty, or forty, years understood a symbol in one sense, will, at the dictation of his Masonic

---

* The Volume of the *Sacred* Law is by the Universalist treated as a volume of "moral" law only.

teacher, at once connect it with some other interpretation. However anxious he might be to adhere to Masonic tenets it would possibly be out of his power to wrench from his mind the, to him, older meaning. The result would probably be, and we believe has been, that the non-Christian brother quietly appropriates the type and becomes a firmer believer than ever in the Universality of Freemasonry, on the ground that the Craft apparently, by its symbolism, supports his own religious belief. This is why we say that there is a danger in our symbols, and that in the East they are liable to be read in a sense foreign to English Freemasonry. This we know has been the general fate of symbols in actual religions, even where they have escaped being eventually treated as possessing in themselves the virtues or qualities which they were only intended to typify. It will be sufficient to instance the Gothic and Heathen Yule-tide, or Winter solstice, festivities and orgies; which now, in a modified form, are part and parcel of our Christmas celebrations.

The Masonic expression "Volume of the Sacred Law" has, we believe, been thus misunderstood. From early times in the history of the present English Fraternity there is evidence that the Volume of the Sacred Law was to be the Bible in England, but that in other Jurisdictions, or in other countries, some other Volume might be esteemed the Volume containing God's law. We believe we are correct in stating that from this has arisen an idea that the Bible, the Volume of the Sacred Law under the English Constitution, is but a symbol in English Freemasonry, and that as such it may be treated as merely typifying or representing the Zend-Avesta to the Parsee, the Shasters to the Hindoo, or the Book of Doctrine and Covenants to the Mormon. From this it follows that a Hindoo can, with complacency, sit in Lodge, treating in his mind the Bible as merely representing a very different code of laws. It is not to be

denied that many most worthy brethren hold such a view, and believe that they thoroughly grasp the principles of Freemasonry whilst entertaining this belief.

That such a position must, sooner or later, prove fatal, can scarcely be disputed. The confusion of ideas is already complete : if not checked it must inevitably lead to a like confusion of the principles of the Order itself.

We have alluded to instances which prove that in India there are brethren who believe that they are acting Masonically, in refusing to recognise the Bible as containing more of God's word and will than any other Volume, even after they have taken all the three Craft Degrees. They so utterly ignore it as to declare that it would have no force with them, when taking the obligation of a Royal Arch Mason. They produce another Volume in the Chapter, and have been allowed to receive the O.B. on it ; thus establishing the fact that, although presumed to have acquired Masonic light under the English Constitution they are still, Masonically, in a state of darkness. The idea is thus spread that a brother is under no necessity whatever to accept the English Great Light : that there is nothing contrary to propriety in his continuing a member of an English Lodge, receiving promotion in it, and even taking the Master's chair, whilst nevertheless an unbeliever in that Lodge's Great Light. It must be evident that did the Eastern brother receive our Great Light he could no longer regard his own Sacred Volumes as containing more of God's Laws than any other book. He would perforce, by acknowledging the Bible as the guide of his life, and by regulating his actions in accordance with its laws, have to renounce at least some part of his former faith. There is no escape from the position that, either the English system must concede something and thus displace the Great Light, or the brother in question must modify his previous religious views.

It is a ridiculously unforeseen phase in Masonry to which we draw attention. The English brother may shut his eyes awhile to the fact that the Institution has members, who are some of its most generous supporters, but who do not accept the English Great Light, and who have no intention of so doing. At present they are content, as is shown in Bombay, to place all sacred volumes on a dead level; they are willing that a Masonic Lodge should be a Pantheon, in which any and every book that any brother esteems sacred shall be equally honoured. That the evil is attributable to Scottish Masonry seems certain. The English system has not yet been brought face to face with a body insisting that any and every volume esteemed sacred shall be raised to one level, the Scottish system *was* so confronted and at once succumbed, allowing its Great Light to lose lustre by the innovation. Masonry has indeed expanded when a Masonic jurisdiction supplies on demand, anything which anyone pleases as the Great Light of its system.

In the contention that no jurisdiction can have more than one Great Light, although it is not to be expected that all will have the same light, we have the complete support of Brother W. J. Hughan. He holds with us that nothing should ever be permitted to stand on terms of equality with the Bible in English Masonry. *To secure a satisfactory obligation* it is rightly conceded that any sacred volume should be permitted in the Lodge, but there the use of that sacred volume ceases, so far as English Masonry is concerned. We know that all cannot accept our Light in the way we would wish them to, but this affords no reason for abandoning it or treating it as one light amongst many, or as merely an abstract idea capable of any concrete interpretation which may appear most convenient at a given moment.

Because the Mahommedan considers that in his book there is more of God's Law than there is any other sacred volume, the *English* Constitution is not

consequently to permit the Bible to be supplanted by the Koran, neither can it concede thereto any "locus standi" whatever, although it is rightly used, when necessary, in the first instance only, for the purpose of obtaining a binding obligation.

If any other sacred volume were entitled to a place in an English Lodge, the Latter-day Saints would have the first claim to consideration. They express their belief with clearness in their 8th Article of Faith :— " We believe the Bible to be the Word of God, as far as it is translated correctly; we also believe the Book of Mormon to be the Word of God." Is any Lodge prepared to see "The Book of Mormon: an account written by the Hand of Mormon, upon Plates taken from the Plates of Nephi," placed side by side with the Bible? If not, then how can it consistently justify Scottish procedure in India? The Hindoo will not concede half such a position for the old Light of Masonry as the Mormon will—there is no sect which will so entirely concede equality for it, as will the believers in the revelations of God to the Prophet Joseph Smith. Probably there is no volume which would raise such a revolt in the minds of English brethren as that which we have named, yet it is honestly believed in by thousands of civilised and educated people. If the principles of Masonry are the ridiculous jumble of ideas, which the Universalist proclaims them to be, there can be no reason why the sacred volume of the Latter-day Saints should not have its duly accredited "Grand Bearer." It is futile trying to shirk the position— either our Volume of the Sacred Law, the Bible, is to be treated as THE Great Light of English Masonry, or it must be relegated to our museum of symbols.

The present Masonic Volume of the Sacred Law is alluded to in many old Masonic MSS. as " ye booke," " swearing on a booke " is also spoken of. We extract the following from Hughan's " Old Charges " with

reference to a MS. at York dated A.D. 1670 :—" It clearly indicates the nature of ye booke on which the apprentices were sworn to secrecy : the document is valuable on that account, because with only two or three exceptions, the various versions simply state that ' It is a great perill for a man to forsweare himselfe on *a* Booke,' whereas this MS. and other York MSS. declare *that* Book to be ye holy Scripture."

When the plea is raised that Freemasonry does not necessitate particular religious observances—for this is what is now often urged—we cannot refrain from asking how can the life of anybody be regulated by the Law contained in any volume esteemed sacred, without some religious observance ? It is true that the Rev. Theophilus Lindsey in 1779 argued that no religion was required by any Scriptural teaching, there is, however, no record that anyone, save himself, assented to this somewhat novel theory.

While entering a protest against placing several volumes variously esteemed in the East as sacred, on a level with the Holy Bible in English Freemasonry, it can hardly be irrelevant to quote Professor Sir Monier Williams' views as to the place they should respectively occupy in the Christian's mind. On the 3rd May last he said—" When I began investigating Hinduism and Buddhism, some well-meaning Christian friends expressed their surprise that I should waste my time by grubbing in the dirty gutters of Heathendom. Well, after a little examination, I found many beautiful gems glittering there—nay, I met with bright coruscations of true light flashing here and there amid the surrounding darkness. Now, fairness in fighting one's opponents is ingrained in every Englishman's nature, and as I prosecuted my researches into these non-Christian systems I began to foster a fancy that they had been unjustly treated. I began to observe and trace out curious coincidences and comparisons with our own Sacred Book

of the East. I began, in short, to be a believer in what is called the Evolution and Growth of Religious Thought. ' These imperfect systems,' I said to myself, ' are clearly steps in the development of man's religious instincts and aspirations. They are interesting efforts of the human mind struggling upwards towards Christianity. Nay, it is probable that they were all intended to lead up to the One True Religion, and that Christianity is, after all, merely the climax, the complement, the fulfilment of them all.'

" Now, there is unquestionably a delightful fascination about such a theory, and, what is more, there are really elements of truth in it. But I am glad of stating publicly that I am persuaded I was misled by its attractiveness, and that its main idea is quite erroneous. The charm and danger of it, I think, lie in its apparent liberality, breadth of view, and toleration. In the *Times* of last October 14 you will find recorded a remarkable conversation between a Lama priest and a Christian traveller, in the course of which the Lama says that, ' Christians describe their religion as the best of all religions ; whereas among the nine rules of conduct for the Buddhist there is one that directs him never either to think or to say that his own religion is the best, considering that sincere men of other religions are deeply attached to them.' Now to express sympathy with this kind of liberality is sure to win applause among a certain class of thinkers.

" We must not forget, too, that our Bible tells us that God has not left Himself without witness, and that in every nation he that feareth God and worketh righteousness is accepted with Him. Yet I contend, notwithstanding, that a limp, flabby, jelly-fish tolerance is utterly incompatible with the nerve, fibre, and backbone that ought to characterise a manly Christian. I maintain that a Christian's character ought to be exactly what the Christian's Bible intends it to be.

" Take that Sacred Book of ours ; handle reverently the whole volume ; search it through and through, from the first chapter to the last, and mark well the spirit that pervades the whole. You will find no limpness, no flabbiness, about its utterances. Even sceptics who dispute its Divinity are ready to admit that it is a thoroughly manly book. Vigour and manhood breathe in every page. It is downright and straightforward, bold and fearless, rigid and uncompromising . . . . If God be God, serve Him. If Baal be God, serve Him. We cannot serve both. We cannot love both. Only one Name is given among men whereby we may be saved. No other name, no other Saviour, more suited to India, to Persia, to China, to Arabia, is ever mentioned, is ever hinted at.

" What ! says the enthusiastic student of the science of religion, do you seriously mean to sweep away as so much worthless waste paper all these thirty stately volumes of Sacred Books of the East just published by the University of Oxford ? No—not at all—nothing of the kind. On the contrary, we welcome these books. We ask every missionary to study their contents, and thankfully lay hold of whatsoever things are true and of good report in them. But we warn him that there can be no greater mistake than to force these non-Christian bibles into conformity with some scientific theory of development, and then point to the Christian's Holy Bible as the crowning product of religious evolution. So far from this, these non-Christian bibles are all developments in the wrong direction. They all begin with some flashes of true light, and end in darkness. Pile them, if you will, on the left side of your study table ; but place your own Holy Bible on the right side —all by itself—all alone—and with a wide gap between.

" And now, with all deference to the able men I see around me, I crave permission to tell you why, or at least to give two good reasons, for venturing to

contravene, in so plain-spoken a manner, the favourite philosophy of the day. Listen to me, ye youthful students of the so-called Sacred Books of the East; search them through and through, and tell me, do they affirm of Vyasa, of Zoroaster, of Confucius, of Buddha, of Muhammad, what our Bible affirms of the Founder of Christianity—that He, a sinless Man, was made sin? Not merely that He is the Eradicator of Sin, but that He, the sinless Son of Man, was Himself made sin. Vyasa and the other founders of Hinduism enjoined severe penances, endless lustral washings, incessant purifications, infinite repetitions of prayers, painful pilgrimages, arduous ritual, and sacrificial observances, all with the one idea of getting rid of sin. All their books say so. But do they say that the very men who exhausted every invention for the eradication of sin were themselves sinless men made sin? Zoroaster, too, and Confucius, and Buddha, and Muhammad, one and all bade men strain every nerve to get rid of sin, or at least of the misery of sin; but do their sacred books say that they themselves were sinless men made sin? Understand me, I do not presume as a layman to interpret the apparently contradictory proposition put forth in our Bible that a sinless man was made sin. All I now contend for is that it stands alone; that it is wholly unparalleled; that it is not to be matched by the shade of a shadow of a similar declaration in any other book claiming to be the exponent of the doctrine of any other religion in the world.

"Once again, ye youthful students of the so-called Sacred Books of the East, search them through and through, and tell me, do they affirm of Vyasa, of Zoroaster, of Confucius, of Buddha, of Muhammad, what our Bible affirms of the Founder of Christianity— that He, a dead and buried Man, was made Life, not merely that He is the Giver of life, but that He, the dead and buried Man, is Life? 'I am the Life.'

K

' When Christ, who is our Life, shall appear.'   ' He that hath the Son hath Life.'   Let me remind you, too, that the blood is the Life, and that our Sacred Book adds this matchless, this unparalleled, this astounding assertion : ' Except ye eat the flesh of the Son of Man and drink his Blood, ye have no Life in you.'   Again, I say, I am not now presuming to interpret so marvellous, so stupendous a statement.   All I contend for is that it is absolutely unique, and I defy you to produce the shade of the shadow of a similar declaration in any other sacred book of the world.   And bear in mind that these two matchless, these two unparalleled, declarations are closely, are intimately, are indissolubly connected with the great central facts and doctrines of our religion —the Incarnation, the Crucifixion, the Resurrection, the Ascension of Christ.   Vyasa, Zoroaster, Confucius, Buddha, Muhammad, all are dead and buried ; and mark this, their bones have crumbled into dust, their flesh is dissolved, their bodies are extinct.   Even their followers admit this.   Christianity alone commemorates the passing in the heavens of its divine Founder, not merely in the spirit, but in the body, and ' with flesh, bones, and all things appertaining to the perfection of man's nature,' to be the eternal source of life to His people. Bear with me a moment longer.

" It requires some courage to appear intolerant—to appear unyielding—in these days of flabby compromise and milk and water concession; but I contend that the two unparalleled declarations quoted by me from our Holy Bible make a gulf between it and the so-called Sacred Books of the East which sever the one from the other utterly, hopelessly, and for ever—not a mere rift which may be easily closed up, not a mere rift across which the Christian and the non-Christian may shake hands and interchange similar ideas in regard to essential truths, but a veritable gulf which cannot be bridged over by any science of religious thought.   Yes,

a bridgeless chasm which no theory of Evolution can ever span.

"Go forth, then, ye missionaries, in your Master's name; go forth into all the world, and after studying all its false religions and philosophies, go forth and fearlessly proclaim to suffering humanity the plain, the unchangeable, the eternal facts of the Gospel—nay, I might almost say the stubborn, the unyielding, the inexorable facts of the Gospel. Dare to be downright with all the uncompromising courage of your own Bible, while with it your watchwords are love, joy, peace, reconciliation. Be fair, be charitable, be Christ-like; but let there be no mistake. Let it be made absolutely clear that Christianity cannot, must not, be watered down to suit the palate of either Hindu, Buddhist, or Muhammadan, and that whosoever wishes to pass from the false religion to the true can never hope to do so by the rickety planks of compromise, or by help of faltering hands held out by half-and-half Christians. He must leap the gulf in faith, and the living Christ will spread His everlasting arms beneath and land him safely on the Eternal Rock."

Making full allowance for Masonic presumption, we are still unable to believe, that Christian brethren who have had an average education, will presume to set up their views as to the value of foreign sacred volumes, in opposition to those of Prof. Monier Williams. There is no trace of any intention to equalise all sacred writings, in our earliest Masonic records, the habit was introduced when Freemasons knew nothing about sacred volumes other than their own, and even then without any authority whatever.

It is not a little remarkable that in Dr. Kloss's celebrated " Bibliographie der Freimaurerei " the " Zend Avesta " is the only foreign Volume of the Sacred Law which receives any notice whatever. It is found in his Chapter XXI., under the heading of *Antiquitäten*,

K 2

Mysterien Cultus. As M. Anquetil du Perron's is the
only French work quoted, and as there is nothing of
later date than 1796 referred to, it is scarcely probable
that Dr. Kloss understood the importance of the Zendavesta, or its real character. Zoroaster is referred to,
but Christ and Mahomet are omitted.

That the Bible had a very recognised position in the
last century is known to most Masonic students. In
the chapter wherein Preston refers to Omdit-ul-Omrah
having initiated his brother Omur-ul-Omrah into the
Craft, he gives a description of a Masonic procession
in Madras on the 7th October, 1787, held to celebrate
the close of a dissension. The Bible is alone mentioned
as having been carried.

Brother Inwood showed, in the last century, how
the Old Testament supplied Masonry with some of its
types and symbols, but that the New furnished the
morality. He states that in the earlier part of the
century, manuscript and, at times, printed copies of
many texts from the Bible, which Masonry had used for
some purpose or other, were freely distributed. Writing
in the present century, Dr. Oliver states he has two such
MSS., one, dated 1764, containing 150 texts with their
references, and the other, dated 1780, with nearly 100
texts, many of them different to those of the first MS.

In the account of the Grand Assembly of Freemasons held on St. John's Day, the 27th December, 1813,
for the Union of the two Grand Lodges of England, two
Bibles are specially mentioned as being carried. The
bearer of that for the " Ancient " Masons was the Grand
Chaplain ; that for the " Moderns " was carried by the
Deputy Grand Chaplain. During the ceremony the
two Grand Masters, *i.e.*, the Dukes of Kent and Sussex,
said " May the Great Architect of the Universe enable
us to uphold the grand edifice of Union, of which this
Ark of the Covenant is the Symbol, which shall contain
within it the instrument of our brotherly love, and bear

upon it the Holy Bible, Square, and Compasses, as the light of our faith and the rule of our works. May he dispose our hearts to make it perpetual."* We find it also recorded that the Bible was kept open during the whole of this ceremony.

At this celebration of the Union, the Royal Arch Degree was declared to be part of genuine Craft Masonry, and if there were ever any real doubt as to the Bible being the only Sacred Volume that English Masonry *could* recognise as its Great Light, this would settle the matter. In this Degree certain portions of the Scriptures have to be read; these are entirely from the Bible, on which the whole tradition of this as well as of the preceding Degrees is based. That the Bible alone is to be the English Mason's Sacred Volume is incontrovertibly established *by the remark* that the first words of the Sacred Volume which contains God's revealed will and word are " In the beginning God created the Heavens and the Earth." We surely need not remind *Christian* Masons that these words constitute the opening statement in our Bible, and although it may be well to recall this fact to those who are *not* Christians, it should be unnecessary, as they cannot find the passage elsewhere. So long as Royal Arch Masonry therefore remains the complement of Craft Masonry, the only book which can be recognised as the English Masons' Trestle-board is THE BIBLE. The Royal Arch Mason will remember that the words quoted are followed by others, announcing in unmistakeable language, the Masonic belief that the same volume contains God's revelation to mankind. There is no mention of any other revelation or of any other sacred volume—their title to consideration is barred by the statements to which we have referred.

Our argument that each jurisdiction can only recognise one light, may be fatal to the advancement of any

---

* Preston's " Illustrations," 14th edition, p. 369.

but Christians in Lodges which are Christian; this cannot be avoided. It is asserted that in some cases the Koran may be considered the Great Light of Masonry, in places for instance where the religion is mainly Mahommedan. This we do not dispute, but we would ask, how could a Christian pass beyond the First Degree in such a Lodge? It is obvious that when he was assured the Koran should be in future the guide of his life, &c., he would naturally refuse to maintain such a principle, and could not therefore be furthered in that Lodge. None the less he would be a properly initiated brother. The position of such an one would be precisely that which the Hindoo or the Parsee occupies in India in an English Lodge. Certain jurists have raised objections to the various Degrees being taken in any Lodge other that that which granted the First, but this is a rule which has perhaps been more honoured in the breach than in the observance, and need not offer any great obstacle to consistency.

It has been a matter of some surprise to us that Chaplains who are officers of English Lodges, have not before this strongly protested against the theory that the Bible may be used to symbolise any other book which may be deemed by non-Christians to contain God's revealed will and word. There must be many who could deal with this subject much more effectively than ourselves. They, at least, might point out that, if Masonic claims to antiquity have any basis, the Koran at all events cannot be admitted into Masonry, as it dates from a time subsequent to the alleged rise of our system, and after the Masonic Sacred Writings were collated and accepted.

If any Englishman, after taking the First Degree, were to state with deliberation that he could not receive the Bible as containing God's word, we doubt if any English Master of a Lodge would dare to confer the Second. Yet a native of India, who has in no way

changed his religious belief or his views as to how God has revealed himself, is allowed to say he will maintain the principles of the First, and to take the Second Degree, still retaining a belief in direct conflict with the Bible.

Innovations in Masonry have always been justified by the plea that a landmark alone is unsusceptible of modification, but that everything else may be altered. The innovator can in this way laugh in his sleeve, for he has a tolerable assurance that, in any discussion on landmarks, there will be no possibility of agreement. Twenty-five Landmarks are commonly quoted and, although there is no exact agreement amongst authorities, there is a reasonable consensus on many points, with a sufficient divergence in most cases to admit of argument.

Mackey says that until 1858 no attempt was made to distinctly enumerate the Landmarks. Oliver, throughout his works, mentions matters which he deems of high importance as Landmarks—they would amount to many more than twenty-five. Mackenzie terms Masonic Landmarks the " leading principles from which there can be no deviation." Peck states " the universal language and the universal laws of Masonry are Landmarks ; " unfortunately it cannot be discovered from his work what these are. Altogether there is no little confusion, therefore we do not claim that any very great importance should be attached to our observations based on reputed Landmarks.

Paton's twenty-first Landmark is the Volume of the Sacred Law. His remarks are almost identical with Mackey's. We shall give them in extenso later on, but here merely the following extract: " The presence of a ' Book of the Law' in the Lodge is strictly a ritualistic Landmark. . . . . . Hence in all Lodges in Christian Countries the ' Book of the Law' is composed of the Old and New Testaments." He admits that in

non-Christian Lodges other books must take its place ; but he makes no provision for mixed Lodges, or for two or more Books of the Law.

" We place the Bible on the Altar as the Great Light of Freemasonry, we carry the Bible in our processions, we read the Bible in our meetings, we offer prayer *in the name of the Lord Jesus Christ.* But Jews who are members of our Order and of our Lodges, object to these things, or to some of them, and their conscientious scruples deserve and receive our regard. When Jews are initiated, they are generally sworn on the Old Testament alone, and Mahommedans are sworn on the Koran, in fact, every one on the Book which he himself receives as that of the Law of God. There is nothing in the Landmarks to hinder Jews, *if Jews exclusively form a whole Lodge,* from having the Old Testament alone set before them as the Great Light; nothing to hinder Mahommedans from giving the same place to the Koran, they acknowledging it as the revelation of the mind of God. Meanwhile it is, however, indisputable that as Freemasonry has for a long time been chiefly cultivated amongst Christians, it has received, in a great degree, a Christian character ; and in nothing is this more marked than in its symbolism. To expound many of the symbols of modern Freemasonry, otherwise than according to Christian beliefs, would be utterly impossible. In the part of this work devoted to them, we have endeavoured to explain them as we find them ; but this implied frequent reference to the Bible—to the New Testament as well as to the Old—and frequent introduction of the distinguishing doctrines of Christianity. *It may be possible for men of other religions to elaborate a similar system for themselves;* but as yet it has not been done, and only the symbols framed by Jewish and Christian Masons are in use in the Fraternity. Where Christians form the great body of the Members of a Masonic Lodge it has been usual for those of other religious beliefs to

accommodate themselves to circumstances, merely refraining from taking part in those religious services which implied or seemed to them to imply, anything contrary to their own religious conditions."*

"Whatever a man's religious creed may be, Freemasonry requires that he shall be sincere and earnest in it, living in the practice of what he owns as religious duties, and adorning his profession by a life of pure morality. Freemasonry demands truth and honesty in all things. There is nothing more inconsistent with it than a religious profession made in mere pretence whilst the man's whole life shows lukewarmness and indifference to religion. Thus if a Freemason professes himself a Christian he must be expected to prove himself a zealous Christian, diligent in the observance of all religious ordinances, and earnest in all those good works which are prescribed for him by what he acknowledges as the Divine Law. It is not enough that the sneer or scoff of infidelity should never be heard from his lips. The professing Christian who gives utterance to anything of the kind proclaims himself a hypocrite and a liar, and cannot be a good and worthy Freemason. His whole life is a lie. But neither can he who manifests in his whole conduct that he lives only for the present world, that he regards Christianity with as much indifference as if it were a mere tissue of idle tales and foolish fancies and the Bible an antiquated book that may be left to old women and weak-minded men, its warnings and threatenings mere bugbears to frighten children, its promises and hopes not worthy to be weighed in the balance against the gains of commerce or the pleasures of the present life; such a man is no more a good and worthy Mason than he is a good Christian."†

Mackenzie says "In all Christian countries the Holy Bible is not only a part of the necessary furniture

---

* "Freemasonry and its Symbolism," by C. I. Paton.   † *Idem.*

of the Lodge, but is esteemed the first Great Light of Masonry." Peck, who does not enumerate the Landmarks, says, under "Book of the Law," that this is the Holy Bible, which is always open in a Lodge, as a symbol that its light should be diffused among the brethren."

From this it will be noted, authorities agree that there is to be one book not many books. It is not anticipated that the Lodge will have a mixed religious belief, or that any Country will have it. But the fact is that both Countries and Lodges are so placed. Mackenzie certainly appears to most nearly approach a settlement when he supposes a Lodge may have a specific religion.* The true way out of the difficulty appears to be by adopting the course which is most in consonance with first principles, and fix a distinct religious teaching to every Jurisdiction.

It is especially noticeable as confirming our remarks elsewhere respecting a tendency to remove religious references from Freemasonry, that the correct Masonic term " Volume of the Sacred Law," is generally abandoned by Masonic lexicographers. " Book of the Law " is substituted by one writer. Another (Mackey), under the head of " Sacred Law," only refers to the tables of stone delivered to Moses, and so on.

Kenning's Masonic Cyclopædia, under " Law, Sacred," refers the reader to " Sacred Law," but there is no such heading. Under " Book of the Law," we read, " Masonically, it means the Holy Bible, which is an indispensable ' Landmark ' in every Anglo-Saxon Lodge." Under the 21st Landmark, the editor (the Rev. A. F. A. Woodford, M.A.) says " The Holy Bible is an essential Landmark in all English Lodges, and we utterly disavow the opinion that, in any English Lodge, under any circumstances, any other book can take the

---

* Article " Landmarks," Royal Masonic Cyclo., p. 439.

place of the Word of God. That we receive in Mahommedan Lodges for instance, or Hindoo Lodges, those who seek admittance in the way most binding on their conscience, is freely admitted; but the Koran and the Vedas cannot take the place of the Bible in an English Lodge, we repeat, nor can any other religious book be substituted for it. The Great Light of Freemasonry can never be banished from a Lodge under the English Constitution, though perhaps another 'Sacred Book' may be used, and is used, as we have already said, to meet the requirements of the candidate."

This opinion as to what *should be* the state of the case is entirely satisfactory, but, unfortunately, what *should be* done, and what *is* done, differ greatly. Our Indian experience extends over more than twenty-one years, sixteen of which have been spent in Masonry, and we are compelled to say that Brother Woodford's view of what occurs is not a correct one. There are no Mahommedan or Hindoo Lodges in India; did any such exist the only question for us would be to decide under what Jurisdiction they should work. What we really have, are Lodges under English and Scottish Constitutions with members of many religions, each brother esteeming a different volume sacred. A Hindoo joining an English Lodge, by reason of his initiation in it, has a certain claim to receive the Second and Third Degrees. We offer no kind of objection to this if the Hindoo will maintain the principles of English Masonry; but this is exactly what he will not do. He wants to be allowed to take his Degrees in an English Lodge and treat the Sacred Volume as a mere symbol totally wanting in that virtue claimed for it by our ritual; and, moreover, he does so. We have asserted that a Parsee will ask to be obligated in the Royal Arch Degree on the Zendavesta. We know cases where this demand has been made and assented to; and we insist, as Brother Woodford assuredly would, that this constitutes

an utter degradation of the Degree. Had these facts been comprehended in England there would have been no necessity for this book.

A rather telling instance of the respect Freemasons formerly entertained for the Bible and the full recognition they accorded to it, is given by the Rev. Moses Margoliouth in his " Vestiges of Genuine Freemasonry." After relating how George Washington was initiated in the Regimental Lodge* attached to the 46th Regiment when in America, he states—" this Lodge offers another proof of the excellence and useful influence of Masonry, ... When in Dominica, in the year 1805, the 46th was attacked by a French force, which it gallantly repelled, but in the action had the misfortune to lose the Masonic chest, which the enemy succeeded in securing on board their fleet without knowing its contents. Three years afterwards, the French Government, at the earnest request of the officers who had commanded the expedition, returned the chest, with several complimentary presents : offering by that act the acknowledgment and homage of an enlightened nation to the purity, value, and usefulness of Masonry."

The Bible of the above Lodge of the 46th Regiment was exhibited in Lodge Virtue, No. 177, Manchester, on the evening of March 16th, 1852, when a printed programme was handed to the brethren, giving directions for the ceremony.

" Programme of the ceremony observed in the Lodge of Virtue, No. 177, Manchester, on Tuesday evening, 16th of March, 1852, on the reception of the Bible used by the Lodge 227, in H.M. 46th Regiment of Infantry, on the initiation into Freemasonry, in that Lodge, of George Washington, afterwards Commander-in-Chief of

---

* No. 227, Irish Constitution. Washington was initiated in Fredericksburg Lodge, Virginia, Nov. 4, 1752, and not in No. 227; but there seems reason to believe that he was *healed* and re-obligated in the latter in order to qualify for admission into a Lodge under the Irish Constitution.

the army of the United States. Brothers Harris and
J. G. Jones (46th Lancers), *sic*, Conductors. Slow
March order of Procession (three times round the
Lodge) :—Inner guard, with sword. Director of cere-
monies. Deacons, with staves. The Bible, borne by
the oldest member of the Lodge. The Chaplain of the
Lodge. Clerical brethren, members of the Lodge.
Military brethren of the 46th Regiment. Visiting
brethren, members of the Lodge. P. Masters of the
Lodge. P.G. officers. S. and J. Wardens of the Lodge.
Stewards of the Lodge with staves. The procession
having passed three times round the Lodge, halts. The
grand honours are given to the Military brethren
accompanying the Bible. The brethren then sing the
following hymn :—

> Holy Bible, book divine!
> Precious treasure! thou art mine;
> Mine to tell me whence I came;
> Mine to tell me what I am.
>
> Mine to chide me when I rove;
> *Mine to show a Saviour's love;*
> Mine art thou to guide my feet;
> Mine to judge, condemn, acquit.
>
> Mine to comfort in distress,
> *If the Holy Spirit bless;*
> Mine to show by living faith,
> Man can triumph over death.
>
> Mine to tell of joys to come,
> And the rebel sinner's doom;
> O thou precious book divine!
> Precious treasure! thou art mine."

If this be a correct account, the members of Lodge
Virtue, No. 177, at all events, as also the visitors to that
Lodge in 1852, did not countenance any abandonment
of the Christian profession.

If any Volume of the Sacred Law was recognised in
the seventeenth century, which saw the birth of English
Speculative Masonry, it could only have been the Bible,
for nothing was then known in Europe of any other
volumes purporting to contain God's revelation to man
—the Koran alone excepted.

The announcement in the ancient charges that Freemasonry severed itself from communion with Rome at the time of the Reformation, renders it very probable that the Craft had a strong religious bias even before it became a speculative science. It is impossible that it could have broken away from a Church if it was never connected with it; and, as the severance took place at the Reformation it almost follows that Freemasonry must have joined in protesting against what others objected to, and that thereby it attached itself to the Protestant party.*

It is only by analogy that some things can be determined, and this is the case in Freemasonry when considering the Sacred Volume. It has been asserted that the Old Testament may alone be accepted by some. We are unable to adopt this view.

It is an undoubted Landmark in Masonry that there should be a belief in the immortality of the soul; the twentieth Landmark is usually given as containing this belief.

Plato taught this doctrine; he died 348 years before Christ. There are reasons to assume that a belief in the resurrection of the dead was fully developed four centuries before Christ, but the Jews, if they had clear conceptions regarding this, did not generally admit the immortality of the soul before the time of Christ. The Sadducees denied it, and the Pharisees confused it with the doctrine of transmigration. In a recent work it has been shown that this teaching is peculiar to the New Testament, there being only the slightest trace, if any, in the Old Testament of a belief in the soul's immortality. It does not, therefore, even in this respect, comply with Masonic requirements. But beyond this, excepting the New Testament, there is no known sacred

---

* The Bible itself was not commonly known until the sixteenth century; and until the Reformation, it could not have been esteemed " a great light " by any institution under Monastic authority.

book which contains an account of an active, ideal, Masonic life. There is no religion save the Christian, which presents as an exemplar a perfect life of activity. The most enthusiastic Mussulman will not claim this even for him whom he reverences as the Prophet of God. The Buddhist admits that Gautama himself felt he could not live a perfect life unless he withdrew from the world's society. No other religion has any example, not even the example of a purely imaginary personage, set down for imitation. Freemasonry teaches that a man may lead a life of activity in this world, and that his daily avocations and every action of his life may draw him nearer to the Great Architect. Yet the modern Mason would abandon the only sacred writings which present for imitation such a perfect life.

"Let our whole deportment testify for us, that we have formed our lives upon the perfect model of God's revealed will, exhibited to us in the Holy Bible; *that this book is the basis of our Craft,* and that it is by this piece of divine furniture, so essential to our Society, we are taught wisdom, to contrive in all our doings, such means as may conduce to His honour, and the Salvation of our immortal souls."*

The subject of the appointment of Chaplains to Lodges is one on which a few words may be appropriately introduced here. A Chaplain has surely some duties or some religious office to fill. It has generally been the custom to appoint a Christian minister to this post; it appears to be doubtful whether it has ever occurred to anybody that there was some measure of incongruity in making such an appointment: yet if Universality is to be accepted in any other than a Christian sense there *is* an element of impropriety in appointing as Chaplain any professor of a particular belief. At all events the religion should be varied on

---

* Charge delivered to a constituted Lodge at King's Arms, Helston, in Cornwall, 21st April, 1752, by Isaac Head.

occasion, and a Jain, a Hindoo, or a Mormon officiate by turns.

It is noticeable that in the Constitutions it is provided that a Private Lodge *may* appoint a Chaplain, that a District Grand Master is *empowered* to appoint one, but that a Grand Master has no volition—the words in his case run " he *shall* appoint" two Grand Chaplains, and this has been the case since 1775, when Hutchinson so distinctly laid down that Freemasonry was a Christian institution.

The Chaplain is the only religious officer of a Lodge, the current Constitutions say that his jewel or badge of office is a book within a triangle surmounting a glory. Curiously enough, although Emulation Ritual cannot be said to side over much with those who would believe in Freemasonry as a Christian system, the jewel of a Chaplain in a Symbolic Lodge is there stated to be " a Bible."

It is not edifying to an English Craftsman to sit in Lodge with a Parsee brother, whilst it is enunciated that the Bible is to rule and govern the faith of a Freemason. He knows the Parsee does not concur in the principle laid down, and that he certainly has no intention of so doing, although he promised, before taking the Second Degree, that he would uphold this doctrine. The system did not provide for the contingencies which have arisen, and it is a cowardly and absolutely un-Masonic subterfuge to assert, that the Bible is not necessarily meant as the Volume of the Sacred Law in English Masonry.

An entirely unforeseen set of circumstances has arisen ; it is highly pleasing that brethren of all creeds should have joined us, but it is also very much to be deplored that the state of the case has not been properly dealt with. Instead of this having been done, contradictory evasions and compromises which cut at the very heart of the Masonic system have been resorted to, and a system which is absurdly anomalous is being evolved. The ties which should exist between a brother

and that which he esteems the Word of God have been, and are being, relaxed, and will soon be entirely severed by the light and careless feeling necessarily engendered by the doctrine, that *any* book is good enough to be esteemed the Volume of the Sacred Law.

A Christian cannot view this state of things with satisfaction. In the words of a well-known writer, " He feels that to reduce our blessed Lord into the category of human seers is practically to dethrone him. Christianity will tolerate no rival. They who wish to raise a tabernacle for some other Master, be it even for the greatest worthies of the old œconomy—a Moses or Elias —must be warned that Christ, and Christ alone, is to be worshipped."*

* Hardwicke, " Christ and other Masters," p. 39.

CHAPTER VII.

THE GROWTH OF UNIVERSALITY.

THE attempt to create an universal system of the most ordinary morality, would, even in the present day, be deemed a sufficiently bold untaking. How much more difficult must it have been for our brethren in the early part of the last century, when so much less of the world was discovered, to erect an institution which, owing to some presumedly common belief, would be universally received. Some of our brethren went still further and asserted, whilst they were absolutely ignorant as to what the majority of the world believed, that the principles of Freemasonry, as formulated in or before 1723, were then universal. Knowing better, as we now do, the many religions of which men in 1723, or even a half century later, were necessarily ignorant, and being conscious that the principles of some foreign religions are still veiled from our view, the claim that any system could have been devised which should include all religious beliefs, may be summarily rejected. When the particular system in question is examined, any such claim must be disallowed, as its principles are found to be incompatible with the known tenets of several religions. The claim was first advanced on the strength of a pure supposition in order to maintain a shadow of the original pretension—advanced in ignorance—and anomalies have necessarily resulted. It is almost needless to say that a tinkering at Universality has not been attended with success.

A patch in one direction has made a rent in another. The more plainly it is shown that the system can admit men of one faith, the clearer it must become that it cannot admit those of a contrary belief. The abandonment of all religious principles—and this is now the aim of some of our members—might possibly get over the difficulty, although we do not say it would: but so long as a fragment of religious belief is required from a candidate it follows that the Masonic system cannot be absolutely Universal. The question as to how widely spread our system may be, is a different one. Wherever seven Christian Masons are met, there it is possible to hold a Lodge, and as Christianity is now to be found represented in all sorts of out-of-the-way places, it may be maintained that in this sense the Craft is Universal. With this view of the subject we have no quarrel.

The question as to whether the Institution originally claimed that which a little later was claimed for it by individuals, is a highly important one; we believe the evidence tends to show that it did not in the first instance pretend to that Universality that is now by some considered to be at the base of the principles of the Order.

The ridicule with which some of the earliest allusions to Universality could be smothered is beside our purpose, for the present at all events. Most Masons are acquainted with an old Charge after initiation, which can be proved to date from the middle of the last century, wherein is stated " the greatest Monarchs in all ages, as well of Asia and Africa, as of Europe, have been encouragers of the Royal Art; and many of them have presided as Grand Masters over the masons in their respective territories," &c. Such foolish pretence might have been expected to disappear in course of time, that it has not done so is only too evident. No one now asserts, it is true, that Freemasonry was found universally spread over the world's surface in 1717 or 1723; yet

L 2

none the less has the Universal claim survived. Annihilated in one form, by one set of facts, it re-appears, subject to a second annihilation, in some other form. The original claim to Universality was upset and refuted by the, perhaps justifiable, vanity of showing how year by year the system was spreading in various lands. The early histories in the Constitutions contain frequent reference to this spreading of Freemasonry, thus supplying unasked a complete refutation of its original Universality.*

Whether we take up Masonic histories or whether we read Bro. Sadler's "Masonic Facts," which we are glad to see has not *much* in common with our old histories, we find one statement constantly repeated, which is, the great spread of Freemasonry which took place in the last century.† If a system was already universal, it is not easy to understand how it could spread? The finite power of the infinite is hardly a more ridiculous expression, nor is it a greater contradiction of terms. But our ancient brethren revelled in contradictions—whilst they asserted that Masonry has ever possessed an universal language, and that Noah and his sons were Masons, they yet attached the most orthodox, old-fashioned meaning to the confusion of tongues at Babel; holding, nevertheles, that they still had, in the eighteenth century, the genuine Masonic cryptographic language of times prior to the Flood.

There is nothing in Anderson's Constitutions of 1723 to justify a belief that any idea of Universality, such as is now claimed, existed when the Grand Lodge of England was founded. Anderson alludes (page 45) to the injury done to Masonry by "Goths and Mahommetans"; he speaks of Masonry as a *British* institution

---

* Preston alludes to the spread of Freemasonry in 1793 and its rapid spread in 1796. He also expresses a hope (p. 367, 9th edition) in 1795 that the Universality of the system may be firmly established.

† Pocket Companion and History of Freemasonry, 1754, p. 275.

(page 47) and, as is elsewhere stated, he specially refers to one of the Charges having been strictly enjoined since the Reformation and the Secession of England from the Church of Rome (page 54).

In the history attached to the 1723 Constitutions we read that the only design of Mahometans is "to convert the world by fire and sword, instead of cultivating the Arts and Sciences."* This was rather injudicious if the Grand Lodge wished to cultivate brotherly feeling with Mahometans.

In writing of Great Britain Dr. Anderson says, "If the disposition for true ancient Masonry prevails, for some time, with Noblemen, Gentlemen, and learned Men (as it is likely it will), this Island will become the Mistress of the Earth, for Designing, Drawing, and Conducting, and capable to instruct all other Nations in all things relating to the Royal Art." From this we may draw two conclusions : the first being that there was some idea that Freemasonry would not thereafter be entirely speculative, but that the operative element would still remain to some extent ; and the second, that there was no intention of changing any ancient principle. The words above quoted are those with which the history concludes.

This intention of retaining the operative element in Freemasonry after the formation of the Grand Lodge in 1717 is, we think, conclusively shown by the appointments made to the Grand Wardenships during the first few years of the Institution. In 1718 we find Mr. Thomas Morrice, *Stonecutter*, was one of the Grand Wardens. In 1719 he was re-appointed. In 1720 Mr. Thomas Hobby, *Stonecutter*, was one Warden, whilst Mr. Rich. Ware, *Mathematician*, was the other. In 1721 we find Mr. Thomas Morrice back in office, and in 1722, Mr. William Hawkins, *Mason*, was one of the two Wardens. It can hardly be contended that this

---

* Page 28, Original Edition of 1723.

was purely accidental, or that it was a mere coincidence. The appointments bear out the idea that, in the first instance, there was no intention of swamping the operative with a speculative element. The old system was, in fact, to be continued.

The foregoing extracts do not lend support to a theory that there was any Universal, new system formulated or Christianity abandoned, but, if there should be any lingering idea regarding this, the next few words in the book must completely remove all doubt. Page 49 of these Constitutions commences with a title which runs " The Charges of a Free-mason, extracted from the ancient records of Lodges beyond Sea, and of those in England, Scotland, and Ireland, *for the use of the Lodges in London.*" The italics are ours. What does this mean save that the Grand Lodge had no idea in the first instance of attempting to extend its jurisdiction beyond Metropolitan limits ? No second set of Charges was ever issued for the Provinces. In the Constitutions of 1784 we find a change, illustrating how the scope of operations had been enlarged. That the word " London " was no oversight, is proved by the heading to the " General Regulations " on page 58 of the 1723 volume. Here we read the Regulations were " for the use of the Lodges in and about London and Westminster."

In 1784 the Grand Lodge had grown somewhat bolder; the Charges were not altered but the title of them was. We now find it run " Constitutions of the Fraternity of Free and Accepted Masons. Part V. Containing the Antient Charges, General Regulations of the Fraternity Necessary Tables, &c." Without any specific statement to show this, the original design—of merely having regularly printed or codified rules for the *London* Lodges—had been extended; we thus have clear evidence that the scope of operations had been enlarged.

But before this it had been taught that the principles of the English Order could not be changed. On page 65 of the 1723 Constitutions we have some evidence what one of the original principles was. " But whether there be a feast for all the Brethren or not, yet the Grand Lodge must meet in some convenient place annually on St. John's Day; or if it be Sunday, then on the next Day, in order to chuse every Year a new Grand Master, Deputy, and Wardens." This again does not fit in with Universality. Further on, page 71, we find additional proof that the jurisdiction was to be a purely local affair, for we here read that " A new Lodge, for avoiding many irregularities, should be solemnly constituted by the Grand Master, with his Deputy and Wardens, or in the Grand Master's absence, the Deputy shall act for his Worship, and shall chuse some Master of a Lodge to assist him; or in case the Deputy is absent, the Grand Master shall call forth some Master of a Lodge to act Deputy pro tempore." From this it is again evident it was not contemplated that long distances would have to be covered. Locomotion in 1723 was not a very easy matter. The Grand Master certainly would not have projected for his Deputy such journies as our Grand Secretary now makes light of. It appears to be clear that this provision applied to a local jurisdiction; the term "absence" further accentuates this. If it was intended to state that the Deputy would undertake a journey provided the Grand Master could not go, the arrangement would have been differently stated. There is absolutely no provision for constituting a provincial Lodge—a foreign one had not been dreamt of.

There is an allusion to wherever Freemasons are " dispers'd over the face of the earth " on page 71, but this obviously refers to English Freemasons who might be resident or travelling in foreign lands.

We do not ourselves know what primary religious principle may be deemed most generally spread over

the earth. The Masonic averment that a belief in one God is everywhere acceptable, and therefore affords a common ground on which all can meet and agree, is open to several objections. Until an accurate census can be obtained of the religious tenets of the world's population, it is perhaps rash to hazard an opinion as to what might prove to be the most prevalent faith. It is, however, certain that a belief in one God is not universal. Neither is there, indeed, any universal idea of God in the world, nor can there be whilst a Buddhist lives. Whilst, therefore, Freemasonry demands assent to even this doctrine it cannot be a truly Universal system.

If Freemasonry has any real claim to be considered an ancient institution, it must of necessity resign all pretensions to Universality. A very few hundred years take us back to a time when nearly all Europe was in slavery. If the present Masonic system was then in existence it must have been a rare absurdity; claiming Universality, whilst its very constitution barred its doors to all but an absolutely insignificant proportion of the population.

Men who were eligible for Masonic election by reason of their completely free birth were not very common in 926, for instance, when the first Grand Lodge of England is *said* to have been held at York. At that time the Gospels were not infrequently used as books to record the manumission of serfs.* There is no reason to suppose that the stipulation which requires a Candidate for Freemasonry to be free by birth is of very modern origin; indeed, the contrary can be satisfactorily established. How then, having regard to the condition of Europe, could Freemasonry have anciently been an Universal society? This particular condition made it a most exclusive one, and there is no doubt in our mind that this was the deliberate intent.

---

* See Add. MS. 9381, British Museum.

The more the history of Masonry is studied, the more will the student be inclined to agree that "the Grand Lodge of England is the original mother of all regular Masonic Lodges of Three Degrees the world over."* The Grand Lodge of England dates from 1717 and at the present time, as the United Grand Lodge, it represents both its original Constitution and other principles received from another Constitution known as the Ancient system.

We have stated our belief that the Grand Lodge did not itself, in the first instance, lay any claim to the Universality of its system. We have to admit that as time passed, we acquire apparent proof of some such claim being put forward. Until 1724 it did not grant warrants to any Lodge "outside the Metropolis, but in that year Bath, Bristol, Norwich, and other Provincial places were visited Masonically and duly honoured with charters for lodges, and then rapidly the principles of the craft spread throughout Great Britain and the civilised world."†

Nor did the York Grand Lodge during its short existence, which terminated in 1790, or thereabouts, grant charters in any such manner as would justify a Universality argument. It never granted a charter outside the Kingdom of Great Britain.

The Constitution of the Ancient Masons prevented its system being anything more than Christianly Universal, for we know that its prayers as used in the Degrees, were such as only a Christian could offer up.‡

Preston states that on the 23rd of May, 1776, Freemasons' Hall was opened "and dedicated to Masonry, Virtue, and Universal Charity and Benevolence"; not to universal Masonry, but universal charity. The distinction is of consequence. A reference to the Univer-

---

* Whytehead's Preface to Hughan's "Origin of the English Rite."
† Hughan's "Origin of the English Rite," p. 2.
‡ See Prayers in all editions of Ahiman Rezon.

sality of any system between 1750 and 1813 must have carried with it an element of absurdity. There were two Masonic bodies in London alone, which were at daggers drawn. The Modern Mason would not at one time enter what was called an Ancient Masons' Lodge, nor would he acknowledge the Ancient Mason as a Mason at all, although in the end they each fully recognised the other and joined forces. Whatever the title of either system to Universality, it could only relate to the possibilities of the future. It at least could not boast an *existing* Universality in the face of the fact that there was another opposing Masonic body. But if it be argued that either body would have been right had it proffered some such claim, it then follows that either, in joining with the other in 1813, must have waived any claim to its Universality in the past. There is no logical escape from this position.

Oliver's assertion that there is no record of any Universal theory prior to the middle of the present century must, however, be received with some caution. Preston, in his celebrated " Illustrations," alludes to " the universality of our system " and to our signs constituting " an universal language." In one place, indeed, he states that in processions "when the Bible is mentioned it applies to whatever is considered to be the Law of God." He says " the universal principles of the art unite, in one indissoluble bond of affection, men of the most opposite tenets, and of the most distant countries." Again, the frontispiece of Scott's Pocket Companion, dated 1754, has a workman holding up a board with " the Constitutions of Masonry universal " inscribed on it.

The following quotations from Ray's " Elements of Freemasonry," Liverpool, 1788, are also in point—

" We are bid to unite with virtuous men, men of the most distant countries and opposite opinions—to unite with them in the firm and pleasing bond of fraternal

love—to regard them with the truest affection. Come then, ye virtuous Jews, Mahometans, ye faithful followers of virtue of every faith and every clime; come to us, and we will, with a brother's arm, receive you. You worship the *Universal Lord of Nature*, the bounteous Giver of all good, in the way you think most pleasing to Him."

Ray quotes a Charge delivered at a Quarterly Communication for Devon at Exeter, some time about the middle of last century. It says of Freemasonry, "Confined by the limits of no country, of no religion, it admits to its privileges the professors of virtue, of every faith, and every clime; and bids us unite as friends, as brethren, with all who regulate their conduct by the Sacred Laws of Morality, and believe in the all-wise Contriver of the Universe, however different from ours their manner of worshipping Him may be."

He also gives " A Prayer to be used at the Closing of the Lodge."

" May the blessing of *the Universal Parent* be upon us and all our brethren. May we be cemented by true affection, and practise out of the Lodge those moral and social virtues which we have been taught in it.— Amen."

" Here reigns Benevolence, whose large embrace,
　Uncircumscrib'd, takes in the human race;
　She sees each narrow tie, each private end
　Indignant—Virtue's *Universal* Friend.
　Scorning each frantic Zealot, bigot tool,
　She stamps on Mason's breast her golden rule."

The following is Ray's address to a foreigner— " You, brother, the native and subject of another, an enlightened kingdom, you, by entering into our Order, have connected yourself by sacred and affectionate ties with thousands of Masons in this and other nations. Ever reflect, that the Order you have entered into bids you always look upon the world as *one great republic*, of

which every nation is a family, and every particular person a child. When, therefore, you are returned to, and settled in, your own country, take care that your progress be not confined to the narrow circle of national connexions, or particular religions, but let it be *universal*, and extend to every branch of the human race. At the same time, always consider, that besides the common types of humanity you have this night entered into," &c.

There can thus be no doubt that about 1750-60, a Universal idea of some sort had taken root. To trace it through lodge orations, printed books, and other paths from its inception to its present development, would be a most interesting pursuit; but this would carry us beyond the limits of our intention.

The Constitutions of 1738 show that the Grand Lodge, after a life of some few years, attempted to assert that the Universality of Freemasonry consisted in the Lodges of Scotland, Ireland, France and Italy working under its patronage. It averred that they only *affected* independency. Later on we find the Institution described as "The ancient and honourable Society of the Free and Accepted Masons established on the Universal System." This is, we believe, the first evidence of the Grand Lodge of England assuming Universality to be a part of the Masonic system. The record of this will be found in "Preston's Illustrations." The occurrence took place in 1755, and is described at foot. We have here not an assertion that the English Constitution was itself Universal, but that it was part of or was based upon some system that was so.* An

---

* "Soon after the election of the Marquis of Carnarvon, the Grand Lodge took into consideration a complaint against certain Brethren, for assembling, without any legal authority, under the denomination of ancient masons; who, as such considered themselves as independent of the Society, and not subject to the laws of the Grand Lodge, or to the control of the Grand Master, Dr. Manningham, the Deputy Grand Master, pointed out the necessity of discouraging their meetings, as being contrary to the laws of the Society, and openly subversive of the

American Mason* has, we think, hit the nail on the head when he says that eventually " the sole aim of the London Grand Lodge was to be esteemed the sole Masonic Government of the Kingdom, and to attain which it resorted to any and all means to render itself popular among all classes of people."

Bro. Sadler, in a very recent work, again reminds us that Freemasons' Hall was dedicated in the ninth Lord Petre's time to " Universal Charity and Benevolence." Why not to Universal Masonry ? We get a telling reason why not four pages further on in Bro. Sadler's book.† He quotes a letter in the Grand Lodge archives from a Mason in Kent to the Grand Secretary in 1791 ; from this we extract the following—

" A person who is a regular Mason under the Grand Lodge of Scotland, applied for admission at the Lodge of Fortitude here, on last St. John's Day—was examined and admitted—was present at a subsequent meeting, and on last lodge night objected to, as having not been made a modern Mason. He stated, that formerly residing in another country, he conceived, that by joining himself to our august Society there, he became a Mason in the most extensive and universal sense of the word, that in the place where he had the honour to be initiated, no difference of that kind was known ; that Masonry considered in its true spirit, entertained no such contracted principles, but in imitation of the Grand Luminary the Sun, diffused its genial rays for the welfare of the brethren in every part of the Globe. That also as a Scotch Mason, he had introduced himself

---

allegiance due to the Grand Master. On this representation the Grand Lodge resolved, that the meeting of any brethren under the denomination of masons, other than as brethren of the ancient and honorable Society of Free and Accepted Masons established upon the universal system, is inconsistent with the honour and interest of the Craft."— Preston, 9th edition, p. 284.

* Leon Hyneman, " Freemasonry in England." York, 1877.

† " Masonic Facts and Fiction," p. 148.

to several lodges in London, to one of which he is actually at this time a subscribing member, that in the course of the many lectures he had attended, had occasion to go through every material part, and, of consequence, considered himself as entitled to admission into any lodge in England, within certain degrees. To all this it was briefly answered that he could not be admitted, unless he would submit to be made in a modern lodge.

"Your thoughts on this subject will honor,

"Sir, your obedt. Servant,

"JOHN COCKBURN."

We do not know what answer was given, neither is it necessary that we should; but this is a striking example that whatever assertions were made regarding Universal brotherhood, or the Universality of the system, there was, in reality, no harmony between even Scotland and England at this time.

This letter tends to support Dermott's statement that there was an Union between the Ancient Masons and the Grand Lodges of Scotland and Ireland. It thereby also offers support to our conviction that England alone had introduced heresy.

Dermott's statement is that the Grand Masters of England, Ireland, and Scotland " wisely and nobly have formed a triple union to support the honour and dignity of the Ancient Craft, for which their lordship's names will be honoured and revered whilst Freemasonry exists in these kingdoms."*

There is little doubt but that the Grand Lodge was at one time prepared to assume all the power it could, and had it not been checked it would have asserted in course of time a more substantial claim that the English system was Universal than is now within its power. In

---

* Ahiman Rezon, 3rd edition. London, 1778.

1769 a Provincial Grand Master for Foreign Lodges was appointed, but in the next year we find the Grand Master of the Netherlands objecting to the constitution of English Lodges in his jurisdiction. He offered, if the English Grand Master would refrain from constituting fresh Lodges in the Netherlands, he would agree to a similar restriction with respect to all parts of the world where the English Grand Lodge was already the recognised superior. The Grand Lodge in London similarly established Lodges under its constitution in districts which were acknowledged to be under the jurisdiction of York, and in various ways showed that it assumed that the world in general was its heritage. It was an early theory that Freemasonry was an Asiatic institution, yet without any hesitation or enquiry, the Grand Lodge granted warrants in India. If Freemasonry had in reality existed in India, or in other parts where the English Fraternity asserted its right to establish Lodges, an act of at least very grave discourtesy to the older Constitutions was committed. The English authorities could have no right to usurp supreme power in any country where Freemasonry already existed as a system. As a matter of fact no usurpation of authority did take place; but it is a curious instance of inconsistency, that an institution, whilst asserting that Freemasonry was diffused amongst all nations, and that the religion of each individual nation should be respected, assumed a right to establish here, there and everywhere, a constitution which by its ritual could not apply to all religions, nor fail, in many instances, to cause offence. The fact seems to be that what has occurred neither was, nor could be, foreseen. There was no Freemasonry in India prior to its introduction by the English. Secret societies there are all the world over, but it is a misuse of words to term any Indian society known to us in the last century, a system of Freemasonry.

The history of Masonic claims to Universality has yet to be written.

The Universal benevolence and charity of Masonry appear to have been among the early assumptions. These could not last long in the face of the very circumscribed charity which became almost a necessity from Freemasonry producing its own crop of beggars.

The universal patronage of Monarchs was another fallacy, which even now has a struggling existence.

Next we find the theory that Freemasonry is common to the world. This has to succumb before any Grand Lodge which wishes to extend its jurisdiction; it is then announced that in some particular spot, some ardent brother has discovered that there is no such thing as Freemasonry known.

A Masonic Universal language is another fallacy.

All these failing, the Mason still insists he must have something or other to bear out the Universal theory, so claims that the principles which are at the base, which are the foundations of the Institution, are Universal; and when you attempt to discover what this principle is, he answers, in effect, " Universality."

CHAPTER VIII.

Is Universality Possible?

WE will now consider whether Freemasonry as it exists to-day can by any means be universally acceptable? or perhaps it would be better to substitute the word " generally " for universally.

This question was discussed in 1853 with some warmth. In the " Freemasons' Magazine " for that year, and on p. 580 we read "The Masonic world has been told that the universality of the Craft means the admission into the Order of all persons, whatever their creed or belief. We deny that this is so, and must emphatically state that no brother, unless he be a hypocrite, can be a Master Mason, or a Royal Arch Mason, as sanctioned by the Grand Lodge and Grand Chapter, without he be a believer in revealed religion as found in the Old Testament." At the present time this will not be disputed in England, and it at once shows that there are other conditions besides the initial requirement of a belief in one God demanded of a Mason who advances in the Order. We propose to show that these requirements are not alone insisted upon from a Master Mason, but that they are in reality exacted from even the Entered Apprentice.

The initial assurance given by a candidate for Masonry is that he believes that God will hear and answer prayer. We need not quote the question and answer, which will at once rise to the mind of every Masonic reader, by which the candidate shows that he acts towards God with this primary belief. Should the

M

candidate assert that he did not pray to God under circumstances of distress, for comfort and relief, his initiation could not be proceeded with. A belief, in God's attention to human prayer, is in other words a belief in it being an attribute of God to listen to human prayer—the candidate attributes this much to God, otherwise his statements are senseless. It is superfluous to argue that a knowledge of, or well founded belief in, any of God's attributes can only be acquired after revelation.* The Deist will not admit that this knowledge exists, he denies that there has ever been any revelation from God to man. The denial of revelation carries with it, as a consequence, denial of a knowledge of God's attributes, and thus a Deist has no faith when addressing the Almighty. In this we but state what Deists will themselves admit—they believe in a Supreme Being but deny that man has ever had conveyed to him any knowledge of that Being. There is every scope for imagination, but a well grounded belief, such as is initially required from a candidate, cannot exist with a consistent Deist. A mere believer in a God is not thus eligible as a Mason; if he believes in Him, and yet does not believe that He will answer prayer, the doors of Masonry remain closed. This point alone brings us to Theism, as opposed to Deism, being a Masonic requirement.

Again a belief in revelation is not the only addition required to a belief in the existence of a God. The Mason in the Third Degree has to learn, by emblematic representation, that it is part of Masonic teaching, that there is a resurrection of the body and that the soul is immortal. It is an anomaly in our rituals that to some of our beliefs an assent is required, and to other equally, or even more, important beliefs no assent is necessary. Thus no man can become a Fellow Craft Mason before

---

* "Let us therefore praise and magnify His Holy Name for the knowledge of Himself which He has vouchsafed unto us." R.A.°

he has promised to maintain the principles inculcated in the First Degree. Until this assent is given any one may remain a Mason and yet have a profound disbelief in the Great Light of Masonry being a light at all. After this assent, the Mason is morally bound to conform to prior Masonic teaching, but previous thereto his sole obligation is to secrecy.

An analysis of Degrees shows that similarly there are other beliefs, regarding which, although most necessary in a Mason, the ritual provides no obligation. The Mason may laugh at them after he has learnt them —he is under no obligation to uphold them. This is the case with the doctrine of resurrection and immortality in the Third Degree, so that a Mason is actually eligible for the Royal Arch Degree, even if he entirely dissents from the teaching in the Third Degree. We term this an anomaly, and consider an unqualified assent should be given to the teaching of one and every Degree before a higher one is conferred. Having studied Masonic Jurisprudence we are at a loss to understand how it is that difficulties have not already arisen from this single circumstance. We are thus placed under the necessity of considering two lines of Masonic belief, the one being obligatory and the other orthodox but not obligatory. In the first category we place a belief in a revelation from God to man, in the second we place a belief in the resurrection of the body and the immortality of the soul.

There is a third belief which we must consider when we are dealing with what may, or may not be, universally accepted. We allude to individuality, creation, and existence. This is an obligatory doctrine in Masonry. To some Brethren we may appear to be writing nonsense when we place this amongst matters for consideration—but we are doing nothing of the kind. Any Constitution which assumes that anything was ever created or that there is such a thing as self, or that a

M 2

Brother must have once existed before a Degree could have been conferred on him, cannot be Universal; inasmuch as it at one swoop refuses to receive any one of the members of the numerically strongest religion on the Globe. Five hundred millions of people believe that nothing ever was created, and that it is an ignorant delusion to think there is such a thing as soul or self.*

There is yet a fourth belief required in the Royal Arch Degree—a belief in the re-discovery of that which was lost. Applied Biblically, a belief in the " Logos " of St. John the Evangelist, or in the second person of the Christian Trinity, is requisite. The symbol of this is a material word to which already we find members who are not Christians have attached a Cabalistic meaning.

We have repeatedly urged that one Constitution cannot be Universal. The first printed Constitutions foretold this by making the statements they did. But this carries with it no denial that the entire system is capable of being an Universal one. We have alluded to the illustration by Preston of a garden made up of parts, the whole forming one harmonious whole. A better example is to be found in the Christian Church. No sect of this body can be universally acceptable, the diversities in points of faith and in particular creeds prevent any one sect attaining such a position. No Christian however can deny that Christianity is an universal religion. Freemasonry draws a line parallel. We cannot all agree in principles, which are as the life blood of a single Constitution, yet we can agree to sink these differences when we treat each different Constitution as but part of a complete system. English Freemasonry either upholds the old doctrines taught by the operative body, after it received members who were not operative, and has thereby a title to be considered an

---

* " Buddhism," by T. W. Rhys-Davids.

ancient institution; or it does not now uphold these principles, and has no title to be so considered. It is by the maintenance alone of the genuinely ancient principles that Freemasonry has any right to stand before the public with a claim to respect, for if it has abandoned ancient principles then it is a fraudulent imposture, as it has never failed to assert its adherence to them. It may be allowable to add something, but assuredly not to take anything away. Although Christian principles have been improperly held in abeyance, to attain some ideal of Universality, yet if it be the case that the original Institution, which present Freemasonry is supposed to represent, was a Christian Society, then the present Society should, nay must, be Christian also.

The mere belief in the existence of one God has been shown to be not the only requirement in a candidate. Above this and of infinitely more importance, is a belief in a revelation from the Almighty, by which men should be enabled to lead lives in accordance with their relationship to God, and which should prepare them for a life hereafter. This and this alone is the object of the Masonic system. It is to make men live with a purpose, to walk honestly before God and man, to practise that which they profess to believe, to act up to their light and to be generally fervent seekers after truth. The absolute sincerity required in every true Mason must necessarily compel him to reject every book, except that in which he is convinced God has revealed more of His sacred word and will than in any other volume.* There can be none of the half-heartedness which would place all books esteemed sacred on a dead level. Masonry teaches that a man should live up to his light, whatever that may be, and prove himself earnest and honest about it; a Mahommedan, we well

---

* "The God of Truth cannot have revealed contradictory doctrines," "Catholic," a pamphlet by the Right Rev. Monsignor Capel, D.D., 4th edition, New York, 1884, p. 5.

know, cannot look upon our Great Light as anything
more than a symbol, if even that; to ask him to do
anything else and yet to not change his religion, is an
absurdity. To ask him to live up to the teaching of
the Koran, if he honestly believes in it, and yet to
accord respect as a great light to other books, is asking
what is impossible. No man can conscientiously hold
that God has revealed most regarding Himself in half a
dozen places. If He has revealed more of Himself in
one volume than He has in another, then the other
contains less, not more, of his revelation. We utterly
deny that any old Masonic teaching enjoins that reverence be paid to any but one sacred volume—produce
another and you detract from the first—you go further
and deny that it, the first, is entitled to the position to
which Masonry originally raised it. In other words,
you have altogether done away with a Great Light.

The introduction by the Parsee, or by the Hindoo,
of their sacred volumes into the Lodge, is both intelligible and consistent so far as they are concerned.
They are not in the position of the Christian, and do
not lose ground by their action. They have to win a
position for their sacred volumes. The elevation of
their books to a level with the Bible is a very distinct
gain. For the Hindoo to get his sacred books placed
on an equality with the Koran is to score a great point,
and all honour to him for his attempt to raise their
status. To acquire for their books equal honour with
the Bible in Masonic estimation is, so far as they are
concerned, most laudable. They at least show they are
sincere, but what about the Christian's Bible—the Great
Masonic Light? has this kept its proper place? The
Hindoo having once got his sacred book firmly placed
will most assuredly never allow it to lose its position.
Was it to gain this end that the English Masonic Constitution was formed, or was it not rather to hold out to
those who might join the Society, in that state of

darkness in which according to Masonic doctrine all are plunged who have not received the Light of the Bible, the true and only Light? What end of the English Constitution would be attained if every sacred volume in the world were crowded into a Lodge-room? Reflection must convince most persons that this was never the design of the English Constitution.

What *is* required is, that the Parsee, the Hindoo and the Sikh should not be content to have their volumes on a level with anything else—if they believe in them they should insist on their receiving the highest place of honour. English Masonry cannot afford this as it now exists, but it might well be considered whether, without surrendering anything in the parent Institution, a society might not be affiliated therewith which could embrace other religions beside that which is based on the Bible.*

That long after the Grand Lodge was formed there was no idea that such a state of things as now exists would come into being can easily be shown.

Preston's "Illustrations" show us that the Craft, in the latter part of the last century, believed that most countries had some one book which was generally esteemed as containing the will or law of God. Possibly most countries have such a volume. India however has no one volume that is so regarded, and what was written on the subject could only have been advanced in ignorance of the actual facts. Writing of the Volume of the Sacred Law Preston states that the Bible is to be used in England, " but in countries where that book is not known, whatever is understood to contain the will or law of God." Here confusion began, and it is continued by modern writers, who should have known more of foreign lands before they essayed to deal with Masonic law. Mackey, Mackenzie, and Paton all help to confuse

---

* To enable an opinion to be formed on this point, certain salient features in Indian religions are given in the next chapter.

matters when they deal with the twenty-first Landmark of Masonry which, we need hardly state, treats of the Sacred Law. For convenience we quote Paton, who in almost identical words expresses Mackey's views.

"It is a landmark that a 'Book of the Law' *shall constitute an indispensable part of the furniture of every Lodge.* The presence of a 'Book of the Law' in a Lodge, as a part of its furniture, is strictly a ritualistic landmark, and the authorities for it will be at once evident to every Mason. It is not absolutely required that everywhere the Old and New Testaments shall be used. The 'Book of the Law' is that volume which, by the religion of the country, is believed to contain the revealed will of the Great Architect of the Universe. Hence, in all Lodges in Christian countries, the 'Book of the Law' is composed of the Old and New Testaments; in a country where Judaism is the prevailing faith, the Old Testament alone is sufficient; and in Mahomedan countries and among Mahomedan Freemasons, the Koran is generally substituted. The author has seen this in Lodges. Freemasonry does not attempt to interfere with the peculiar religious faith of its members, except so far as relates to belief in the existence of God and the Resurrection, with what necessarily results from such belief. On the subject of the religious, or, rather, the doctrinal, requirements of Masonry, the Old Charges utter the following explicit language: 'Though in ancient times Masons were charged in every country to be of the religion of that country or nation, whatever it was, yet it is now thought expedient only to oblige them to that religion in which all men agree, leaving their particular opinions to themselves.' The 'Book of the Law' is to the Speculative Mason his trestleboard, without this he cannot labour; whatever he believes to be the revealed will of the Great Architect constitutes to him his trestle-board, and must ever be before him in his hours of speculative labour, to be the rule and guide

of his conduct. The landmark, therefore, requires that a 'Book of the Law,' a religious code of some kind, purporting to exhibit the revealed will of God, shall form an essential part of the furniture of every Lodge."*

This opinion of Paton's has never, we believe, been questioned heretofore, yet its utter inapplicability to India must be evident to anyone who has the most casual acquaintance with that country. Preston's ignorance that what he wrote might cause confusion is excusable, but we are hardly inclined to say the same regarding jurists of the present day. When Preston wrote, the condition of India was very much as it now is, so far as relates to the distribution of religious beliefs. The religion of the country, taking India as a whole, is without doubt, if considered numerically, Hindoo. Are we, however, to deal with India as one country? If so, then by Masonic law as laid down by most jurists, the Bible should be removed from every Lodge of Freemasonry in India, and replaced by some Hindoo sacred volume to be henceforth esteemed the great light of Masonry. If we are not to deal with India as one nation, what is the division to be? It will be evident that on the geographical or political division depends what our Indian great light is to be? Are we to deal with Bombay as one nation? Madras as another, Burmah as a third? The religion of Burmah is Buddhist, this belief denies the existence of a soul or a Creator, and of a future life. Is this to be the Masonic belief of Burmah? Paton says it is to be so. He states the religion of the country governs the case. Here indeed we have got back to the old position laid down in the Constitutions of the last century, where every Mason is expected to be of the religion of any country in which he chances to be resident. According to this, an English Mason on arrival in Bombay is to accept the

---

* "Freemasonry and its Jurisprudence," by Chalmers I. Paton. London, 1872.

Shasters as his great light (it goes without saying the Parsee brother is to give up his Zendavesta). Our brother proceeds to Secunderabad, which is in the State of Hyderabad, here he is to receive the Koran. He is ordered to Burmah, and his Masonic attainments —truly cosmopolitan—immediately enable him to subscribe to the doctrine of annihilation without a murmur. This is Masonic law according to Mackey and Paton.

Mackenzie differs, but does not render the position any easier for our Indian brethren. He states the Book of the Law need not be the Bible; but according to the religious faith of the Lodge, it may be the Koran, the Zendavesta, or the Vedas and Shasters. What is the religion of a Lodge which has an equal number of members of three different religions? Perhaps Bro. Mackenzie will enlighten us.

But assuming that the majority have a right to impose on a minority any sacred volume they please, how is the minority to deal with the great light? Is the difficulty to be solved by considering one light as good as another, and that the Lodge's adopted great light is nothing more than a symbol?* Proceeding still further on the assumption that a majority has a right to decide what the religion, and consequently what the great light of a Lodge shall be, we have by no means exhausted all the difficulties. A party in the majority one month may be in a minority the next, especially so in India with its fluctuating population. If a majority have a right to alter the religion of a Lodge, a Hindoo Master who has been elected by a Hindoo majority, may find himself in the embarrassing position of having to assure a Parsee initiate that the "Grunth," the sacred volume of the Sikhs, contains more of God's revealed word and will than any other book. All this would be far from making the system consistent.

---

* In Mackey and Peck's Lexicon the Bible is stated to be a symbol, *vide* p. 37, Seventh Edition, London.

It is assumed by others that a Lodge should follow the religion and great light of the Constitution under which it works. We ourselves see no other thoroughly consistent line which can be adopted. But if this be so, we must take a stand and forbid any but the Constitution's sacred volume being represented in the Lodge, save for the purpose of obtaining a satisfactory obligation at initiation—never thereafter.

It is tolerably certain that the difficulties and strange combinations which might arise in a country such as India, were not foreseen at the time when brethren first began to treat the system as one which could be Universal.

The Scottish Constitution has got over the difficulties created, or thinks it has, by giving up the Bible as the Great Light of all its members. The danger therefore of our own Constitution being expected to do the same is imminent and cannot longer be unrecognised.

There are brethren who so cling to the Universality of the system that, to attain it, they would even allow the English Constitution to proceed to greater lengths than the Scottish has already gone to. Their idea is that some great injury would be done by the Society recognising that its operations must be restricted to some extent. To them, if Universality is removed, but little is left. They have, in fact, already thrown away the Great Light that the Almighty gave them, and that English Masonry adopted, to chase an " Ignis fatuus;" so long as they still believe it can be caught they are happy; they have wilfully extinguished a true light, all hope in that direction has gone, their only hope now is in the will-o'-the-wisp. This disappears and Freemasonry is then enlightened by—nothing.

CHAPTER IX.

Is Universality Possible?

THE object of this Chapter is to point out to the Freemason certain peculiarities in some of the leading Asiatic religions which have a definite bearing on the principles of Freemasonry.

Apart from any difficulties in the way of the *English* Constitution being universally acceptable, there are insuperable objections to the Masonic system ever being generally accepted in all countries. It might easily be shown that as at this very day we do not know all the languages of Asia, it is preposterous to assert that any system whatever can be accepted by all Asiatics. We know neither the language nor the religion of many large populations in the immediate vicinity of British India at the present time.

Putting this aside, we do know that the conditions of Masonry preclude the system ever being universal, save in the sense that Christianity is so.

Craft Freemasonry, in its complete Degrees, insists on a belief

   1st—In a revelation from God to man.
   2nd—In a resurrection.
   3rd—In the immortality of the soul.
   4th—In the Logos of St. John.

We know that these conditions can *not* be accepted by many. That great religion, which is numerically the strongest in the world, the Buddhist, rejects every one of them; we cannot with certainty assert that any

known religion, except the Christian, accepts all of them. The Parsee belief is perhaps that which approximates closest to our requirements.

It has been remarked in a previous chapter, that there could hardly have been an intention in the seventeenth or even eighteenth century, of forming an institution which should embrace believers in all religions, for the exceedingly simple reason that no comprehensive knowledge of all religions then existed in England, or on the continent of Europe.

This argument can be illustrated to any extent desirable, but for the present it may be pertinent to enquire what the recognised authorities on Masonic subjects know regarding the Parsee's volume of the sacred law. Our respect for Masonic authorities is not enhanced by the enquiry.

"The Zendavesta is the scripture of the modern Parsee; and hence for the Parsee Mason, of whom there are not a few, it constitutes the Book of the Law, or Trestle-Board. Unfortunately, however, to the Parsee it is a sealed book, for, being written in the old Zend language, which is now extinct, its contents cannot be understood. But the Parsees recognise the Zendavesta as of Divine authority, and say in the catechism, or compendium of doctrines in use among them: 'We consider these books as heavenly books, because God sent the tidings of these books to us through the Holy Prophet Zurthost.'"*

The foregoing displays the knowledge of the greatest American authority on this subject, and here is what the English authority says—

"The entire teachings of Zarathustra are to be found in the Zendavesta where Avesta means the text, and Zend the commentary. A great portion of this work has been lost, and all that we at present possess consists of the Vendidad, comprising twenty chapters;

---

* Mackey's " Encyclop. of Freemasonry."

the Vendidad Sadé, fragments of the Yasna and the Vespered; together with another fragmentary collection termed the Yasht Sadé. This work is to the Parsee what the Bible is to the Christian; but being in the Zend language, now extinct, it is a sealed book, except to scholars. The Parsees, however, honour it with great reverence, and say in their catechism or compendium—‘We consider these books as heavenly books, because God sent the tidings of these books to us through the Holy Prophet Zurthost.’ Zurthost is the name given to their prophet by the modern Parsees, and their community they termed the Zurthosti Community.”*

The latter quotation appears to have been inspired to some extent by the former. But Bro. Mackenzie apparently knows, as evidenced by another part of his article on the Zendavesta, what it would appear Bro. Mackey did not know, or he would in all probability have mentioned the fact, that the Parsee believer in the Zendavesta complies with all the conditions required in English Freemasonry in the First Degree. Both writers concur that the Parsee’s sacred volume is a closed book to all but scholars. Under such circumstances it is difficult to conceive how either could consider the Zendavesta as affording Masonic light to all Parsees. The Freemason is nowhere taught to treat the Lodge’s sacred volume as a fetish to be superstitiously worshipped. In the Masonic system, whatever the sacred volume may be, it is intended that it shall be *a guide* to the Mason’s life. In it he is to discover his duty to his God, his neighbour, and himself. In it he is to find God’s revelation to mankind. He is enjoined to diligently study the sacred writings and strive to live up to the divine principles they contain. The Masonic authorities quoted clearly think the Parsee’s veneration for his sacred volume is not greatly removed from fetish worship.

---

* Mackenzie’s “Royal Masonic Cyclop.”

What is the belief of the Parsee of the present day, as based on the writings regarded by him as sacred?

The authority of the following cannot be disputed—

" All that have been living, and will be living, subsist by means of His bounty only. *The soul of the righteous* attains to immortality, but that of the wicked man has everlasting punishment. Such is the rule of Ahuramazda whose the creatures are." (Gatha Ushtavaiti.)

" This splendour attaches itself to the hero (who is to rise out of the number) of prophets (called *Saoshyantó*) and to his companions, in order to make life everlasting, undecaying, imperishable, imputrescible, incorruptible, for ever existing, for ever vigorous, full of power (at the time) when the dead shall rise again, and imperishableness of life shall commence, making life lasting by itself (without further support.) (Gatha Ushtavaiti.)

" The belief in the Resurrection of the body at the time of the last judgment also forms one of the Zoroastrian dogmas. In consequence of Burnouf's inquiries into the phrase *Yavâecha Yavatâtaêcha* (which had been translated by Anquetil 'till the resurrection,' but which means nothing but 'for ever and ever') the existence of such a doctrine in the Zendavesta was lately doubted. But there is not the slightest reason for doubting it, as any one may convince himself—it is clearly stated that the dead shall rise again. That the resurrection of the dead was a common belief of the Magi, long before the commencement of our era, may be learned from the statement of Theopompos. Now the question arises, had Spitama Zarathushtra already pronounced this doctrine, which is one of the chief dogmas of Christianity, and of the Jewish and Mahommedan religions, or is it of later, perhaps foreign origin?

" Though in the Gathas there is no particular statement made of the resurrection of the dead, yet we find

a phrase used which was afterwards always applied to signify the time of resurrection, and the restoration of all life that has been lost during the duration of creation. This is the expression *frashem kerenaon ahûm*, 'they make the life lasting,' *i.e.*, they perpetuate the life. Out of this phrase the substantive *frashô-kereti*, 'perpetuation of life,' was formed, by which, in all the later Avesta books, the whole period of resurrection and palingenesia at the end of time is to be understood. The resurrection forms only a part of it. That this event was really included in the term of *frashô-kereti* one may distinctly infer from Vend xviii., 51, where *Spenta-armaiti* (the earth) is involved to restore 'at the triumphant reduration' of creation the lost progeny in the form of one 'knowing the Gathas, knowing the Yasna, and attending to the discourses.'

"According to these statements, there can be no doubt that this important doctrine is a genuine Zoroastrian dogma, which developed itself naturally, from Spitama Zarathushtra's sayings. There is not the slightest trace of its being borrowed from a foreign source. Besides these direct proofs of its forming a genuine and original part of Zoroastrian theology, it agrees completely with the spirit and tendency of the Parsi religion."

We offer no comment on the above, none is necessary to the Masonic student.

It is somewhat curious that in the few allusions to religion which are to be found in old Masonic songs some are to the Parsi religion. An allusion to the Magi resembling grand columns is to be found in a song, entitled, "By the foregoing hand." Another song (No. 17 in a "Collection of songs to be sung by Freemasons") intimates that Masonry was derived from the Magi. These songs were in existence when there

---

* Haug's "Essay on the Parsis."

was no knowledge in England of the tenets of Parsi belief.

The Parsees number a few hundred thousand souls. The Buddhists number several hundred millions of souls ; the following extracts will therefore be instructive to those who believe Freemasonry can be Universal.

Professor Max Muller shall speak first—

" In no religion are we so constantly reminded of our own as in Buddhism, and yet in no religion have men been drawn away so far from truth as in the religion of Buddha. Buddhism and Christianity are indeed the two opposite poles with regard to the most essential points of religion : Buddhism ignoring all feeling of depend-dence on a higher power, and therefore denying *the very existence of a Supreme Deity.*"*

The following are extracts from a printed Catechism which is largely a compilation from the works of T. W. Rhys Davids, Bishop Bigaudet, Sir Coomara Swamy, B. C. Childers and the Revs. Samuel Beal and R. Spence Hardy ; and in a few cases their exact language is used. The Catechism is sold all over Ceylon.

" A very incomplete popular notion of what orthodox Buddhism is seems to prevail in western countries. The folk-lore and fairy stories upon which some of our prin-cipal Orientalists have mainly based their commentaries are no more orthodox Buddhism than the wild monkish tales of the middle ages are orthodox Christianity. Only the authenticated utterances of Sakya Muni him-self are admitted as orthodox."

Here follow the questions and answers from which we quote—

Question.—What is a Buddhist ?

Answer.—One who professes to be a follower of our Lord Buddha and accepts his doctrine.

Q.—Was Buddha a God ?

A.—No.

---

* Max Muller, Introduction to the Science of Religion.

N

Q.—Was Buddha his name ?

A.—No. It is the name of a condition or state of mind.

Q.—Its meaning ?

A.—Enlightened ; or, he who has the perfect wisdom.

Q.—What was Buddha's real name then ?

A.—Siddartha was his royal name, and Gautama or Gotama, his family name.   He was Prince of Kapilvastu.

Q.—Who were his father and mother ?

A.—King Suddhodna and Queen Maya.

Q.—What people did this king reign over ?

A.—The Sakyas ; an Aryan tribe.

Q.—Where was Kapilvastu ?

A.—In India 100 miles north-east of the city of Benares, and about 40 miles from the Himalaya mountains.

Q.—What is the light that can dispel this ignorance of ours and remove all sorrows ?

A.—The knowledge of the " Four Noble Truths," as Buddha called them.

Q.—Name these Four Noble Truths ?

A.—1st, The miseries of existence ; 2nd, The cause productive of misery, which is the desire, ever renewed, of satisfying one's self without being ever able to secure that end ; 3rd, The destruction of that desire, or the estranging of one's self from it ; 4th, The means of obtaining this destruction of desire.

Q.—How may we gain such conquest ?

A.—By following in the Noble Eight-fold Path which Buddha discovered and pointed out.

Q.—What do you mean by that word ; what is this Noble Eight-fold Path ?

A.—The eight paths of this path are called angas ; they are—1, Right Belief ; 2, Right Thought ; 3, Right Speech ; 4, Right Doctrine ; 5, Right Means of Livelihood ; 6, Right Endeavour ; 7, Right Memory ; 8, Right Meditation.   The man who keeps these angas in mind

and follows them will be free from sorrow and may reach salvation.

Q.—Salvation from what ?

A.—Salvation from the miseries of existence and of rebirths, all of which are due to ignorance and impure lusts and cravings.

A.—And when this salvation is attained, what do we reach ?

A.—Nirvana.

Q.—What is Nirvana ?

A.—A condition of total cessation of changes, of perfect rest ; of the absence of desire, and illusion, and sorrow, of the total obliteration of everything that goes to make up the physical man.   Before reaching Nirvana man is constantly being re-born : and when he reaches Nirvana he is re-born no more.

Q.—Who or what are the "Three Guides" that a Buddhist is supposed to follow ?

A.—They are disclosed in the formula called the Tisarana :—"I follow Buddha as my Guide : I follow the Law as my Guide : I follow the Order as my Guide."

Q.—What does he mean when repeating this formula ?

A.—He means that he regards the Lord Buddha as his all-wise Teacher and Exemplar ; the Law or Doctrine, as containing the essential and immutable principles of Justice and Truth and the path that leads to Summum bonum ; and the Order as the teachers and expounders of that excellent Law revealed by Buddha.

Q.—In what book is written all the most excellent wisdom of Buddha's teachings ?

A.—In the three collections of books called Tripitikas.

Q.—What are the names of the three Pitakas, or groups of books ?

A.—The Vinaya Pitaka, the Sutta Pitaka, and the Abidhamma Pitaka.

N 2

Q.—What do they respectively contain ?

A.—The first contains rules of discipline, for the government of the Priests ; the second contains instructive discourses for the laity ; the third explains the metaphysics of Buddhism.

Q.—Do Buddhists believe these books to be inspired in the sense that Christians believe their Bible to be ?

A.—No : but they revere them as containing all the parts of that Most Excellent Law, by the knowing of which man may save himself.

Q.—Do Buddhists consider Buddha as one who by his own virtue can save us from the consequences of our individual sins ?

A.—Not at all. No man can be saved by another, he must save himself.

Q.—What, then, was Buddha to us and all other beings.

A.—An all-seeing, all-wise counsellor ; one who discovered the safe path and pointed it out ; one who showed the cause of, and the only cure for human suffering. In pointing to the road, in showing us how to escape dangers, he became our Guide. And as one leading a blind man across a narrow bridge, over a swift and deep stream saves his life, so in showing us, who were blind from ignorance the way to salvation, Buddha may well be called our " Saviour."

Q.—How many people are there supposed to be living on this earth ?

A.—About 1,300 millions.

Q.—Of these how many are Buddhists ?

A.—About 500 millions ; not quite half.

Q.—How do Buddhist priests differ from the priests of other religions ?

A.—In other religions the priests claim to be intercessors between man and God, to help to obtain pardon of sins ; the Buddhist priests *do not acknowledge or expect anything from a Divine Power,* but they ought to govern

their lives according to the Doctrine of Buddha and teach the true path to others. *A personal God Buddhists regard as only a gigantic shadow thrown upon the void of space by the imagination of ignorant men.*

Q.—Do they accept the theory of every thing having been formed out of nothing by a Creator?

A.—Buddha taught that two things are eternal, viz: "Akasa," and "Nirvana:" every thing has come out of Akasa in obedience to a law of motion inherent in it, and, after a certain existence passes away. Nothing ever comes out of nothing. We do not believe in miracles; *hence we deny creation and cannot conceive of a Creator.*

Q.—What striking contrasts are there between Buddhism and what may be properly called religions?

A.—Among others these: *It teaches the highest goodness without a God: a continued existence without what goes by the name of "soul;" a happiness without an objective Heaven; a method of salvation without a vicarious Saviour;* a redemption by ourselves as the Redeemer, and without rites, prayers, penances, priests or intercessory saints; and a summum bonum attainable in this life and in this world.

Q.—Are there any dogmas in Buddhism which we are required to accept on faith?

No: *we are earnestly enjoined to accept nothing whatever on faith;* whether it be written in books, handed down from our ancestors, or taught by the sages. Our Lord Buddha has said that we must not believe in a thing said merely because it is said; nor in traditions because they have been handed down from antiquity; nor rumours, as such; nor writings by sages, because sages wrote them: nor fancies that we may suspect to have been inspired in us by a Deva (that is in presumed spiritual inspiration); nor from inferences drawn from some haphazard assumption we may have made; nor because of what seems an analogical necessity; nor on

the mere authority of our teachers or masters. But we are to believe when the writing, doctrine, or saying is corroborated by our own reason and consciousness. "For this," says he in concluding, "I taught you not to believe merely because you have heard, but when you believed of your own consciousness, then to act accordingly and abundantly."

The Buddhist population in the year 1717 must have very largely exceeded the world's Christian population.* The most ardent Freemason can hardly pretend that the Masonic belief in the resurrection of the dead, and an eternal life, are doctrines which any Buddhist can accept. But, judging from what has occurred in the past, we may in the future expect some enthusiastic believer in Universality to propose that all allusions to a life hereafter shall be banished from the Third Degree, as they must give offence to any Buddhist. Such a proposal is strictly in accordance with the concessions already made to the Hebrew and other faiths. If Freemasonry is only to contain that in which all men agree, the character of the Third Degree must be entirely changed. Probably half the population of the world does not at this time believe in an eternal life; certainly many hundreds of millions do not.

The Buddhists claim that their co-religionists represent 5-13ths of the population of the world.† Rhys Davids gives the following table of Buddhist religions :—

SOUTHERN BUDDHISTS.

Ceylon ...	..	...	...	...	...	1,520,575
British Burmah		...	..	...	...	2,447,831
Burmah ...	...	...	...	...	...	3,000,000
Siam	...	...	...	...	...	10,000,000
Annam ...	...	...	...	...	...	12,000,000
(Jains) ...	...	...	...	..	...	485,026
Total about			...	...	...	30,000,000

* Which, even to-day, is never put much over 300,000,000.

† The Encyclopædia Britannica says that more than one-third of the human race are Buddhists.

NORTHERN BUDDHISTS.

Dutch Possessions and Bali	50,000
British Possessions	500,000
Russian Possessions	600,000
Lieu Khen Islands	1,000,000
Korea	8,000,000
Butan and Sikhim	1,000,000
Kashmir...	200,000
Tibet	6,000,000
Mongolia	2,000,000
Mantchuria	3,000,000
Japan	32,794,897
Nepal	500,000
China proper (18 Provinces)	414,686,994
Total about	470,000,000

Mr. T. W. Rhys Davids is a recognised authority on Buddhism. Writing recently, he states that it may well be doubted, whether the present knowledge of that religion is sufficiently advanced to enable even a proficient like himself to state clearly, in a popular treatise, what Buddhism really is.* Only a very small part of the Southern Canon, which is identical with the Ceylon Pitakas, has been published.

To be thoroughly consistent, a revising and reforming Freemason should omit all reference to the resurrection of the body and to the immortality of the soul. These doctrines are rank heresies to the pious Buddhist, and are not acceptable to many others. All mention of individuality and creation should also be excised from the Masonic Ritual. Five hundred millions do not believe anything ever was created, and that it is a mere delusion to think there is either a soul or self.

We have noticed in England the prevalence of a feeling, that a Freemason who has resided for any length of time in India, should know with precision what a Hindoo really believes regarding God. The subject is, however, attended with many difficulties, not the least of them being the contrary opinions expressed by those who should be best acquainted with the facts. If we were

---

* Buddhism by T. W. Rhys Davids, pp. 8–11.

to accept the following, which is from a lecture delivered by the Dewan of Mysore, at Bangalore, on the 28th of March, 1885, we should be satisfied that all Hindoos could consistently take the First Degree if not the others.

Dewan Bahadur R. Ragonauth Rayo then said—"The Hindoo religion expects every Hindoo to observe the following duties unconditionally, namely, 1st to pray and worship the Supreme Ruler of the Universe; 2ndly to obey the Rulers of the land whom a Hindoo is supposed to regard as the representatives of God on earth; and hence the lecturer pointed out the steadfast loyalty of 250 millions of native subjects to our Gracious Sovereign, Empress of India; 3rdly to follow the dictates of our conscience as our true guide."*

Against this we have the fact that the members of the Brahma Samaj, in 1878, treated Hindoo customs, if not the religion itself, as idolatrous. In that year their great leader Keshub Chunder Sen, betrothed his daughter to the Maharajah of Kuch Behar, who recently visited England. The following was a resolution passed at the Brahma Mandir, "That in the opinion of the members of the congregation of the Bharatvarshiya Brahma Mandir, assembled at this meeting, Babu Keshub Chunder Sen, the Minister of the Mandir, by countenancing the premature marriage of his daughter, has violated principles accepted by himself and the Brahma Samaj of India, and, by allowing Hindoo rites to be observed in connection with that marriage, has sanctioned an idolatrous marriage; consequently in the opinion of this meeting he cannot continue in the office of the minister."† From this it is tolerably clear what the enlightened Hindoo, who has not renounced, but has tried to purify his religion, thinks of ordinary Hindooism.

---

* "Madras Mail," 2nd April, 1885.
† Leonard's History of the Brahma Samaj.

The assertion is constantly made that there is a pure monotheism at the base of Hindooism. It would be easy to quote the opinion of scholars to this effect, but the contrary could also be supported. Professor Sir Monier Williams, for instance, states that the manifestations believed in are pure Pantheism. If he be correct, how could a Masonic system be based on the religion of India? The plain state of the case is that at even this late date we do not know what the majority of Hindoos really do believe.

Sir Monier Williams says, "Only a few hymns of the Vedas appear to contain the simple conception of one divine self-existent, omnipresent being; and even in these the idea of one God, present in all nature, is somewhat nebulous and undefined"* " When charged with Polytheism, and of violating the primary law respecting the unity of God, they (Hindus) reply that Brahma, Vishnu, Siva, &c., are only manifestations of the Supreme Brama,"† whom they describe as one without a second.

There is a sect known as the Brahma Samaj, which worships the Supreme Brahma, or God, alone. Wilkins calls this a theistic sect, as does Sir M. Williams. Sir A. Lyall ‡ describes it, on the other hand, as professing an exalted Deism, imported from Europe by its founder about fifty years ago. Sir M. Williams states its creed may be described as "a belief in the Fatherhood of God and the Brotherhood of mankind," and " its theology might be well expressed by the first part of the first Article of the Church of England, 'There is but one living and true God—everlasting, without body, parts, or passions, of infinite power, wisdom and goodness, the maker and preserver of all things.' " He also notices the Arya Samaj, but, while admitting the good

* " Indian Wisdom."
† Wilkins's " Hindu Mythology," edition of 1882.
‡ " Asiatic Studies."

this and other similar societies must do, by uncompromising opposition to caste and idolatry, states that he fears that, with the exception of the Brahma Samaj, they are not free from Pantheistic proclivities.*

We will now deal briefly with this Hindoo sect of reformers which is doing so much good in India at the present time, and whose verdict respecting the idolatrous nature of Hindoo marriages we have already quoted. We do not for one moment decry the doctrines of other bodies which are earnestly striving to purify Hindoo belief—our quotation is merely given because it is from the most celebrated oriental scholar of the day, and is illustrative of other reforming sects among the Hindoos.

Our excerpt is a summary, by Professor Max Muller, of the Doctrines of the Brahma Samáj.

" 1. The Book of Nature and Intuition form the basis of the Brâhmaic faith.

" 2. Although the Brâhmas do not consider any book, written by man, as the basis of their religion, yet they do accept, with respect and pleasure, any truth contained in any book.

" 3. The Brâhmas believe that the religious condition of man is progressive, like the other parts of his condition in this world.

" 4. They believe that the fundamental doctrines of their religion are at the basis of every religion followed by man.

" 5. They believe in the existence of One Supreme God, a God endowed with a distinct personality, moral attributes equal to His nature, and intelligence befitting the governor of the Universe, and worship Him—Him alone. They do not believe in His incarnation.

" 6. They believe in the immortality and progressive state of the soul, and declare that there is a

---

* " Hinduism."

state of conscious existence succeeding life in this world, and supplementary to it, as respects the action of the universal moral government.

" 7. They believe that repentance is the only way to atonement and salvation. They do not recognise any other mode of reconcilement to the offended but loving Father.

" 8. They pray for spiritual welfare, and believe in the efficiency of such prayers.

" 9. They believe in the Providential care of the Divine Father.

" 10. They avow that love towards Him, and performing the works He loves, constitutes His worship.

" 11. They recognise the necessity of public worship but do not believe that they cannot hold communion with the Great Father without resorting to any fixed place at any fixed time. They maintain that we can adore Him at any time and at any place, provided that time and that place are calculated to compose and direct the mind towards Him.

" 12. They do not believe in pilgrimages, but declare that holiness can be attained by elevating and purifying the mind.

" 13. They do not perform any rites or ceremonies or believe in penances as instrumental in obtaining the grace of God. They declare that moral righteousness, the gaining of wisdom, divine contemplation, charity, and the cultivation of devotional feelings are their rites and ceremonies. They further say, — govern and regulate your feelings, discharge your duties to God and to man and you will gain everlasting blessedness. Purify your heart, cultivate devotional feelings, and you will see Him who is unseen.

" 14. Theoretically there is no distinction of caste among the Brâhmas. They declare that we are the children of God, and therefore must consider ourselves brothers and sisters."

Professor Max Muller states of Rajah Rammohun Raj, the great religious reformer of India, the founder of the Brahma Samaj—a sect which should restore the old religion of India, as contained in the Veda: " He never became a Mohammedan, he never became a Christian, but he remained to the end a Brahmin, a believer in the Veda and in the one God, who, as he maintained, had been revealed in the Veda, and especially in the Vedânta, long before he revealed himself in the Bible or in the Koran*" The Trust deed of an Educational Institution he founded in Jessore contains, amongst other stipulations, the following most Masonic one :— †

" The hall is to be used as a place of public meeting of all sorts and descriptions of people, without distinction, as shall behave and conduct themselves in an orderly, religious and devout manner for the worship and adoration of the eternal, unsearchable, and immutable Being, who is the Author and Preserver of the Universe; but not under or by any other name, designation, or title peculiarly used for and applied to any particular being or beings by any man or set of men whatsoever ; and that no graven image, statue, or sculpture, carving, painting, picture, portrait, or the likeness of anything, shall be admitted within the said messuage, building, land, tenements, hereditaments, and premises, &c., &c..

Sir Alfred Lyall says,‡ concerning Indian religions what we think may well be applied to Masonry. He illustrates how the status of even first-class Indian gods has usually been human and exceedingly humble and obscure. When from accidental or other circumstances any divinity has become famous and popular, none of his worshippers will accept the humble origin which

---

* " Biographical Essays," p. 23.
† " Biographical Essays," p. 27 (foot-note).
‡ " Asiatic Studies," p. 24. This work may be studied to the greatest advantage by Masons, whether young or of long standing.

has been so successfully developed. They devoutly credit a picturesque theory of mythical evolution, usually supplied by one possessing more ability than his fellows.

"Thus," says Sir Alfred, "successful thaumaturgy, with lapse of time sufficient to evaporate the lingering flavour of mortal origin, are the two qualifications which lead to a high status among gods. But interest and a good connection open out short cuts to distinction for gods as well as for men. When the original saint or hero belonged in the flesh to a particular tribe, caste, or profession, in such case he may become the tutelary deity of that community, and is less dependent on continual proof of his efficacy, because the worship of him by his constituents is a point of honour, tradition, and *esprit de corps.*"

Having no desire to overload our argument we do not give further quotations from works on Indian or Asiatic beliefs. Freemasons who are unacquainted with them will probably peruse the foregoing sketches with pleasure. We trust it will be believed that we would not have drawn attention to the points we have attempted to elucidate, had we the least intention of proposing any severance in Masonry, or anything in the least derogatory to the Indian Mason. No one can more firmly believe than we do, that in the majority of cases (chiefly we think by reason of the Oriental naturally being of a more religious cast of mind than the European) there are more elements in the native of India for the formation of an ideal Freemason, than can be looked for in the average Englishman. An outspoken Madrassee once said to us "the European is a fine man to teach ; but what a d—d bad Christian he is." There was no intention of being sarcastic. Whilst fighting for the principle that the English Constitution cannot make the least atom of concession regarding the Bible to the natives of India, we are compelled to admit our

belief that they generally lead more consistently Masonic lives than we Europeans do. We do not anticipate that any offence will be given by the position being clearly defined to natives—we have grave doubts as to the respect they entertain for a body of men, who have already sacrificed something of principle in a vain effort to attain the impossible.

The Freemasons of India at this time are entirely under English, Scottish, or Irish Constitutions, neither is there any authentic record of indigenous Freemasonry. We have heard of certain secret societies amongst the Sikhs, described as bearing some affinity to Masonry, but have never been able to ascertain any particulars in support of this statement. If the old Masonic assertion that, wherever civilization has flourished there Masonry has also flourished were true, we might expect to find some trace of it in China. Yet what is understood by Freemasonry, in Europe, has never been found in China, the only society supposed to approach it is purely revolutionary in character, and has no such aims as Freemasonry. We believe the result of any enquiry will be to show that all Masonry in India, if not in Asia, has been imported from England. Scottish Masonry is perhaps better suited to natives than English, as it is notorious that there is a laxity in the former that happily is not common to the English system.

Whilst denying the possibility of the Universality that has been claimed for the Masonic system we yet admit its extreme Catholicity.*

---

* CATHOLIC (Gr. καθολικός, general, universal), a designation adopted at a very early period by the Christian Church to indicate its world-wide universality in contrast with the national particularism of Judaism. It has also been used by ecclesiastical writers, from Ignatius downwards, to denote the Church as the depository of universally-received doctrine (*quod semper, quod ubique, et quod ab omnibus*) in contrast with heretical sects. In the latter or exclusive sense it is still claimed on the ground of historic continuity by the Roman Catholic Church; but the claim, in so far as it is exclusive, is, of course, not recognised by other Christian denominations."— Enclyclopædia Britannica, 9th Edition.

Dr. Oliver stated that Freemasonry was first described as Catholic because it originally embodied the genuine principles of Christianity.*

"If we grant," says Hardwick,† "that in as far as our domestic instincts are concerned, a parallel is found among the other orders of creation, it is no less obvious, that wherever such (faculties) exist in man, their character is uniform, their operation is identical, while in that loftier province of his being where he is immediately connected with the 'God of the spirits of all flesh' the traces of a common nature are peculiarly discernible. . . . .

"Even where the human type is lowest, where it reaches the extreme of degradation, bordering almost on brutality, as, for example, in the natives of Australia, the philanthropist is, notwithstanding, cheered by frequent glimpses of the same distinctive nature, and enabled to detect at least the groundwork of a desecrated temple. . . . .

"Wherever it (Christianity) has penetrated the Lord Shepherd's voice is heard, and wakes an echo in the consciences of men, and what in every case attracts them to his fold, is also that which makes them truly conscious of the universal brotherhood subsisting in all nations.

"Christianity came fresh from Heaven, it rested on a series of objective revelations, it was active and diffusive as the light, and all-embracing as the firmament of Heaven, it dealt with man as man, and never faltered in its claim to be regarded as a veritable 'world religion.'"

"The Church is called Catholic, because it is throughout the world, from one end of the earth to the other; and because it teaches universally and completely all the truths which ought to come to men's

---

* Discrepancies, p. 175.
† "Christ and other Masters," pp. 57-58.

knowledge, concerning things both visible and invisible, heavenly and earthly; and because it subjugates, in order to godliness, every class of men, governors and governed, learned and unlearned; and because it universally treats and heals every sort of sins which are committed by soul or body, and possesses in itself every form of virtue which is named."*

That Preston's ideas agreed with Oliver's, the following passage plainly shows—

"Masons have ever paid due obedience to the moral law, and inculcated its precepts with powerful energy on their disciples. Hence the doctrine of a God, the Creator, and Preserver of the Universe, has been their firm belief in every age; and under the influence of that doctrine, their conduct has been regulated for a succession of years. The progress of knowledge and philosophy, *aided by Divine revelation*† [the italics are ours throughout this passage], having enlightened the minds of men with the knowledge of the true God, *and the sacred truths of the Christian* faith, Masons have readily acquiesced in a religion so wisely calculated to make men happy."

We have seen that it was formerly stated in the Constitutions that Freemasons were enjoined to change their religion with their residence—a somewhat odd notion for reconciling a sincere Christian, or any other pious brother, to Freemasonry; there is room to doubt whether this was ever seriously enjoined. A more reasonable theory is that the statement in Anderson's Constitutions is correct, and that brethren were enjoined to conform to the variations in Christianity itself, practised in various countries, and that by this, ancient Freemasons considered Universality was attained. In

---

* "St. Cyril," Catechetical Lectures, xviii., 23.

† The idea of a revelation from God is especially Christian, but not peculiar to Christianity alone. The Brahmins believe that each nation has had imparted to it the doctrines most suitable for it. Bjornstjerna: Theogony of the Hindoos, p. 67.

other words, their ideas of Universality did not extend beyond various phases of Christian belief. Oliver argues that the Church of Christ is so variously represented in different countries by various establishments suited to the genius and disposition of their people,* that it has a superior claim to Universality than any other religion. All mankind may embrace Christianity, but there are, as we shall see further on, hindrances to many of them joining Fremasonry. Women being excluded tends to spoil this idea of Universality : private soldiers are barred from its privileges ; its somewhat heavy fees and subscriptions close the door to a large part of the world. Of this more anon.

In the "Emulation" Lectures it is asserted (properly no doubt), that learning originated in the East, and spread to the West. Now, how could such a ritual be Universally used ? Take China or India ; there is no doubt that learning arose *with* them, or in countries to the *west* of them, and spread still further west. But the ritual, with all its claims to superior wisdom, comes *from* the West, and is designed to enlighten the East, as all the world beside. It simply shows that it was never even dreamed in the earlier days that Masonry would be practised in Asia.

The writer unhesitatingly ascribes many of the errors which have crept into Freemasonry to the claim put forth on behalf of Universality. There is no reference made in early charges to it ; while the existence of Masonry from the beginning of time is asserted, in the early charges of the 18th century there is not a word about it.† It seems certain that the doctrine was first promulgated by a brother, Dunckerley, who never foresaw what it would all lead to.

The Universality of the system is nowhere alluded to in any Landmark, as given by any Masonic authority. If it had been the intention, when the Landmarks were

---

* " Discrepancies," p. 214.   † *Ibid.*, p. 216.

O

first collected, to make an Universal system, or if it was then considered to be Universal, how is it that the Landmarks are devoid of any allusion to it?

Oliver urges that to be Universal, a system must be inclusive, and that Freemasonry is, in its very essence, exclusive in its ritual observances and general plan. Doubtless, on the other hand, some idea that Freemasonry would spread, as it has spread, gradually arose in the minds of many intelligent Brethren, as the world became known to them by the progress of exploration, conquest, and adventure, and that it might in this sense become a Universal institution in the end. To be precise, Masonry may be and is Universal in this sense only—that it is found in every part of the habitable globe. In the same sense Christianity is Universal; because both Christians and Freemasons have settled everywhere; but neither the Society—nor the religion of which it is the handmaid, can be universally embracing, till all men be converted Christians. It is Masonically orthodox to spread the light, and the great Masonic light in English practice is the Bible, the study of which we see so repeatedly enjoined. Believing, as does the writer, that English Masonry was originally a pure and creedless form of Christianity, remembering that the Great Architect enjoined that the Gospel which the Bible contains should be placed before all nations, he believes that Freemasonry *should* be—nay, *will* be—Universal, although at present there are so many obstacles in the way. That every encouragement should be offered to all people to lead more earnest and truer lives, lives of honest purpose and endeavour, is a religious truism. It cannot be doubted that the observance of any reasonably pure religion would conduce to this end, and if they will not accept Christianity as their belief, and the Bible as their guide, then let them get what good they can from their own religious systems. But why should the Christian Mason abandon or shamefacedly

hide his belief to gain a Hindoo, or any other member, for the Craft? It is purchasing too dearly: it is creating contempt for our poltroonry: it is being false to all our professions, to in any way allow a shadow to overcast our Great Light.

Among the irreconcileable points of Freemasonry with Universality, the following stand out prominently.

The Invocation on the Consecration of a Lodge is to the "God of Israel." How can this be reconciled with Universality?

The 23rd Landmark is commonly stated to emphasize the Secrecy of the Institution. Can an institution be Universal and secret at the same time?

Let the reader study the articles on "Quaker" and "Affirmation" in Mackey's Lexicon, and he will see that at least the God-fearing and upright Quaker is excluded from the benefits of this vaunted Universality.*

The poor have no chance of entering Masonry.† Should a comparatively poor man join the English Brotherhood, he will probably soon find that the ordinary expenses are beyond his means. How many men do we not know who have been compelled to neglect Freemasonry owing to their means not being equal to the calls made upon them? The customs and regulations of the Order have often prevented Masons from taking part in many Craft matters, to their loss as regards both profit and enjoyment. Extremely poor men—an expression which describes by far the larger part of the world's male population, must always be excluded. By the present conditions, no man can be initiated in England under £5 5s., or abroad for less than £3 10s. 6d. In the United States the expenses

---

* We are aware that in English practice, a Quaker's affirmation has been accepted, and that in many German jurisdictions no form of oath is ever administered: but in America, Mackey's ruling would hold good. Peck's Edition of Mackey is in error as regards the Society of *Friends*.

† *Vide* p. 269 of "The Golden Remains of the Early Masonic Writers," by Dr. Oliver (quoting Calcott).

are very greatly in excess of these rates. Add to these sums the dues payable on joining, and quarterage, and it will be at once perceived that Freemasonry is not for the poor. In India, the payment of 50 Rupees would be impossible to millions upon millions : the possession of far less money than that in many parts constitutes a fairly well-to-do native.

The claim is not that Freemasonry will some day be an Universal system, but that it is so now, and that a belief in God is all that is required of a Candidate, whereas, in many cases, a prohibitive amount of money is equally necessary—an amount, in all probability, not possessed by the male individuals of half India's population.

A Lewis, or son of a Mason, can be initiated at the age of 18 years, while all other Candidates must be 21 years of age*. The Order in some countries thus closes its doors for three years to all those who are not sons of Masons, and who may die between 18 and 21; they can never enter the earthly heaven of Masonry. Dr. Farr's life tables are now somewhat out of date, and Dr. Ogle's are generally accepted. By these it is shown that between these ages 14,900 males die out of every million born. These 14,900 may rightly complain that the Universal character of Freemasonry did not affect their case.

Admittance into the Order is denied to all who cannot write. Thus the *Universal* Light of Freemasonry is denied to those who most require it !

The Ballot is another refutation of Universality. It is certain that many believers in the One God, and otherwise excellent men, have been refused admittance to our Order by the operation of the ballot-box. It is

---

* This is the popular idea everywhere, and is acted on in America and some Jurisdictions. The notion is prevalent in England, but founded on a delusion. The Lewis can claim no advantage beyond that of being initiated first of several Candidates at any meeting. On the other hand, any man may be initiated under age, by dispensation, on good cause being shown.

true that all men may stand the ballot, but this hardly supports the Masonic doctrine of " Universality—with but one condition." There are *many* conditions.

The Candidate must be "physically perfect." Mark this rather exacting demand and grandiloquent description which, in reality, requires that the person presenting himself must be something more than the Apollo Belvidere—must be able to pass the tests of the anatomist, physiologist, and physician, as well as the artist and professor of athletics! How many shall we find to "fill the bill?" "When found, make a note of." But seriously, what proportion in the world are in even reasonably physical health—perfectly sound in limb and wind? Were we to say that half the world's population complied with these conditions, we should overshoot the mark. Every other person has some physical defect or blemish, or actual disease, slight or severe, as the case may be. Poor cripples! " ye cannot enter here," but must seek some easier Universal system.*

Modern Freemasons assert that there is an Universal religion: that there is some one point on which all religions agree, *i.e.*, in a belief in the true and living God, the Great Architect of the Universe. Were this true, there would certainly be a good starting point for Freemasonry, but it is utterly incorrect. The greatest religion in the world, so far as mere numbers are concerned, is Buddhism, and must therefore be heard on this point. What does it tell us? Why, that *nothing* ever was created, and that there is no *God*. Neither Buddhist nor Hindu has any such clear conception of God as is required by Freemasonry: that is to say, approximately one half the population of the world is debarred from joining our *Universal* Institution.

* Here, again, Americans are more stringent than Englishmen. Nowhere, of course, can physical *perfection* be insisted on; but "the maimed, the halt, and the blind" are rejected in the United States, whilst in England they are admitted, and in Germany even eunuchs have attained our privileges.

To the Masons who believe in the very early birth of our system we would urge, that an Universal system could not have existed in the time of Solomon by reason of the fact, generally admitted, that any pure monotheistic faith must then have been antagonistic to the religions by which it was surrounded, and could never have been kept alive except by the exercise of intolerance towards them.*

Those writers of the last century who attempted to trace the History of Freemasonry up to Adam, although they asserted much that was absurd, still had one definite aim in view; viz., to create an idea of the connection between the existing Masonic system and "a primeval preternatural revelation" communicated to mankind in its infancy.

One of the first claims regarding Universality in Freemasonry, appears to have been that it possessed an Universal language ! Whether Masonry ever did possess anything beyond a few cryptographic alphabets, signs, and tokens, is very doubtful. Anyhow, no claim to universal language could be sustained, for it would not be more than—if so much as—common to the Craft.

The idea of the possibility of an Universal religion has had many supporters. The Persian Mani in the fourth century compared the teachings of Zoroaster, Buddha, and Christ, and finding what he deemed the same divine ingredients in all, though variously modified, proposed a reconciliation of the three systems, "or rather to incorporate the older creeds with what had been more recently revealed in Christianity."†

In the present day one of the greatest thinkers in Germany—Eduard von Hartmann—believes the religion of the future will be a "synthesis of the Eastern and Western religious Developments."‡

---

* Newman's "Hebrew Monarchy," p. 26, 2nd edition.
† Hardwick's "Christ and other Masters."
‡ *Westminster Review,* July, 1886.

Dr. Cudworth, while engaged on his great work,* was extremely anxious to confute Atheism, by producing all the evidence he could as to the universal existence of a belief in one God. In dealing with Japan, India, and China, he had reluctantly to admit that too little was then known regarding the ruling faith in those countries to draw any definite conclusion whether or not a clear belief in one God prevailed there.

In further support of our argument that an acquaintance with all religions did not exist even at the time of the Masonic Union, we quote Professor Tiele, who,† in undertaking as late as 1877, to write universally regarding religion states, he has to deliberately exclude the natural religion of Japan, as so much is dubious and vague regarding it.

Yet we are asked by some Masons to accept as a fact that even two hundred years ago, or certainly in 1717, our Institution was so framed and constituted as to be Universal in its character and operations. If this were so in 1717, a very profound knowledge of religious systems must then have existed. Before such a position could be admitted by any thinking man, he would demand precise information as to the tenets of at least the principal faiths of the world. We know that this knowledge was not available in 1717. It is even open to question whether, at the Union in 1813, the fundamental tenets of the chief religions of the world were known by Masons; certainly no such comprehensive knowledge could have existed as to justify a statement that all men could subscribe to the Masonic system. An examination of the dates when Europe became acquainted with the principles of the Buddhist, the Jain, the Sikh, and the Parsee religions will show conclusively that if Freemasonry did originally advance the

---

* The first edition of his work, " The Intellectual System of the Universe," was published in 1678.

† " Outlines of the History of Religion."

pretensions with which it is now credited, it was a piece of presumption and nothing more. At the present time it is impossible to be confident that any initial form of religious belief affords a common point of union for even half the human race.*

The following tables, the one regarding religions and religious compliances, and the other touching the education of the people of India will afford some food for thought, as to how far Freemasonry can be Universal in India.

---

* The languages of all the tribes on the Indian frontiers are not yet known. As recently as 1886 a work on the Bargastá language, previously quite unknown, was published.

TABLE OF COMPLIANCE, IN RELIGIOUS SYSTEMS, WITH ENGLISH MASONIC CONDITIONS (APART FROM CHRISTIAN), IN THE FIRST THREE DEGREES.

Religious Belief.	Is there belief in one God.	Is there belief in Revelation.	Is there belief in Resurrection.	Is there belief in Immortality of the soul.	Is there belief in the Logos of St. John.	Estimated number of Religionists.	Remarks.
VARIOUS FORMS OF CHRISTIANITY	Yes.	Yes.	Yes.	Yes.	Yes.	About 327 to 330 millions.	Berghaus' and Keith Johnston's estimate.
HINDOO (ORDINARY)	No.	Yes.	Yes.	?	No. }	About 188 millions.	Census of 1881.
,, (BRAHMIN)	Yes.	Yes.	Yes.	Yes.	No. }		
MOHAMMEDAN	Yes.	Yes.	Yes.	Yes.	No.	About 155 millions.	Keith Johnston's estimate.
BUDDHIST	No.	No.	No.	No.	No.	About 500 millions.	All authorities agree on 500 millions.
JAIN	Yes.	Yes.	Doubtful	Doubtful	No.	About 1·2 millions.	Census of 1881.
SIKH	Yes.	Yes.	Yes.	Yes.	No.	About 1·8 millions.	Census of 1881.
PARSEE	Doubtful	Yes.	Yes.	Yes.	No.	About 150,000.	
SHINTO	Doubtful	No.	Doubtful	Doubtful	No.		
TAO	No.	No.	Doubtful	Doubtful	No.		
CONFUCIAN	No.*	No.	Yes.	Yes.	No.		* Shangte is worshipped by some as a God.
MORMON	Yes.	Yes.	Yes.	Yes.	Yes.		
ATHEISTIC	No.	No.	Various.	Various.	No.		
DEISTIC	Yes.	No.	Various.	Various.	No.	3 to 4 millions. Rev. Hugh Miller places Jews at 7 millions.	
HEBREW	Yes.	Yes.	Yes.	Yes.	†		† A belief in the loss, but not the recovery.

UNABLE TO READ AND WRITE IN INDA.

(Extracted from the Census of 1881).

ABORIGINES	4,878,013
HINDUS	158,841,634
MUHAMMEDANS	46,899,098
BUDDHISTS	2,440,876
SIKHS	1,764,570
JAINS	589,007
PARSIS	38,088
JEWS	7,089
CHRISTIANS	887,694
VARIOUS RELIGIONS	825,215
	217,171,284

Out of a total population of 253,891,821 souls.

In Armenia there is a religious sect called " Yezidis," who worship the Devil and yet so comply with all Masonic conditions that a Universalist Freemason would have to admit them to initiation. They believe their Devil-god to be a true and living god, they supplicate and put their trust in him, they possess a volume of the sacred law, they even possess an ineffable name. All this is much more than the Universalist requires; the first qualification is ALL he demands. The following cutting from the *St. James's Gazette*, of 26th February, 1887, will show our Universalist friends what manner of man is eligible, according to them, for initiation. No objection can be taken to their want of good morals. Morality is a question of usage, they are doubtless moral according to their special religion. If our own standard of morals is to be our guide, how can we admit the polygamous Oriental?

" THE DEVIL-WORSHIPPERS OF MESOPOTAMIA."

" Not far from Mosul, in Mesopotamia, there are a few Kurdish villages where one finds neither mosque nor minaret, synagogue nor medrash, church nor meeting-house. Moslems—saving an occasional Government official—are rarely seen there, travellers not at all. Ordinarily there is nothing in the appearance of these places or the people to attract the attention of wayfarers,

apart from the white dresses of the women and the vests of the men. But one day in the year the villages assume quite a holiday aspect in preparation for a strange ceremony annually enacted there. The houses are plentifully decked with garlands of yellow flowers, and the people take up positions outside—the women in spotless gowns, the men with a twisted black cord round their necks. Then a procession of some thirty persons emerges from the residence of the 'pir' or priest, and begins slowly to perambulate the village. In front march half a dozen weird-looking personages in long black robes and strange black head-gear; then come half a score of 'kawals,' in yellow mantles and white turbans, chanting religious hymns in an outlandish tongue; and behind them as many more, playing an accompaniment to the singers on reedy flutes and tambourines. Following these is the white-robed priest, bearing upon his shoulders a kind of epaulette, and holding aloft the bronze figure of a bird, guarded on either side by a fierce-looking Kurd with a perfect arsenal of small arms about his person. In the rear rides the white-turbaned sheikh of the district, with a second batch of 'black-heads' to wind up the procession. The party makes the round of the village, the people raising their hands towards the brazen bird as it passes, and then halts in front of the priest's house. Here a sheep is in readiness; it is cut open, and the heart is torn from it and thrown down at the feet of the black-robed figures. The procession then re-enters the dwelling, while the sheep is made ready for the pot; and, in honour of the day, the residents afterwards dine together as soon as their 'stew' is ready. These Kurdish villagers are the 'Yezidis' or 'devil-worshippers' of Mesopotamia; and their annual procession —known as the 'Showing of the King-Bird,' the Melik Taous or 'Peacock King'—is the only ceremonial of their mystic cult.

" This strange sect is by no means confined to the vicinity of Mosul, though the hereditary religious head of the community resides there. There are numerous Yezidi villages in the country stretching from the Euphrates to Aleppo, and the devil-worshippers are found in Asiatic Russia as well as in Persia. They are all Kurds, and use only the Kurdish language in their homes. Once in the course of every year they are visited by their sheikh with the sacred ' king-bird ; ' but on all matters connected with their religion, their rites, and their traditions, they preserve the most obstinate silence. Their deity is denominated ' Khoda,' and they reverence the devil; but the more immediate object of their worship is Adi, the son of Mussafer, who lived in the sixth century and in whom the deity became incarnate. For religious purposes they are formed into five clans or divisions, each under the rule of an ecclesiastical sheikh descended in a miraculous way from the prophet Adi. The saint was himself un-married and had no children; but, in order that the Yezidis might not be without authoritative rulers, he created a son for himself who subsequently had five others, the progenitors of the existing religious chiefs. These sheikhs are regarded as semi-divine, and are not allowed to marry out of their own line; in fact, inter-marriage with a common Yezidi entails the punishment of death upon both parties. The chiefs assert that they are in possession of an inspired volume, called the ' Jalaoo,' and a commentary upon it by the prophet Adi, known as the ' Mashafi Bashe' or ' Black-Book ; ' but no stranger has ever yet set eyes on these works. They are forbidden to learn either reading or writing, except-ing a single family which has charge of their sacred writings. The patriarch of the sect—like the ' Kak ' near Aleppo, and the Emir—is unable to read; but he claims for himself and his family the gifts of clair-voyance and second-sight, as well as the power of

prophecy. The devil-worshippers accept no proselytes: 'A Yezidi,' they say, 'must be born a Yezidi; he cannot be made.' They have no ceremonial ablutions, or attach no importance to them, and are allowed to use nothing coloured blue. They will not sit down on a sofa having a blue tassel, or enter a room containing an article of furniture covered with blue cloth. Their religion prohibits them from serving as soldiers, though there appears to be nothing to prevent them from cutting throats on their own account. They baptize boys and girls; and, when old enough, every member has to make choice of a sister or brother who is to be his or her companion for eternity. Adultery, where consent is given, is lawful, and intercourse between the sexes is regulated by no conventional restraints. The sheikhs and their families, as well as the subordinate priests known as 'pirs,' are entirely supported by the voluntary gifts of the villagers, whom they visit regularly three times a year; such gifts being regarded in the light of offerings to the semi-divine prophet from whom their rulers claim descent. The Yezidis may everywhere be distinguished from the Moslem inhabitants of the country by the vests they wear closed up in the neck. They certainly bear a secret mark upon their persons, like some Indian sectaries; for they will never bare their breasts; and under no circumstances will a Yezidi ever utter the word 'sheitan'—that is, 'devil'—or in any way refer to the central object of his secret adoration.

"The most important personages — and the most highly venerated — in the hierarchy of the devil-worshippers are the brotherhood of ascetics whom the Moslem peasants designate the 'Karabash' or black-heads. They are a kind of devotee or fakir, who dress entirely in black, with a curious over-mantel of yellow which gives them a very uncanny appearance. They form a distinct class among the Yezidis, and take

precedence of everybody. On the occasion of any public solemnity or religious ceremonial the Emir himself makes way for the 'Karabash,' whose hand he reverently kisses. These ascetics are usually of the sheikh families, and aspirants must be introduced by one already belonging to the brotherhood. For forty days prior to his initiation the novice has to live alone in a retreat specially appointed, and he fasts every day from morning till night. He must not speak a word during this period, and is not allowed to look upon a human face. None may go near him, saving the fakir or devotee who brings him his food each evening. When the time of probation has expired he is conducted to his village by six companions. The residents assemble in front of the priest's house, the 'king-bird' is brought out, a sheep is slain, and the neophyte sprinkled with blood. Then, one by one, his brother fakirs dress him in the sombre garments of the order: a long black woollen gown, a vest that may be of any colour save blue, and black head-gear, which may not be of cotton and is bound to be the work of his own hands. Last of all he receives the symbolical 'mahak' or 'bridle,' a cord that goes round his neck and is never afterwards, be the wearer living or dead, removed from its place. When travelling from village to village the Karabash carries suspended from his neck a 'kashkul,' or wooden bowl, in which the well-disposed deposit any gifts intended for the order. The person of the fakir is sacred while alive, and when dead none may touch his body, excepting a member of the fakir fraternity—not the Emir, sheikh, or chief. His *confrères* take charge of the corpse, envelop it in a black cloth, and so inter it in certain caves allotted to them near a holy shrine. The ascetics are under the immediate orders of their own chief, the 'Kak,' who resides at a well-known 'mazar' or pilgrim resort not very far from Aleppo. He has also control of the 'kawals' or Yezidi singers; who travel from village to village with

the image of the sacred 'bird-king,' chanting hymns which they only know, and which have been transmitted to them orally—so they assert—from their progenitors, who themselves served the prophet Adi.

"In the secret cult of the Yezidis an important part is borne by the 'Fakraya,' an order of 'female devotees' attached to the shrine of the saint near the Hakkariya Mountains. There are about fifty of them, in the charge of an elderly woman designated 'Kabana' or chief of the fakiresses. A few are middle-aged persons, whose duty it is to trim the lamp of Adi and burn incense at his tomb every evening. The remainder are mostly well-favoured and comely young persons whose status is that of the 'kadeshoth' attached in ancient times to the Temples of Baal and Astarte. Every year there is a great festival at the shrine, attended by numbers of Yezidis from every district where they live; and as the devil-worshippers have inherited the traditions of the ancient 'love rituals' and the gnostic 'agape' or 'love-feasts,' the existence of the 'Fakraya' in connection with Yezidi-worship is understood and accounted for. The morning ritual on the occasion of the yearly gathering is simple enough. In the shrine-chamber, a plain whitewashed hall, the 'kawals' chant a few hymns; and the 'farash' or keeper goes round with a large bowl of oil, in which a lighted wick is floating. The worshippers, in turn, hold their hands above the flame, stroke their faces gently, and then bend over to inhale the odour of the sacred light. But the secret ceremonies of the Yezidi sectaries are performed at night, in a cavern beneath the shrine, with subterranean passages leading in and out, carefully guarded by the 'tshavish' or permanent officials of the place. Here, in total darkness and in the bowels of the earth, secure from all possibility of observation, they celebrate those mystic rites, designed to propitiate the arch-enemy of man, which have gained for the followers

of Adi the designation of devil-worshippers and which no stranger has ever yet witnessed."

One of the most scientific of our writers on "The Science of Religion," makes the following statement in one of his lectures :—" In exploring together the ancient archives of language, we found that the highest God had received the same name in the ancient mythology of India, Greece, Italy, and Germany, and had retained that name whether worshipped on the Himalayan mountains, or among the oaks of Dodona, on the Capitol, or in the forests of Germany. I pointed out that his name was *Dyaus* in Sanskrit, *Zeus* in Greek, *Jovis* in Latin, *Tiu* in German; but I hardly dwelt with sufficient strength on the startling nature of this discovery. These names are not mere names . . . . these words are not mere words, but they bring before us, with all the vividness of an event which we witnessed ourselves but yesterday, the ancestors of the whole Aryan race, thousands of years it may be before Homer and Veda, worshipping an unseen being, under the self same name, the best, the most exalted name they could find in their vocabulary—under the name of Light and Sky." This expresses a Masonic belief, but we ask Freemasons, even if this view be correct, is their system one which would commend itself to a Buddhist ?

The denial of God's existence by Buddhists is affirmed by all great writers on the subject* and by themselves.

This was not known in 1717. We also find that in the catechism already quoted, Buddhism teaches the possibility of the highest goodness, *without a God.*†

Is therefore Universality (in the sense usually understood) POSSIBLE?

And now let us return to our main argument. Has this effort to suppress Christian allusions and connections

---

* *Vide* Prof. Kuenen in his Hibbert lectures, 1882.

† Students may be referred to Hardy's "Manual of Buddhism."

been attended by any good? Has it even helped to make a more consistent universal system? These points may well be inquired into.

On the one hand the Christian has stifled his feelings, he has cancelled and done away with Christian allusions, so as not to cause offence to others, and to obtain Universality. On the other hand the Hebrew appropriates to himself the Royal Arch Degree, which the Christian has thoughtlessly turned adrift. Again, on the one side the Christian refrains from speaking of Christ as his Saviour, and on the other hand our Hindoo brethren openly assert that Jesus Christ's position is on a mere level with "Zoroaster, Mahomed, Krishna, Rama, and others."* It is not easy to discover what good has been wrought by this; the Christian is distinctly the sufferer by the result. He alone has abandoned his religion, whilst the brethren of all other beliefs have asserted theirs.†

---

* *Vide* p. 91, vol. xv., "Masonic Record."

† At Masonic meetings in Bombay the Grand Zendavesta Bearer, the Koran Bearer, &c., are often present, but not the Bible Bearer; if he be present the notices of the Scottish meetings are strangely silent regarding him.

CHAPTER X.

Opinions of Masonic Writers.

WE are not aware that anyone has tried in any systematic manner to show that Freemasonry evinces throughout its history, its ritual, and its records, strong traces of its Christian origin, and of its utter irreconcileability with any other interpretation. Many authors have expressed their views on this point, and have dealt with individual details, showing, to at least their own satisfaction, the Christian connection. Some, imbued with what we deem to be the true spirit of Masonry, have openly expressed their conviction that English Freemasonry cannot be separated from Christianity. A complete collection of such dicta would fill many volumes. Masonic works teem with clear enunciations on this point. In this chapter we give the views of some of the most eminent Masonic writers, who, in nearly every instance, were in their day considered authorities.

One of the earliest writers after the Grand Lodge was formed was the Rev. Charles Brockwell, A.M., Chaplain to George II. He wrote: " In some points, or rather modes of worship, we may differ or dissent from each other, yet still the Lodge reconciles even these. . . . . Thus we are united, though distinguished : united in the same grand Christian fundamentals, though distinguished by some circumstances."* We are unable

---

* Sermon at Christ's Church, Boston, on 27th December, 1749, by the Rev. Charles Brockwell, A.M., His Majesty's Chaplain. Published at the request of the Grand Officers.

ourselves to construe this as meaning anything else than that, at the time Bro. Brockwell wrote, Christians only, but of all shades of that religion, were Freemasons. We may be mistaken, but so it reads to us.

Speaking of the character of a Mason, Bro. Brockwell said : " He is under the strictest obligation to be a good man, a true Christian, and to act with honour and honesty, however distinguished by different opinions in the circumstantials of religion."* This, again, reads to us as we have before stated.

We will now quote from three of the best known authors of the last century. These are Calcott, who published his "Candid Disquisition," in 1769, Preston, who wrote his "Illustrations of Masonry" in 1772, and Hutchinson, who issued his first edition of "The Spirit of Masonry" in 1775. Numerous editions of all these books have been issued both in America and England.

Of the last-named work Mackey says it contains the first philosophical explanation of the Symbolism of the Order, and that it still remains a priceless boon to the Masonic student. Writing of Calcott's book, Mackey states, it "was the first extended effort to illustrate philosophically the science of Masonry, and was followed a few years after by Hutchinson's admirable work ; so that Oliver justly says that Calcott opened the mine of Masonry and Hutchinson worked it." In these three works we have at least the generally accepted views of the Craft in the latter part of the last century, regarding the esoteric teaching of Freemasonry. Two of these writers teach that Masonry is a Christian system.

Calcott speaks of *Our Saviour* on several occasions.† He speaks of the Bible as being the Mason's spiritual trestle-board. His references to the necessity of the Mason observing certain Masonic teachings because they are Christian doctrine, are repeated over and over

---

* *Ibid.*
† Pages 71 and 182 original edition.

P 2

again.* After giving certain advice, he says that, if it be followed, the world will be convinced "that we are lovers of Him who said, 'If ye love me keep my commandment, that ye love one another as I have loved you.'" He gives a prayer to be used at the admission of a brother as follows, "endue him with divine wisdom, that he may, with the secrets of Masonry, be able to unfold the mysteries of godliness and Christianity." The prayer concludes "This we humbly beg in the name, and for the sake of Jesus Christ, our Lord and Saviour. Amen."

We are, in fact, unable to conceive how Calcott could have more explicitly expressed his conviction that Freemasonry was a Christian system.

In an address to the Palladian Lodge, Hereford, presumably about 1767, will be found the following remarks. In referring to certain disreputable Brethren, Bro. Calcott declared them to be " no ways qualified for a Society founded upon wisdom, and cemented by morality and Christian love." Speaking of temperance, he said: " This virtue has many powerful arguments in its favour, for, as we value our health, wealth, reputation, family, and friends, our character as men, as Christians, as members of Society in general, and as Freemasons in particular." He then emphasises that *Masonic* are *Christian* virtues, and that they should be exercised for this reason. He concludes by stating: " this will convince the scoffer and slanderer that we are lovers of Him who said ' If ye love me, keep my commandments ; and this is my commandment, that ye love one another, as I have loved you.' This will prove to our enemies that a good Mason is a good man and a good Christian."

Although our author holds religious discussions in Lodge to be un-Masonic, yet are there frequent references to St. Peter, St. Paul, and to *our Saviour* in the Charges, &c., quoted by him, and said to have been used

---

* Pages 161, 164, 169, 183, and elsewhere.

in Lodges in the last century. Reading this book, the only conclusion that can be drawn is, that although no discussion of religious subjects was allowed in Lodges, it was then considered perfectly proper to continually remind the Members that they were, as Freemasons, members of a Christian association. There does not appear to have been any inclination to dispute this point; it apparently never entered anybody's head to deny it.

Calcott quotes the well-known invocation of the Old Charges, which commences: "The Mighty God and Father of Heaven, with the wisdom of his Glorious Son," as a prayer formerly used.

We have mentioned that Hutchinson carried on the explanations commenced by Calcott. The "Spirit of Masonry" was issued with the sanction and approval of the Grand Master, his Deputy, the Grand Wardens, the Grand Treasurer, and the Grand Secretary, who jointly *recommended* it to the Fraternity. This they did after stating that they had read the book. We could thus hardly have a more authoritative work. Hutchinson commences with an explanation of the design of Freemasonry; he has hardly entered upon his subject before he asserts that the Society is at once religious and civil.* He is not vague when defining what the religion of an English Freemason is, or rather was, in 1775. On his eighteenth page he says "It is not to be presumed that we are a set of men professing religious principles contrary to the revelations and doctrines of the Son of God, reverencing a Deity by the denomination of the God of Nature, and denying that mediation which is graciously offered to all true believers. The members of our Society at this day, in the third stage of Masonry, confess themselves to be Christians," "the veil of the Temple is rent—the builder is smitten—and we are raised from the tomb of transgression."

* Page 9 original edition.

After writing regarding the origin of Freemasonry and giving views generally entertained, Hutchinson states that finally we obtained our teaching and rules from " the propagators of the Christian doctrine, who brought with them the principles of the Master's Order, and taught the converted those sacred mysteries which are typical of the Christian faith, and professional of the hope of the resurrection of the body and the life of regeneration. Yet I fear few among us are equal to the character we have assumed."

The foregoing is sufficiently distinct, but Brother Hutchinson evidently was prepared to go further and enunciate that a Master Mason could *only* be a Christian, for he wrote* "The Master Mason's Order, under its present principles, is adapted to every sect of Christians. It originated from the earliest era of Christianity, in honour to, or in confession of, the religion and faith of Christians, before the poison of sectaries was diffused over the Church."

Space will not allow us to further quote the opinions of these two brethren; any study of their works will but more clearly prove the entire acceptance by them of Masonry as a Christian institution. We do not think it is all-important to prove they were correct in their view; we maintain that the universal acceptance thereof at the time it was expressed, is sufficient proof that the fraternity acknowledged Freemasonry as Christian.

We now go back to Preston's work. This was more an historical narrative than an exposition of principles. We must here warn readers who may only be able to peruse Preston's Illustrations as edited by Oliver, that it is almost impossible to distinguish by any internal evidence what is Preston's writing and what is Oliver's. If any of Oliver's reprints are taken, an enormous mass of quotations could be given in support of our

---

* Page 225 original edition.

contention. These would not, however, be Preston's views, and for the sake of safety we quote only from the twelfth edition, which was edited by Preston himself. If Preston is not read with some care it is conceivable that erroneous opinions might be formed as to the doctrines he is explaining. We are inclined to believe that it was the vagueness of Preston which may have induced Hutchinson to write as he did. If the student will refer to the former's remarks on the second section of the second lecture, it will be seen that he alludes repeatedly to the " author of nature," " nature's work," to " nature's God," and so on. We think this may have induced Hutchinson to write, as he did three years later, that Masons should not be treated as a set of men " reverencing a Deity by the denomination of the God of nature." But there is evidence in Preston that in reality he was not in conflict with either Calcott or Hutchinson. The following is unmistakeable on this head : " Masons have ever paid due obedience to the moral law, and inculcated its precepts with powerful energy on their disciples. Hence the doctrine of a God, the creator and preserver of the universe, has been their firm belief in every age ; and under the influence of that doctrine their conduct has been regulated through a succession of years. The progress of knowledge and philosophy, aided by Divine revelation, having enlightened the minds of men with the knowledge of the true God and the sacred tenets of the Christian faith, Masons have readily acquiesced in a religion so widely calculated to make men happy ; but in those countries where the Gospel has not reached, or Christianity displayed her beauties, they have inculcated the universal religion, or the religion of nature : that is, to be good men and true, by whatever denomination or persuasion they are distinguished ; and by this universal system their conduct has always been regulated. A cheerful compliance with the established religion of the

country in which they live is earnestly recommended in the assemblies of Masons." Here we see that Preston believed that English Freemasonry, or certainly Freemasonry in England, was a Christian institution, whatever it might be elsewhere. This passage was Preston's commentary on one of the questions in the MS. attributed to Locke, which ran : " Whatte artes haueth the Maçonnes techedde mankynde ? " Preston writes : " It appears to have surprised the learned annotator that religion should have been ranked among the fraternity; but it may be observed that religion is the only tie which can bind men, and that where there is no religion there can be no Masonry." Further on, Preston says : " Enthusiastical sects have been perpetually inventing new forms of religion in various countries by working on the passions of the ignorant and unwary, and deriving their rules of faith and manners from the fallacious suggestions of a warm imagination, rather than from the clear and infallible dictates of the word of God. One set of men has covered religion with a tawdry habit of type and allegory, while another has converted it into an instrument of dissension and discord. The discerning mind, however, may easily trace the unhappy consequences of departing from the Divine simplicity of the Gospel, and loading its pure and heavenly doctrines with the inventions and commandments of men." How far Preston would have approved of appointing bearers of all sorts of volumes for which sanctity was claimed, is tolerably clear from a remark of his that multiplying honorary distinctions among Masons infallibly lessens the importance of the original holders of office.*

The extent of Preston's acquaintance with religions only to be found in Asia, is not easily ascertained, but we may admit his belief that Freemasonry was a widely-spread institution. English Freemasonry is,

---

* Page 276 Preston's Illustrations, 12th Edition, 1812.

however, but a part of the whole. This fact appears sometimes to be overlooked, one Jurisdiction being treated as the whole system.

The entire Masonic system is not, and cannot be, embraced by one single Constitution, neither was there ever any *original* intention that a single Constitution should assume to be all-embracing. A part is not the whole ; Freemasonry is built up of parts. Each part is, or should be, in harmony with the rest, but each must remain separate and distinct for many reasons.

There is no novelty in this view, indeed, it is a very old one, for our writer, in his very first illustration, drew an emblem of Freemasonry from a garden. Each part was seemingly complete in itself, and reflected new beauties on the other parts, all contributed to form a harmoniously beautiful whole. After dealing with the art displayed in the formation of a garden, Preston passed on to Nature unassisted by Art, and showed how the system of the Universe is a moral lesson to the Masonic student. He dwelt much on the value of association and friendship, and his second section concludes thus—

" Though friendship appears divine when employed in preserving the liberties of our country, it shines with equal splendour in more tranquil scenes. Before it rises into the noble flame of patriotism, aiming destruction at the heads of tyrants, thundering for liberty, and courting danger in defence of rights, we behold it calm and moderate, burning with an even glow, improving the soft hours of peace and heightening the relish for virtue. In those happy moments contracts are formed, societies are instituted, and the vacant hours of life are employed in the cultivation of social and polished manners. *On this general plan the Universality of our system is established*," &c. There is a great deal more to the same purport as this in Preston. His idea is, although he does not express it as clearly as he might have done, that Freemasonry arose from feelings, principles, and

circumstances which are common to the human race. Some of his illustrations are directed to show that at a very early period in the world's history the principles of Freemasonry were recognised, and that the wants, wishes, and aspirations of mankind necessarily eventuated in a Masonic system.

No one can deny that looked at in this light Freemasonry is Universal. It may be confidently stated that there is not one word in Preston's celebrated book which in any way countenances the modern theories which, in effect, do away with all consistency in matters relating to religion.

The Rev. Dr. Ashe is perhaps the next Masonic writer whom we should be expected to quote from. He has been accused of plagiarism, and apparently with some good reason; still his "Masonic Manual" has been often reprinted and quoted, and it is not unfair on our part to give his views. He wrote in 1813, the year of the Union, " Christians in religion, sons of liberty and loyal subjects, we have adopted rules, orders, emblems, and symbols, which enjoin us to live a life of morality . . . . and to strengthen our faith, we have enlightened our lodge with the emblem of the Trinity." He expresses his opinion that the spirit of the enterprise, *i.e.*, Freemasonry, sprang from the Christian faith. He avers that it originated to honour the religion and faith of Christians.

Dr. Ashe followed on in the lines laid down by Calcott in the first instance; his book teems with allusions to the connection between Christianity and Freemasonry; and it is not of serious importance for us to enquire whether in every case he gave additional currency to the words of others, in which he acquiesced, or whether what he published were his own views for the first time expressed. His work was dedicated to the Duke of Sussex, the Grand Master, and was issued designedly to " plainly and completely tell the Craft their eternal and temporal obligations."

He expressed his belief that some of the truths of Masonry have always been preserved unpolluted by the Magi in Persia, the Brahmins in India, and others. These truths, he states, were also common to the leaders of many ancient religions and philosophies. In this way he believed in the Universality of Masonic doctrine, but he held that the knowledge of truth itself only approached perfection under the Christian dispensation. He explained many Masonic emblems as being purely Christian. The star he alluded to as proclaiming the nativity of the Son of God; the lights, he says, are typical of the Holy Trinity.* He refers to Christ in speaking of the white apron of the First Degree. He states that the usual Masonic dedication to St. John arose from his having proclaimed salvation by Christ. He wrote, "In the name of St. John the Evangelist, we acknowledge the testimonies which he gives, and the Divine logos, or word, which he makes manifest." He goes beyond this, and insists that the Master Mason's Degree is typical of the Christian faith, and, consequently, of Christian hope.† He says Masons are Christians in religion,‡ and he emphatically affirms that Freemasonry "originated from the earliest influence of Christianity, in honour to, or in confession of, the religion and faith of Christians." He asserts we derive our doctrines from the Christian revelation. The work (*The Masonic Manual*) in which all this was published received the approval of the then Grand Master of English Freemasonry; the dedication was written in the very year of the Union of the two English Grand Lodges.

"A true Christian faith is the substance of things hoped for, the evidence of things not seen. If we with true devotion maintain our Masonic profession, our faith will become a beam of light, and bring us to those blessed mansions, where we shall be eternally happy

---

* Page 119, 2nd Edition.　　† Page 161.　　‡ Page 162.

with God, the Grand Architect of the Universe, whose
Son died for us, and rose again, that we might be
justified through faith in His blood." Thus wrote Ashe
in the first years of this century. He held, and it has
never been disputed, so far as his writings are concerned,
that the true faith of a Freemason was the faith of a
Christian. This to an Universalist may appear rank
heresy. Our reply is, Freemasonry in its principles is
unalterable; if, therefore, Ashe was right in his views
seventy-five years ago, the faith of a Freemason is at
this day what it then was, and the heresy is with those
who would make it anything else. Would the dedication
to the Duke of Sussex have been allowed if Ashe was
introducing new doctrine? In his preface he states that
he is indebted to Preston, Smith, Furnough (*sic*)—Brother
Hughan has pointed out to the writer that this should
be Turnough—and Calcott for the doctrines he sets
forth (see his address at opening). He should have
added Hutchinson's name. All these authorities are
treated as of no account by the Universalist.*

We have long thought Ashe has not had justice done
to him; he had the clearest perception of the only consistent position which the English Freemason can
assume, and the whole tenor of this book is in complete
harmony with our views. He wrote, or quoted (?)
" Whilst, as Christians, we worship God through Jesus
Christ, we believe that in every nation he that feareth
God and worketh righteousness is accepted of Him.
All Masons, therefore, whether Christians, Jews, or
Mahomedans, who violate not the rule of right written
by the Almighty upon the tables of the heart, who do
fear Him and work righteousness, we are to acknowledge
as brethren, *and though we take different roads*, we are

---

* That the Universalist ideas are very modern is proved to some
extent by a small book called the " Desideratum for the Age," published
in London in 1851. In this work Masonic Universalism is fully discussed, but there is no reference whatever to English Freemasonry
being anything else than pure Christianity.

not to be angry with or persecute each other on that account. We know that the end of our journey is the same."

Ashe never imagined that to make the English Jurisdiction a large one it would eventually be proposed to abandon Christianity. He saw that different Constitutions of necessity would be in conflict in esoteric teaching. He completely recognised that different systems would travel different roads, but that the goal for which all would make was, and always would be, the same. He saw that to remove the fixed religious belief of any Constitution would be to take from it its life-blood, and therefore he thus strenuously insisted on the Christianity of the English system or Constitution. He had no idea that the Great Light of any system might be *any* book, if only it was considered sacred somewhere or other. He held the Bible, and the Bible only, as the Great Light under the English Constitution. It is for this clearness of perception that we esteem his work so highly.

The four authors already quoted are known to all Masons by name, at least, but there are other authors whom we consider even more eminent, but whose names are perhaps not equally familiar to the ordinary reader. Thomas Dunckerley was such an one. He was born in 1724 and died in 1795. To him is attributed the removal of the true word of the Master Mason from the Third to the Royal Arch Degree. He did not write much, yet his influence on the esoteric teaching of the last century was without parallel. The American authority Mackey places him in an inferior position to Preston and Hutchinson, although in a superior one to Anderson or Desaguliers, but he, with others, admits the enormous influence of Dunckerley on Masonic teaching in the last century. This is what Brother Dunckerley said in a lecture on Masonic Light delivered in 1757 at Plymouth : " The sacred writings confirm what I assert, the sublime

part of our ancient mystery being there to be found, nor can any Christian brother be a perfect Mason that does not make the word of God his study. Indeed, we own all Masons as brothers, be they Christians, Jews, or Mahometans (for Masonry is universal, and not strictly confined to any particular faith, sect, or mode of worship); all Masons, I say, of whatever religious denomination, who rule their passions and affections, and square their actions accordingly, are acknowledged by us as brothers; but, for our parts, the Holy Scripture is to be studied." The prayer to be used at the initiation of a candidate, quoted previously, is attributed to Brother Dunckerley.

We now come to an anonymous writer, but one who is so well known that we have a right to treat him as an authority. We allude to the unknown author of that exceedingly rare work, " Multa Paucis," said by all booksellers to be the rarest work of Masonry in the book market. Part One of " Multa Paucis" commences thus : " A scriptural and historical Account of Geometry and Masonry, from the creation of the World to the Resurrection of Jesus Christ, the GRAND ARCHITECT of the Christian Church." The Architect of the Universe and the Architect of the Christian Church are treated as one and the same. This work was published about 1763. The conclusion of the first part can hardly be curtailed, so we give all but the last paragraph. " The appointed time, Genesis, Chap. xlix., ver. 10, the Sceptre shall not depart from Judah, nor a Lawgiver from between his Feet, until Shiloh comes, was now fulfilled; for in the 34th Year of the Reign of Herod, and the 26th Year of Augustus, the Messiah, Jesus Christ, the Grand Architect of the Christian Church, was born at Bethlehem, in Judea, of the Virgin Mary, a lineal Heir of the Tribe of Judah.

" The Tidings thereof were soon brought to Herod, who, knowing himself an Usurper, and fearing the Loss

of his Crown and Dignity, ordered all the Male Children of two Years and under to be murdered. But the Angel before warned Mary to go into Egypt, where she continued till after the Death of Herod, which happened but a few months after, then she returned and dwelt in the City of Nazareth.

" After the Death of Herod, Rome arrived to that glorious perfection by the noble Art of Masonry, that when Augustus was a-dying, he very justly said, I found Rome built of Bricks, but I leave it built of Marble.

" A.M. 3963, A.D. 15. Tiberius succeeded Augustus, and in his Reign the LORD JESUS CHRIST was crucified without the Walls of Jerusalem by Pontius Pilate, the Roman Governour of Judea, for the Remission of our Sins, and rose again on the third Day for the Justification of all that believe in him. Tiberius was a very just Monarch, and when he heard of the partial Judgment of Pontius Pilate, he banished him for the injustice done to CHRIST."

We have here the strongest confirmation that in the middle of the last century the Great Architect of the Masonic system was considered to be Christ. Oliver always insisted on this, and he received not a little censure from certain quarters for his openly expressed opinions. Not only this, but we have here evidence that the Masonic system was considered to be part and parcel of the Christian Church. We raise no theory of our own, but we insist that over one hundred and twenty years ago the Masonic and the Christian systems were treated as one and the same, *or* that " Multa Paucis " expressed a view which was then already untenable. No one has yet pointed out that it contained any inaccuracy of this nature : doubtless it will *now* be denied that it correctly expressed Masonic belief, but it is rather late in the day to discover this after a lapse of some one hundred and twenty years. There is nothing in " Multa

Paucis" to justify the present Universal theories. Its estimation as a Masonic work is proved by a complete copy readily realising from £5 to £10. We paid £2 2s. for a very imperfect one, and I have never heard of a lower price.*

In 1686, Dr. Plot published a history of Staffordshire, and wrote rather disrespectfully of Freemasonry and its pretensions to an ancient history. We do not know with precision when he was first replied to, but it was apparently after his death in 1696. The only date we can authenticate is 1754, when "a detection" of his errors was published. Dr. Plot fell foul of St. Alban and St. Amphibalus as Masonic patrons. The reply, if it means anything at all, attributes their position as patrons of the Craft to their being the first Christian martyrs under the Diocletian persecution in England. We have no intention of discussing this point, but, as this was the reason assigned in 1754 for their enrolment as Masons, it follows that Freemasonry was then considered a Christian institution.

In a work entitled "The Principles and Practice of Masonry," published in 1786, it is stated that one of the causes why Freemasonry is a secret institution is that it was necessary, when the Christians took up arms against the infidels who held the Holy Sepulchre that each might know his companion by signs, signals, and watch-words unknown to the Mahomedans. We attach no importance to this, beyond that it must be evident no such Christian origin of Masonry would have been given in 1786 if theories now entertained had then had any existence. This same work, whilst admitting

---

* The following is from a recent catalogue issued by George Kenning, the Masonic publisher and jeweller: "Complete Freemason, or Multa Paucis, for Lovers of Secrets, 1763 (circa) £5 5s. 0d. (This is one of the rarest and most curious historical works on Freemasonry, and is scarcely ever to be met with. As a matter of fact, its value is beyond that of the Constitutions of 1723)." Catalogue No. 2, October, 1886.

that Jews and Mahomedans may be made Masons, particularly argues that Masons should follow Masonic teaching by showing that its laws are *Christian* laws. It speaks of a Mason's character as *Christian*, and never as of any other religious belief.

Amongst other writers of the last century who spoke with clearness on the subject which we have attempted to elucidate is the Rev. James Watson. In 1794* he showed how Masonry, which primarily inculcates morality and a natural religion, derived its brightness from "the light of revelation and the *Sun of righteousness.*" He also treated Freemasonry as a *Christian* brotherhood.

In 1795, he wrote as follows :

" As the darkness of heathenism, or natural religion, preceded the Divine revelation vouchsafed to the favourite people of God, so, by our initiation into the SECOND DEGREE, we advance still further into the *dawn* figured out by the Mosaic dispensation, which preceded the more perfect CHRISTIAN DAY. Here the noviciate is brought to light, to behold and handle tools of a more artificial and ingenious construction, and emblematic of sublimer moral truths. By these he learns to reduce rude matter into due form, and rude manners into the more polished shape of moral and religious rectitude, becoming thereby a more harmonious corner-stone of symmetry in the structure of human society, until he is made a glorified corner-stone in the Temple of God, *made without hands, eternal in the Heavens.* Here he learns to apply the SQUARE of Justice to all his actions ; the LEVEL of Humility and Benevolence to all his Brother Men ; and, by the PLUMB LINE of Fortitude, to support himself through all the dangers and difficulties of this, our fallen, feeble state. Here, instead of the *casual* Lodge as before, like the vagrant tabernacle in the wilderness, he first becomes acquainted with the

---

* Address delivered to brethren of St. John's Lodge, No. 534, Lancaster, Dec. 27th, 1794.

Q

construction of the glorious Temple of King Solomon, whose magnificent proportions were dictated by the oracular instruction of God, and are figurative of celestial perfection.

"The THIRD DEGREE brings the Masonic enquirer into a state representing the meridian light of the last and fullest revelation, from Heaven to man upon earth, by the eternal SON OF GOD, through whose resurrection and ascension he is raised from darkness and death to the certainty of life and immortality.

"Such is the Masonic economy. Such are the outlines of that system, which is justly compared to an *equilateral triangle*, the perfect emblem of universal harmony, and the sublimest symbol of the incomprehensible Deity, whose radiant throne may we all hereafter encircle with songs and choral hallelujahs for evermore! Amen, so mote it be!"*

In 1794 or 1795, he reiterated this doctrine in a Masonic address at Lancaster: "The three degrees in Masonry seem to have an obvious and apt coincidence with the three progressive stages of mankind, from the creation to the end of time. The first is emblematical of man's state of nature, from his first disobedience to the time of God's covenant with Abraham, and the establishment of the Jewish economy. The second, from that period to the era of the last, full, and perfect revelation from Heaven to mankind, made by our Great Redeemer. The third, comprehending the glorious interval of the Christian dispensation down to the consummation of all things."

"The religious ritual of Masonry is unexceptionally orthodox, and scripturally Catholic." Such is the opinion of an anonymous writer in a work on the principles of Freemasonry published by Bro. John Hogg, and such is the present writer's opinion. The Universality of English Freemasonry lies in its orthodox

---

* Address delivered St. John's Lodge, 534, Dec. 28th, 1795.

Catholicity. The abandonment of every Christian allusion does not make the system more, but less, Universal, and it is from a mistaken conception of this point that serious anomalies have arisen. Being completely Catholic, Freemasonry takes no heed of sects, whatever their Christian pretensions may be. It maintains that the English Bible is all sufficient for the English Mason to build his religious belief upon. There is nothing inconsistent with this when it receives as a Brother a Parsee, a Hindoo, or any other believer in a Supreme Being. It would not be a Catholic system if it excluded such candidates; but this affords no grounds for any abandonment of the English Masons' Great Light—the Bible. The English system should teach the Parsee or the Hindoo what the English system is, it should not allow those who are in a state of Masonic darkness to remain in that condition.

All Masonic students know the name of the Rev. Jethro Inwood; here are a few of his words—" The world of mankind is one family, is one brotherhood. As the redeemed of the Almighty God, the Saviour of the world, all are Brethren, and Christ, the eternal God, is our elder Brother. Yes, he is the corner-stone." . . . . " As the redeemed of the Eternal and Just God, the universal world is a brotherhood." . . . . " Masonic secrecy is Christian virtue, and the precepts of the Gospel are universally the principles of Masonry."*

" And in the sequel of my discourse I shall endeavour to join him in this opinion, and prove that the science of Masonry in this country cannot lawfully admit, much less can it ever encourage, either any member, or any opinion that is irreligious, impious, *or at all disaffected to our Church,* to our King, or to our Constitution."†

---

* Inwood's Sermons to the P.G. Lodge of Kent, June 5, 1797.

† Inwood's Sermon preached before the Prov. Grand Lodge of Kent, 1798.

Q 2

" In a particular manner at this time would we sup-plicate Thy divine favour and blessing upon this small portion of a large community, now worshipping before Thy glorious throne ; sanction with Thy divine grace and heavenly benediction all the pious endeavours and all the benevolent intentions of this our sacred unity with each other ; make all, and each of us, useful and ornamental members of this our very affectionate attachment ; give to us universally the true fear of Thy Holy Name, that Thy glory may ever rest upon us ; give us that true brotherly affection for each other, that shall lead us to the exercise of every Christian charity, every masonic benevolence ; inspire us with true Christian and British loyalty, that upon all occasions we may, if ever called upon, be found good and steadfast subjects to our king and constitution—and, above all, make us devout and zealous members of the church of Christ ; that having thus laboured in the earthly lodge of masonic piety, charity, and integrity ; we may be trans-lated into that perfect lodge of eternal felicity, whose builder and maker is the everlasting Jehovah ; we beg all for the sake of our Lord and Saviour Jesus Christ."*

" Freemasonry as it is practised at the present day commemorates particularly five great events in the history of the world, each typical of the Messiah. These are—the vision of Jacob ; the offering of Isaac ; the deliverance from Egyptian bondage ; the offering of David ; and the building of the Temple. Now these extraordinary events, which unequivocally point to our Saviour Jesus Christ, are the principal historical events contained in our lectures. It follows then that Masonry was intended to perpetuate that most important fact, the salvation of souls through the atonement of Christ. To accomplish this design more perfectly, the most prominent types as they arose were incorporated by wise

---

* Inwood's Sermon preached before the Prov. Grand Lodge of Kent in 1794.

and pious brethren into the original system until it contained a perfect chain of evidence, which could neither be effaced nor misunderstood, illustrative of this fact, so essential to the future welfare of mankind."*

The following are remarks made by the Rev. Jethro Inwood, Chaplain to the Prov. Grand Lodge of Kent, in 1799.

"Masonry is truly the sister of religion; for she boasts her efficacy in all its native influence; and is continually the assistant promoter of like principles and of like actions. The central point of all her innumerable lines, squares, and circles, is the love of God. And upon this central point she builds her faith; from it she derives her hope of glory here and hereafter; and by it she squares her conduct in strict justice and universal charity. The central point of all true Christanity and of all true Masonry is, the love of God." .... "Masonry is dedicated only to the Gospel." .... "It has nothing in its institution but what both the law of Moses and of Christ will fully allow and universally sanction."

Inwood, in more than one place, gives clear intimation what his idea of Masonic Universality was. He states in almost the following words that as Christ, the Eternal God, is our elder Brother the world is an universal Brotherhood and that Freemasonry, by recognising this, therefore becomes an universal institution. His sole view of Universality was this and this only, and he preached this doctrine, year after year, to the Provincial Grand Meetings of Kentish Masons at the close of the last century. We have no record that anyone then asserted that such teaching was contrary to the principles of the Institution. There is on the contrary every reason to believe that his views were those generally entertained by his audiences. At the present time Inwood's sermons are well known and are readily

* Inwood's Sermon before the Prov. Grand Lodge of Kent, 1796.

bought up whenever copies are offered for sale, and, if it really is the case that they contain Masonic heresy, how is it that no one has drawn attention to the fact?

The Rev. James Hart, in a sermon preached at Durham in the year 1772, says, " Masonry is founded on that sure rock, against which let the waves and billows of temporal persecution never so strongly dash, it will stand erect and secure, because that rock is Christ."

One of the most determined modern English champions of the Christianity of Masonry was the Rev. Moses Margoliouth, B.A., and we need offer no apology for giving extracts from one of his works at some length. The following are from " Genuine Freemasonry indissolubly connected with Revelation. A Lecture delivered in the Worthy and Worshipful Lodge of Virtue, 177, Manchester, by the Rev. Moses Margoliouth, B.A., in the year 1852—"

" I shall proceed, therefore," he says, " to prove, for the especial benefit of the brotherhood, that ' Masonry is' not only ' a beautiful system of morality,' but also a peculiar system of revealed religion, ' veiled in allegory and illustrated by symbols.' " . . . .

" Brethren, look towards the east—towards the pedestal of the W.M. Does not yon unfolded sacred volume bear ample testimony to the correctness of my statement? Does not that holy code, though silent, speak most eloquently to your heart of hearts, that the basis of Masonry is such a foundation as no other Order can boast of? Nor does the Bible lie open simply as a matter of form and no further allusion made to it. On the contrary, this book of books is our constant theme. Listen to the charge of the W.M. to a brother who had just past the portals of our lodge—' As a Mason, I would first recommend to your most serious contemplation the volume of the Sacred Law, charging you to consider it as the unerring standard of truth and justice, and to

regulate your actions by the Divine precepts it contains. Therein you will be taught the important duties you owe to God, to your neighbour, and to yourself. *To God,* by never mentioning his name but with that awe and reverence which are due from the creature to his Creator; by imploring his aid on all your lawful undertakings, and by looking up to him in every emergency for comfort and support. *To your neighbour,* by acting with him upon the square; by rendering him every kind office which justice or mercy may require; by relieving his distresses and soothing his afflictions; and by doing to him as, in similar cases, you would wish he should do to you.

" But let us take a bird's-eye view of the ceremony of initiation, as practised in worthy and worshipful lodges, and we shall soon behold how beautifully and indissolubly are Masonry and Revelation linked together. The candidate who has not been as yet admitted as a child of LIGHT is, as a matter of course, represented in a state of darkness, just as chaos was before 'the Spirit of God moved upon the face of the waters.' The poor candidate in that state obtains the most practical view of himself, without the benign influence of that Spirit; and when he makes the confession that he stands in need of the blessing of light, all the brethren join in the ceremony . . . . . which gives a fair notion of the statement made by the inspired recorder :—' And the earth was without form and void, and darkness was upon the face of the deep. And the Spirit of God moved upon the face of the waters.'* And whilst the brethren are in the act of representing the operation of the Spirit, the W.M., in some lodges, repeats :—' And God said, Let there be light : and there was light. And God saw the light, that it was good : and God divided the light from the darkness.'†

---

* Genesis i., 2.   † Genesis, i., 3, 4

. . . " In other lodges, again, the W.M. repeats, during the representation of the operation of the Spirit —as was the case in the lodge in which I was made— 'In him was life; and the life was the light of men. And the light shineth in darkness; and the darkness comprehended it not. That was the true Light, which lighteth every man that cometh into the world.'*

" The Prophet Amos, when speaking of the events which are to take place in the latter days, introduces the Almighty as the Great Architect of the Universe, repairing the way of communication between earth and heaven, which was demolished with the fall of man. The passage, as it stands in the authorised version, reads thus :—' It is He that buildeth His stories in the heavens, and hath founded His troop in the earth.' † But this does by no means convey the sense of the original. It should have been translated thus :—' It is He that buildeth His ascent in the heavens, and founded its adhesion on the earth,' which illustrates the purport of Jacob's dream, at Bethel, most felicitously. The ladder was a most appropriate symbol of the resti- tution of all things, when heaven and earth shall no more be severed, but that a road which shall safely lead from one to the other all those whose aim shall be to reach the Grand Lodge above. This symbol was beautifully illustrated by the Great Architect of the Universe in his answer to Nathaniel :—' Jesus answered and said unto him, Because I said unto thee, I saw thee under the fig tree, believest thou? though shalt see greater things than these. And he saith unto him, Verily, verily, I say unto you, Hereafter ye shall see heaven open, and the angels of God ascending and descending upon the Son of man.' ‡

" One of the most cogent arguments, to my mind, for the antiquity and holiness of our Order is drawn

---

* John i., 4, 5, 9.   † Amos ix., 6.   ‡ John i., 50, 51.

from the circumstance that all our tests of merit, or pass-words, consist of expressions borrowed from the sacred tongue, from the Hebrew Scriptures. The tests of merit have been so wisely chosen as to express proper names, and also to convey most significant communications. But what is most singular in connection with our pass-words is, that scarcely any of the brethren know the *real* import of those words, and, consequently, a great deal that is beautiful and august is lost to Freemasons. I venture, therefore, to give you the following new translations, which I conceive to be the oldest that could ever have been given, of those words.

"The test of merit entrusted at the conferring of the First Degree signifies, THE MIGHTY ONE HAS COME; that at the Second Degree signifies, THE LORD THE BRANCH; that at the Third Degree signifies, THOU SHALT BE LED TO THY POSSESSION. The two solemn sentences which are given in a whisper signify, when properly rendered, THE SON WAS SLAIN—WISDOM HAS DEPARTED.

"The allegory and symbol of the Third Degree are not only most solemn lessons in the history of our redemption, but are also august and sublime. The name H. A. introduced to our notice, is one which does not occur in the whole volume of the sacred law; there is not the slightest allusion to the history of His 'untimely death,' as related in the course of the lecture on the occasion. But if you bear in mind that 'Masonry is a system of morality (and religion) veiled in allegory and illustrated by symbols,' the difficulty vanishes. . . . . The name given to Him who personifies our Grand Master, who is said to have met with an untimely death from the hands of three ruffians, is important; inasmuch as the appellation signifies, HE WAS EXALTED TO HIS FATHER.

"The tools by which His death was effected, viz., the Level, Plumb-rule, and Mallet, are also remarkable, as the two former, when placed one above the other,

present the figure of a cross. The Mallet is a necessary tool for fastening anything to the cross, and hence we have the whole of the instruments by which the death of H. A.—of him who **was** exalted to His Father—was caused."

The following is a quotation in the above work from a letter written by Bro. E. G. Willoughby, of Tranmere:—

" You are aware that my opinion is that every mark, character, and emblem depicted in a lodge has a reference to the Christian system. It is said in our lodge lectures that all squares, levels, and perpendiculars are true and proper signs to know a Mason by. The same may be said of Christians, externally; the cross is a figure which consists of all squares, etc., and at baptism the same symbol is applied to the forehead as an outward and visible sign, etc. . . . . But that part of our ceremonies to which I may have referred when speaking to you about the symbol of the cross is in the Third Degree. You may remember that the candidate is reminded that the instruments with which our Grand Master was slain were the plumb-rule, the level, and the setting-maul. These are generally thrown promiscuously . . . . and are also depicted on the tracing-board. And if the level is placed in a regular position and the plumb-rule placed immediately under it they will form the cross, and evidently allude to the instrumentality by which Christ, the Grand Master of the Universe, or, as He is styled in the oldest Book of Constitution, the Grand Architect of the Christian Church, was slain."

If the reader wishes for any more of Bro. Margoliouth's views he can obtain them by consulting " Vestiges of Genuine Freemasonry amongst the Ruins of Asia, Africa, etc.," published in 1852.

Scotland as well as England supplies opinions of Masonic writers that Freemasonry is essentially and entirely a Christian system. The Rev. A. C. L. Arnold

wrote in 1866*—"We do not hesitate, therefore, to say that we regard Freemasonry as the truest expression of the mind and thought of Christ this age is destined to witness. *Christianity is its central idea*, and at the same time the foundation and corollary of our Temple. Nay, Masonry is Christianity—Christianity applied to life—made actual in the arrangements of society—Christianity realised in man's relations one with another," and Brother Arnold concludes by asserting that Freemasonry "stands one of the very first among the Christian institutions of the day."

An address,† delivered by the R.W.P.G.M. for the Province of Glasgow, the late Sir Archibald Alison, at a Masonic festival, contains the following passage:—"Where would they find a remedy for this state of society, in which the angry and selfish passions had acquired so great a preponderance? He had no hesitation in saying that it could only be found in the spread and increased influence of the principles of Freemasonry.

"Let them recollect that the fate of the world had been changed by a faith which began from still smaller numbers. Eighteen hundred years ago, principles were preached on the shores of Galilee, which then had the most unpromising of all appearances, for they were surrounded by hostility on every side. Where were these principles now, and where were the powers that endeavoured to oppose them? The principles of Freemasonry were the principles of the Gospel."

Although the Grand Lodge of Scotland has been the first to officially recognise other volumes than the Bible as the Volume of the Sacred Law, or as volumes having Masonically, within its jurisdiction, a standing equal to that of the Bible, still it is somewhat curious that by

---

* "History and Philosophy of Freemasonry," Edinbro', 1866.
† Taylor's "Masonic Gatherings," p. 36.

a kind of side wind we learn from its Constitutions that the absolute connection of Freemasonry with Christianity has, perhaps, been more distinctly admitted by the Grand Lodge of Scotland than by any other Grand Lodge.

This connection is discussed in the introduction to the Scottish Constitutions of 1848, and although the remark is there made that Dr. Oliver's Christian views are, "we think, exaggerated," still a close connection is admitted, and, what is more, certain probable reasons for the relationship are given. Oliver never pointed out a more extraordinary anomaly than this.

The view which was taken in Germany at the close of the last century and the commencement of this is shown by Gædicke's article on the Bible:—"Amongst the three Great Lights, the Bible is the greatest; it directs and rules our faith; without this Light we can find no altar; without it no Lodge is held. No one can enter the Order unless he acknowledges and touches with his hands this Great and Holy Light. (Oliver's rendering of this runs, 'unless he supports and is supported by that blessed Book.') The square and compasses stimulate one still more to reverence this Great Light, for justice and all-comprehensive love are thus maintained. It teaches us, In the beginning was the word; the Sacred Book is a symbol that we should be united by brotherly love and an universal charity, as gentle John, whom Jesus loved, says in his Gospel. Here, in this Book, is the gauge for all Christians, no matter whether they be Lutherans, Reformers, Catholics, or modern Greeks. He who is a Christian may swear by the Gospel of John, and is able to allow these holy truths to enter his heart. He who is not a Christian neither may nor can do this. . . . ."*
Further on we find this in Gædicke:—"The true and

---

* Freimaurer Lexicon. Berlin, 1818.

genuine Freemasons' Lodges permit no Jew in their body, for such cannot, according to his creed, lay his hand upon the Gospel of St. John as a proof of truth. Also, the doctrine of the Triune God is the most important difference between Christianity and Judaism, and it is the chief doctrine of Christians, so that no Jew can acknowledge that symbolical number so sacred to Masons.*

Gædicke was apparently as opposed to Jews as the rest of his nation when he wrote, for, under his article on "Religion," we read: "The ancient lodges only initiated, as members of the Order, believers in Jesus Christ, either Christians of the English, Catholic, Lutheran, Reformed, or Modern Greek Church. Mahometans, Jews, &c., are excluded, for none of them admit the New Testament to be sacred writing. In modern times, under Napoleon Buonaparte, some French lodges have received even Jews; but these cannot be recognised by ancient lodges as Freemasons."

Regarding this reference to Napoleon, it may be noted that in 1806 he summoned a sanhedrim of the Jews to assemble at Paris. It assembled in 1807. The result, as stated by Dean Milman, was that in France, as in other countries, "the Jew became a citizen, with all the rights and duties of the Order.†

Let us now turn to America.

A former Grand Chaplain of Massachusetts has left behind him a series of discourses which very emphatically demonstrate what view was entertained in America during the latter part of last and early in this century, of religion in connection with Masonry. The Rev. T. M. Harris was not only once Grand Chaplain, but he was also once Deputy Grand Master, and was specially deputed, owing to his great Masonic knowledge, to revise the American Constitutions.

---

* *Ibid.* Article "Jews."
† History of the Jews, Vol. 3, page 12.

In the first year of the present century he published
a series of discourses which he had previously delivered
on public occasions, several being before the Grand
Lodge. His publication was avowedly to convince the
world in general "of the sacred character" of Freemasonry.

Whilst acknowledging that Masonry does not usurp
any religion, he preached on St. John the Baptist's Day,
1795, before his Grand Lodge, that he stood as the
representative of Him who " came for a witness to bear
witness."*

In his discourses to various Masonic bodies he
invariably termed the brethren Christians. He alludes to
Masonry existing in various lands, but it never seems to
have entered into his mind that an American Mason
could be anything except a Christian. He wrote of the
sacred character of Freemasonry, and dwelt much upon
the necessity of a Mason showing by the goodness of
his life that he was a Christian.† He delivered discourses of this nature for half a century, and was universally credited with teaching sound Masonic doctrine.
Mackey, who generally expresses unqualified disapproval
of Christianising Freemasonry, states that Harris' Discourses form a valuable portion of the Masonic classic
literature of America. Harris' addresses are so full of
Christian allusions that selection is difficult, but here is
one sentence from an oration delivered to a Royal Arch
Chapter, " Then shall we not only have fellowship with
one another," but " our fellowship will be with the
Father, and with his Son Jesus Christ." " Let the
hopes of meeting with this great reward animate us,"
etc. Again, here is another of his remarks delivered at
the consecration of a Lodge, " These observations and
counsels are equally applicable to us all, my respected

* Harris's Masonic Discourses, p. 259.
† Discourses No. VII.

hearers, both as Christians and Masons; and I feel a peculiar pleasure in affirming the intimate connection between the two characters. We are alike 'built upon the foundations of the prophets *and apostles*, Jesus Christ himself being the chief corner-stone.'"

When delivering a discourse, at which the representatives of *two* Grand Lodges were present, Bro. Harris stated that "Freemasonry would be less necessary" if professing Christians acted up to their principles —or, in other words, that Christianity had become so degraded that modern Freemasonry became a necessity. Can Freemasonry take this position in the present day? He concluded by expressing a hope that in future " May we all love fervently as Christians and as Brethren."

At another discourse, delivered before a Masonic body in 1798, he treated Freemasonry and Christianity as virtually one and the same thing, and spoke to Masons of their duties arising from the injunctions of the New Testament,* stating that Freemasonry "seeks to intwine the cardinal virtues and the Christian graces in the web of the affections and the drapery of the conduct." He added, "Piety towards God" was one of the immoveable pillars which supported Masonry, and that the Masonic was Christian character.

In a sermon delivered before a Chapter of Royal Arch Masons, which he published under the title of " Freemasonry Glorified," he gave expression to views still more distinctly claiming that in Christ were all the treasures of wisdom and knowledge, and intimated that, " the stone which bears 'the mystic word' is legible only by those who have been taught the interpretation (*i.e.*, Christian interpretation)." He concludes this sermon by stating that one of the privileges that members of our glorious Society could look forward to, *and which arose from their relation to the Society,* was

---

* Page 47.

that they would have fellowship "with the Father, and with His Son, Jesus Christ."

In alluding to the attack on Freemasonry made by Barruel, Bro. Harris said that a Mason's duty was "piety towards God and faith in the Lord Jesus Christ."

We hardly know where this chapter would end if we attempted to exhaust the Rev. Brother's utterances, which laid down, as pure Masonic doctrine, the identity of Freemasonry with Christianity. Of more importance than his speeches is the fact that when he delivered these discourses the American and the English Masonic publics were in entire agreement with Bro. Harris. It was never urged that he overstepped just limits; on the contrary, he was held in high estimation as a preacher of sound Masonic doctrine. What harmony is there between his teaching and the Masonic teaching of the advanced school at the present time? Are doctrines which harmonize with the entire ritual of our Degrees, with all their symbolism, and, above all, with common sense, to be rejected in order to assist brethren in their attempts to convert a Christian Society into a purely Theistic one, or something worse?

Another worthy American Mason, the Rev. William H. Hart, spoke out with an equal plainness early in the present century. In a sermon preached before the Masonic Societies of Richmond and Manchester, on St. John's day, 1818, he said "This auspicious day, distinguished in the annals of Masonry and sacred to the memory of an exalted patron of our Order, and apostle of our Lord Jesus Christ;" and, continuing in the same strain he declared, "Masonry takes for its first great light the Word of God—the book of books—the Bible; and from thence, as from an inexhaustible quarry, it draws forth all the exquisite materials which compose its sacred edifice. Although that fair structure, which was projected and reared by the wisest of men upon the mountain of Zion (assisted by him whose name is ever

dear to the Mason's heart) has long since crumbled into ruin—though nation after nation has successively flourished and decayed—though the proudest monuments of art and industry lie prostrate in the dust, yet this remains. This has defied the lapse of time, and continues to flourish in undiminished splendour.

"Thus have we received it from the hands of our forefathers, and it is our duty—our bounden duty—to transmit it to our posterity with untarnished lustre. It is a sacred deposit committed to our hands, and every individual of our Order should consider its interests as entrusted to his peculiar care." We offer no comment whatever on these utterances beyond that which we have before insisted on—*i.e.*, that these opinions were once deemed comprehensively Masonic. We believe that in the hands of any ordinarily skilful literary man the works of the few authors we have quoted from would prove, as Bro. Hart says, an inexhaustible quarry of materials, to refute the Masons who believe that Freemasonry is other than a Christan system.

Later on in the present century we find Dr. Robert Morris supporting the opinions of the foregoing writers. Dr. Morris is at this day treated as a high authority. In his Lights and Shadows of Freemasonry he quotes the dying speech or words of a Freemason to illustrate Masonic principles, and alludes to the Messiah having taught the doctrine of Masonic resurrection.* He refers in more than one place to the Lion of the tribe of Judah, particularly in a Masonic funeral song, where he states that the Masonic emblems employed in the service are used to intimate that Judah's Lion will prevail over death.† In other places he introduces Christ as "the Mason's righteousness"‡ or as "the Saviour."§

---

* "Lights and Shadows of Freemasonry," by Robt. Morris, LL.D. Louisville, 1852. He died whilst these sheets are going through the press, 31st July, 1888, much lamented.

  † *Ibid.*   ‡ *Ibid.*   § *Ibid.*

R

This American author, poet, and Freemason is fully as positive on the connection of Freemasonry with Christianity as Dr. Oliver was. Under the various heads of blasphemy, discipline, sabbath-breaking and offences, Dr. Rob. Morris makes remarks, or assertions, to the following purport—He considers it right to divide Masonic offences into four classes, 1. Those which contravene the constitutional rules or edicts of Grand Lodge or bye-laws in question; 2. The unwritten laws of Masonry; 3. The laws of the land; 4. The laws of God. He states the following catalogue of offences will will serve most practical purposes — 1. Assault; 2. Blasphemy; 3. Contumacy; 4. Disobedience; 5. Gambling; 6. Homicide; 7. Intoxication; 8. Libertinism; 9. Murder; 10. Perjury; 11. Robbery; 12. Sabbath-breaking; 13. Secret-breaking; 14. Slander; 15. Theft.

Regarding the Second offence of Blasphemy, Dr. Morris shows that it is contrary to the teaching and, indeed, the Ritual, of the first two Degrees.

What, according to Dr. Morris, blasphemy would be, is evident when he writes of Freemasonry, "Its conquest over ignorance, idolatry, and vice in every form, will eventually secure for it the approbation of the historian who ignores it and the Christian moralist who stands aloof from it. It will be found not an adversary of *the world's Saviour*, as has been foolishly charged against it, but the handmaid and servant of Him who 'went about doing good,' whose teachings are equally adapted to all peoples and all times, and whose heaven is broad enough for every cast of mind." From this it is evident that Dr. Morris saw no inconsistency in Freemasonry claiming to be both a Christian and an Universal Institution. It is shown elsewhere that this is the view entertained of English Freemasonry by other eminent brethren. It is the object of this book to prove that no other view is consistently tenable, that the allegories, symbols, and teaching cannot otherwise

be reconciled, neither can the Ritual have any other meaning in a Christian community.

The works of Robert Macoy are well-known in the United States, if not in England. In his "True Masonic Guide" he quotes an address given in the First Degree; and, without conceding the least weight to the theory involved regarding the antiquity of Masonry, we do attach considerable importance to the address itself, as showing what was the tenor of Masonic teaching in America only some thirty or forty years ago. From it we extract the following :—"Many brethren of our Ancient Craft also went forth to aid in redeeming the sepulchre of the Saviour from the hands of the infidel; between these and the Knights of St. John there existed a reciprocal feeling of kindness and brotherly love; strengthened by long association and continued struggles in their sacred mission on the Plains of Jerusalem, they entered into a solemn compact of friendship; and it was mutually agreed between them that from thenceforward all lodges, whose members acknowledged the divinity of Christ, should be dedicated to St. John the Baptist and St. John the Evangelist (who were two eminent Christian patrons of Freemasonry), reserving to our Jewish brethren the right of dedicating their lodges to King Solomon." Robert Macoy is a very distinguished Craftsman; he was Deputy Grand Master of the Grand Lodge of New York, he inscribed his book to the Grand Lodge and its officers, and he asserts that he only republished the lectures and teaching of some dozen authorities, whom he names. That the opinion quoted is no accident is proved by what he writes of the Third Degree, where he says— "Thus we close the explanation of the emblems upon the solemn thought of death, which, without revelation, is dark and gloomy; but the Christian is suddenly revived by the evergreen and everliving sprig of faith in the merits of the Lion of the Tribe of Judah."

R 2

Other instances can readily be afforded that Macoy firmly expressed belief in the Christianity of Free-masonry as derived from England. We are unaware what his views may now be.

Bro. Chalmers Paton, in his "Origin of Free-masonry," enquires why, if Masonry was a mere common Craft in the seventeenth century, or if it was merely a moral system, was there any necessity to so much insist upon using no manner of error or heresy? He asks what other Craft has ever had such rules? Indeed what, we may well enquire, has a simple morality to do with "heresy?"

Paton* further points out that Germany, as well as England, demanded a profession of religion from candi-dates, "and a conduct consistent with that profession." He says, "They did not, however, demand the highest orthodoxy of the Church. Their system was too free for that, and during the Middle Ages a continual protest may be said to have been kept up by the Masons in favour of a liberality which had no other existence in those times. The Masons of Germany, in the days of their most flourishing existence, even protected the Members of their Order from persecution, and opposed the Inquisition with success."

We may here add that Bro. Paton's idea also is that, as the introduction of a "brotherhood amongst men" is peculiarly Christian, this part of our system arose from Christianity itself.†

Brother Paton's works are circulated at the present day, we therefore call attention to a remarkable passage of his, where he states :—"I have written as a Christian, and perhaps, therefore, the work may be deemed more suitable to Freemasons who are Christians than to those of other religions. It would have been wrong, and contrary to the laws of Christianity and of Freemasonry,

---

* Origin of Freemasonry, p. 52.   † *Ibid*, p. 56.

for me to disguise or conceal my religious sentiments. And whilst Freemasonry delights in opening its portals to all—whatever their religious creed—who hold the great fundamental principles of religion already mentioned, yet, as it has for many ages prevailed chiefly amongst Christian nations, its teachings have been very largely imbued with Christianity, and very many symbols are in general use which admit of no explanation apart from that religion, and from the Holy Bible, which in Christian countries is placed upon the altar of every Lodge, read at every meeting, carried in every Masonic procession, and acknowledged as the Great Light of Freemasonry. If the present work, therefore, should be found more entirely suited to the views of Christian Freemasons than of others, I entertain a perfect confidence that it contains nothing which any Brother—Jew, Mahomedan, or Parsee—can deem offensive."*

Paton justly remarks that "many symbols are in use (in Freemasonry) which admit of no explanation save Christianity."

The works of a great number of minor writers could be brought forward in support of our argument, but as we have already perhaps too highly taxed the endurance of the reader, we will close this section after giving one more author's views. This writer is the Rev. Dr. G. Oliver, and we frankly admit we would have preferred not to introduce him. Did we not do so, however, we should assuredly be blamed for not alluding to the Brother who, above all others, so persistently advanced that position which we ourselves maintain. The rev. doctor is by some held in great disrepute, whilst others believe in him as the greatest Masonic authority there has yet been. Our own particular objection to him we have not seen elsewhere advanced as a reason for disregarding his opinions.

* Paton's " Freemasonry, its Symbolism," &c.

We think that whilst he undoubtedly held correct ideas regarding the principles of Freemasonry, he at the same time held very improper notions as to how those ideas should be disseminated. The absolute impossibility of discovering in many instances, which are his personal views, and which those of the authors whom the rev. doctor is supposed to be only editing, illustrates our meaning. Any student who attempts to discover what is Preston, and what Oliver, in the latter's editions of the former will not think that we treat him harshly in saying what we do. Still, Oliver is an authority with many, and his opinion carries weight. He wrote more on Masonic subjects than any other man has, or, we trust, ever will. He took the Christian side. Some of his arguments are of great interest, and even value. A mere summary of his various contentions would fill all our space, and although we give more matter from his works than we do from other writers, for the reasons given, it is after all but a drop in the ocean of his written opinions on this head.

The Rev. Dr. Oliver never had any hesitation in expressing his views as to the Christianity of genuine English Freemasonry. Here are some of his opinions : " Freemasonry is a Christian Institution, established by Christian men, and embracing Christian principles ; a truth which may, indeed, be gathered from any of my numerous publications on the subject of Masonry. My faith in this respect commenced at my Initiation, when I was only 18 years of age, and has remained unshaken through a long and eventful life; and I rejoice in the opportunity of publicly professing the same faith at the age of eighty-five years."* He expressly stated his conviction that it was not even a latitudinarian institution, but that it was identical in principle and design with Christianity. He had no sort of doubt that Freemasonry was intended to picture " the co-equal and

* Oliver's " Origin of the Royal Arch."

co-eternal existence of the adorable persons in the Sacred Trinity." He rightly argued that if we still have genuine ancient Freemasonry, the old prayers known to have been used are still applicable to Masonic belief. He quoted the oldest known Masonic prayer, which was used before Freemasonry was speculative only: "The mighty God and Father of Heaven, with the wisdom of His Glorious Son, through the goodness of the Holy Ghost, three persons in one Godhead, be with us at our beginning, give us grace to govern us in our living here, that we may come to His bliss that shall never have an end." He asked, "Does this sound like disowning Christ."*

He expressed his opinion that English Freemasonry was in early times *exclusively* a Christian society, adding that it is only in very recent times that this important fact has been questioned. He denied that any alteration was sanctioned at the time of the Union, *as it was expressly stipulated that no alteration whatever was to be permitted*, and he affirmed that no general Masonic idea as to the non-connection of English Freemasonry with Christianity was given expression to until 1858.† He pointed out that if at the Union in 1813 any such disseverance occurred, the fact was certainly concealed with great success for half a century.

"A Christian" says Oliver,‡ "is bound to practise Masonry as a Christian Institution. All other Masons are equally bound to adore the one God, the Creator of heaven and earth; for an infidel or an atheist is ineligible for admission. Even the spurious Freemasonry had a similar requisition; and all the great heathen philosophers admitted the existence of a Supreme Being, who created and governed the world."

The following comprise a number of quotations from Dr. Oliver's paper "Star in the East." In the preface

---

* *Ibid.*   † *Ibid.*   ‡ " Masonic Institutes."

he says that Freemasonry is "a science, which inculcates the chief doctrines and morality of Christianity, and assumes as an universal axiom the broad tenet of unrestrained union and brotherly love."

"Freemasonry, as practised at the present day, commemorates particularly five great events in the history of the world, *each typical of the Messiah*. These are, the *vision of Jacob*, when he beheld the celebrated ladder, reaching from earth to heaven; the *offering of Isaac* upon Mount Moriah, when it pleased the Lord to substitute a more agreeable victim in his stead; the *miraculous deliverance from Egyptian bondage* under the conduct of Moses; *the offering of David* on the threshing-floor of Araunah the Jebusite; and the *building of Solomon's Temple*. Now, these extraordinary events, which unequivocally point to our Saviour Jesus Christ, are the principal historical events contained in our lectures.* This coincidence could not have been accidental, and must, therefore, have been designed. It follows, then, that Masonry was intended to perpetuate in the mind of man that most important fact, the salvation of his soul through the sacrifice of Jesus." †

"The precepts of the gospel are universally the principles of Masonry."

"*The great pedestal of Masonry* is religion."

"We cannot help noticing," says Dr. Oliver, "the strange obliquity of vision in the revisers of the lectures, both of Craft and Royal Arch Masonry, that could induce them to omit direct reference to that religion which was figured in the Old, and revealed in the New Testament, although by it alone can the

---

* In a note he says, "In the lectures of Freemasonry there is no direct reference to Christianity; but its types and symbols clearly point to a perfect dispensation which should supersede all the ancient systems of religion, and, bring all mankind into one fold under one shepherd."

† This whole passage is, however, taken and enlarged from Inwood's Sermon, 1796, cf. ante.

symbols and doctrines of all Degrees be harmoniously assimilated. It is now understood by a great majority of the Craft that Christianity constitutes part of our civilization, and without it neither Freemasonry nor any other institution will be allowed to make visible progress in this country.

"As to the idol, 'Universality,' which has been set up as the substitute for the cross of Christ, it is a bubble of froth—($\pi o\mu\phi\acute{o}\lambda\upsilon\xi$)—a shadow without substance. We repudiate it altogether. We are of those who cannot be prevailed on to concede an iota of the Christian character of Freemasonry in favour of any other principle. Place the cross of Christ in one scale and the whole world in the other, we shall not hesitate to proclaim our choice. We know that the heathen nations had their mysteries, and we do not envy them. But they were not our mysteries. They were dedicated to idols, while ours are dedicated to Jehovah; and the Jehovah of the Old Testament is Jesus Christ, the Redeemer of mankind."

"The historical part of its lectures bears an undoubted reference to our pure religion; and this coincidence is so remarkably striking that it would almost convince an unprejudiced mind that Masonry was formed as an exclusive companion for Christianity. The strength of this testimony is increased by the nature and tendency of its symbolical instruction, by the peculiar cast of its morality, and by the very extraordinary nature of its allegorical mechanism; extraordinary on any other principle than with a reference to Christianity."*

"The first lesson which Masonry teaches is to persevere in the constant study of the Holy Bible as the sacred source of *our faith*, and containing the only certain information on a subject the most interesting to a responsible agent in this probationary state; and the

---

* " The Star in the East."

next is an admonition to *practise* the three great duties of morality, one of which is the duty to God. As its instructions proceed, we learn that our groundwork is sanctified by the efficacy of Three Religious Offerings, which are typical of the great sacrifice of atonement by Jesus Christ."*

The following is from an American Masonic lecture (quoted in Dr. Oliver's " Golden Remains of the Early Masonic Writers," Vol. I.) :—

" As our lectures admonish, let us imitate the Christian in his virtuous and amiable conduct; in his unfeigned piety to God; in his inflexible fidelity to his trust; that we may welcome the grim tyrant Death, and receive him as a kind messenger sent from our Supreme Grand Master to translate us from this imperfect to that all-perfect, glorious, and celestial lodge above, where the Supreme Architect of the Universe presides."

" The lectures," says Oliver, " define Freemasonry to be a ' science which includes all others; which inculcates human and divine knowledge, and teaches man his duty to God, his neighbour, and himself.' "

" Every well-governed Lodge is *furnished* with the *Holy Bible*, the *square*, and the *compass*. The Bible points out the path that leads to happiness, and is dedicated to God; the square teaches to regulate our conduct by the principles of morality and virtue, and is dedicated to the Master; the compass teaches to limit our desires in every station, and is dedicated to the brethren. The Bible is dedicated to the service of God, because it is the inestimable gift of God to man; the square to the Master, because, being the proper Masonic emblem of his office, it is constantly to remind him of the duty he owes to the Lodge over which he is appointed to preside; and the compass to the Craft, because by a due attention to its use they are taught to

* " The Star in the East," p. 15-16.

regulate their desires and keep their passions within due bounds."*

"*That Book* (the Bible), *which is never closed in any Lodge,* reveals the duties which the Great Master of All exacts from us."†

"In all regularly constituted Lodges there is represented a certain *point within a circle;* the point representing an individual Brother, the circle representing the boundary line of his duty to God and man, beyond which he is never to suffer his passions, prejudices, or interests to betray him on any occasion. This circle is embordered by two perpendicular parallel lines, representing St. John the Baptist and St. John the Evangelist, who were perfect parallels in Christianity as well as Masonry, and upon the vertex rests the Book of the Holy Scriptures, which point out the whole duty of man. In going round this circle we necessarily touch upon these two lines as well as on the Holy Scriptures; and whilst a Mason keeps himself thus circumscribed, it is impossible that he should materially err."‡

"To the Holy Scriptures the Lectures frequently refer. The Masonic ladder, say they, stands firmly with its foot on the Holy Bible, whilst its summit is lost amidst the clouds of Heaven. Can anything be founded on the Bible, and have no connection with religion? Impossible! This ladder, by which we all hope to ascend to the glorious *arch of Heaven* at the final consummation of all things, is a direct type of religion."

"The first important act which takes place at the establishment of a Masonic Lodge is the business of dedication and consecration. This act is a solemn appropriation of Masonry to God; as the Lodge is, at the same time, inscribed to St. John the Evangelist, who finished by his learning what the Baptist began by his

---

* E. A. P. Lecture, sect. 5, from Webb.   † *Ibid.*

‡ *Ibid.* Oliver states that he cites the *Lectures* as they existed before the revision of Dr. Hemming.

zeal; and these are the two burning and shining Lights on earth, which illuminate our journey as we travel on to attain to the third Great Light in Heaven."

"The Lodge being opened with solemn prayer, and impressed with the conviction that the *All-seeing Eye* above observes and notes our actions, we proceed to the initiation of candidates by progressive steps or degrees. This plan of gradual admission to our privileges is sanctioned by the practice of every system of true religion which has flourished in the world. The patriarchal scheme had its three separate degrees of perfection. The Jews had their three sorts of proselytes, and three orders of the priesthood; and the early Christians their Rulers, Believers, and Catechumens, each corresponding with the Three Degrees of Masonry."

"The admission into the First Degree is on a certain text of Scripture, sanctified by a firm reliance on the protection of God. The reception is by prayer; the candidate is bound by solemn obligations to keep faith with his Brethren; and the *illumination* is performed in the name of the Divinity. The aspirant, with his face to the east, fancies he beholds, in succession, the place where Adam enjoyed the happiest period of his existence; the place where Christianity was revealed to man; the place where the star proclaimed the birth of Jesus; the place where Christ was crucified; and the place where He ascended into heaven. . . . . A white apron, made of the purest lambskin, is presented to him, which he is told derives its distinction from the purity of its colour, emblematical of innocence. . . . . But it possesses a still higher and more glorious reference: it is a symbol of the innocence and perfection of the Christian life which makes *the Lamb without spot* a model for its imitation, and looks to futurity for a *crown* of glory and a *sceptre* of peace. The early catechumens, when they were admitted to the first degree of Christianity, were invested with a white garment,

accompanied by this solemn charge : ' Receive the white and undefiled garment, and produce it without spot before the tribunal of our Lord Jesus Christ, that you may obtain eternal life.' "

Although the following passages occur in Hutchinson's "Spirit of Masonry," as now commonly procurable, they are, we believe, largely Dr. Oliver's own writing.

" The light and doctrines which we possess are derived from the begining of time, and have descended through this long succession of ages uncorrupted; but our modes and manners are deduced from the different eras of paradise, the building of the temple at Jerusalem and the Christian revelation." *

" It has been pointed out to you that the furnitures of the Lodge are emblems excitive of morality and good government; prudence shines in the centre; or if you would apply this object to more sacred principles, it represents the blazing star which conducted the wise men to Bethlehem, and proclaimed the presence of the Son of God." †

" In this assembly of Christians, it is no wise requisite to attempt an argument on the necessity which there was upon the earth for a Mediator and Saviour for man; in the rubbish, superstitions, ceremonials, and faith of the Jewish temple, the true worship of God was buried and confounded, and innocence became only the ornaments of its monument. Then it was that the Divinity, looking down with an eye of commiseration on the deplorable state of man, in His mercy and love sent us a Preceptor and Mediator, who should teach to us the doctrine of regeneration, and raise us from the sepulchre of sin to which the human race had resigned themselves; He gave to us the precepts of that acceptable service wherewith his Father should be well pleased;

---

* Hutchinson's Spirit of Masonry. Editions edited by Oliver.
† *Ibid.*

He made the sacrifice of expiation, and, becoming the first fruits of them that slept, manifested to mankind the resurrection of the body and the life everlasting. In the Master's order this whole doctrine is symbolised, and the Christian conduct is by types presented to us."*

"Lastly we have attempted to examine into the origin of our Society and in many instances, wandering without evidence, have been left to probability in conjecture only. It doth not now seem material to us what our originals and predecessors were, if we occupy ourselves in the true spirit of Masonry; in that Divine spirit which inspired the patriarchs when they erected altars unto the Lord; if we are true servants to our being, faithful and true to our chartered liberties, Christians in profession and in practice; and to each other, and mankind in general, affectionate and upright." †

"In regard to the doctrine of our Saviour and the Christian revelation, it proceeded from the last. The star which proclaimed the birth of the Son of God appeared in the east. The east was an expression used by the prophets to denote the Redeemer. From thence it may well be conceived that we should profess our progress to be from thence; if we profess by being Masons, that we are a society of the servants of that divinity, whose abode is with the Father co-eternal, in the centre of the Heavens. But if we profess no such matter, then why should not we have alleged our progress to have been from the north and the regions of chaos and darkness?" ‡

"Under the influence of this doctrine, the conduct of the Fraternity has been regulated through a succession of ages. The progress of knowledge and philosophy, aided by divine revelation, having abolished many of the vain superstitions of antiquity, and enlightened the mind of the men with the knowledge of the true

---

* *Ibid.*   † *Ibid.*   ‡ *Ibid.*

God and the sacred mysteries of the Christian faith, Masons have always acquiesced in, and zealously pursued, every measure which might promote that holy religion so wisely calculated to make men happy. In those countries, however, where the gospel has not reached, and Christianity displayed her beauties, the Masons have pursued the universal religion of nature; that is, to be good men and true, by whatever denomination or persuasion they have been distinguished. A cheerful compliance with the established religion of the country in which they live, so far as it corresponds with, and is agreeable to, the tenets of Masonry, is earnestly recommended in all their assemblies. This universal conformity, notwithstanding private sentiment and opinion, answers the laudable purpose of conciliating true friendship among men."*

In discourses by the Rev. W. Fenn, the Rev. Delanoy, Bro. Robert Green, Bro. J. Wright, and others, all that is advanced in this work will be found to receive support.

If any Brother, previously unacquainted with the many writings on the subject of the Christianity of Masonry, should wish to further study opinions, he can readily obtain them in any of the various volumes published by Dr. Oliver, entitled " Golden Remains of the Early Masonic Writers."

We have no wish to ascribe more value to these opinions than they actually possess. They very largely refer to the esoteric teaching of the Order ; they are impressions derived from that teaching, and reflections arising from it, and as such are important. The writers are not like Lessing, who on being asked, after he became a Mason, if he found any evil principles in the system, replied, he only wished he had, as then at least he would have found *something* in it.

---

* *Ibid.*

Following the old custom of closing Masonic work with songs illustrative of Masonry, we here give two verses which some Masons may not know.

> Fair virtue and friendship, religion and love,
> The motives of this noble science still prove;
> 'Tis the key, and the lock, of Christ'anity's rules."

In a later book than that from which we quote; " Christ'anity's " is altered to " Godly." In this song " the reverend crozier" is alluded to.

This, again a plain allusion to our Saviour, is taken from the article " Corner Stone," in Peck's appendix to Mackey's " Lexicon."

> Within this stone there lie conceal'd,
>   What future ages may disclose,
> The sacred truths to us reveal'd,
>   By Him who fell by ruthless foes.

> *   *   *   *   *   *

> On Him, this corner stone, we build,
>   To Him this edifice erect,
> And still until this work's fulfilled
>   May Heaven the Workman's way direct.

CHAPTER XI.

CONCLUSION.

WE trust that some consideration has been accorded us during the perusal of the foregoing chapters, from a remembrance of the peculiar conditions imposed by Masonic law. We are forbidden, wisely so, to discuss any matter relating to religion within a Lodge, or any secret teaching in public. A complete refutation of error, either within or without a Lodge, is thus impossible, owing to the laws and esoteric nature of the system.

We have attempted to show that mistakes have been made, as we opine, through forgetting or ignoring that the religious belief of the First Degree is not the final teaching of Freemasonry; it is not indeed teaching at all, *it is a belief prior to initiation.* The belief required in a candidate is treated as but darkness which needs illumination. This is often forgotten, and it is accordingly thought that a brother has Masonic Light because he professes a belief in God. The truth, of course, is, that even with this initial faith he is still in a state of Masonic darkness. Masonry has not given him this belief, he had it before. The candidate is, by the possession thereof, Masonically fit to receive Light—he is not yet in possession of it.

The First Degree states that a certain material volume is an emblem of the Masonic Spiritual Light. If in the First Degree the full Light were given, no further Degree would be required; but we know that even in

the Third or Master Masons' Degree, the Light finally afforded is but darkness visible. The study of the material words of the Bible has given a mere glimmering ray of Light. This is the teaching of the Degrees, it is not our individual teaching alone; we see no other rational interpretation of them. The recognised ceremonies since the Union have always taught this.

The Master Masons' Degree, therefore, gives no sufficient Light, it merely prepares the mind for the reception of truth. The Degrees are, throughout, supposed to have raised the conceptions, or increased the capabilities for the reception, of the final truth to be disclosed. A strict Biblical development is followed, in which material facts emblematically represent spiritual truths.

In the Royal Arch Degree the statement is repeated that the true Light has yet to be found, and the want of Light is here again symbolised. The non-existence of it, in the symbolism which is employed, prevents even him who holds the truth from knowing that he does so. The search for truth has been successful—yet nevertheless, he who has found it knows it not. Twice is it stated in the ritual of this Degree that the Light can only come by the acceptance of revelation, and that this revelation is the final grand reward. The ritual does not speak of *any* revelation, nor of *a* revelation, but of *the* revelation. Herein the Universalist may find ample food for thought.

We are forbidden to enter into a description which would display the full importance of that which follows. But it may be said in general terms that a threefold explanation of that word,* which is supposed to be again given to the world, emphasises in language not to be mistaken, that the Great Light which has been so

---

* We are aware it is denied that there is any such Hebrew interpretation of the word as is Masonically stated to exist. This is of no importance to our argument; it is the interpretation that is actually given which is alone of consequence.

appropriately symbolised by the Bible is the Light to which no one can consistently attach aught but a Christian interpretation. Let any Royal Arch Mason remember the combinations of the sacred words which are presented to the newly-exalted companion, and there need be no further contention that the great mystery which is unfolded, the aim and end of English Freemasonry, is purely and entirely Christian.

Nevertheless, we have small expectations of carrying conviction to any Brother who has imbibed the idea that Freemasonry has no connection with religion. Such a theory, to us, is incomprehensible, there being nothing in the way of evidence to support it. It is, however, the teaching of a modern and aggressive school. We yet cherish the hope that those who view Masonry as having a close connection with religion—and here we shall have many non-Christians with us—will be induced to see that the question, *what volume* shall be the emblematic Masonic Light? is of serious importance.

It should, at least, be in the power of the Master of a Lodge, when referring, as he does, to a specific sacred book, to be able to say what that book is. So long as the ritual remains as it now stands, the Master cannot refer to the Bible as the symbol of any and every sacred book. He is obliged to refer to it as the emblem of a Spiritual Light, and as containing God's revelation to man. It can hardly be denied that the Bible has been the emblematic Light of the English Constitution, nor that when Light is asked for under it, only the Light of that particular Constitution should be given.

We do not propose as a remedy for further inconsistency, any innovation in Masonry. We have shown that an assumption has long existed that there are Lodges where the Koran, the Shasters, or some other book esteemed as sacred, is treated as the Great Light. This supposition to some extent supports the contention that every Masonic Lodge must of necessity have *one*

s 2

Great Light, not *many*. For a long series of years the existence of Mahommedan and Hindoo Lodges has been assumed, and the proposal to realise this supposition cannot, therefore, consistently be found fault with. Our proposition amounts to no more than this. Let that which has been supposed to exist, but which never has existed, now be established.

We will not enter into the question as to whether the English ritual is suitable for non-Christian Lodges —that is not our concern but theirs; all we wish to do is to make our own part of the system less of an anomaly. We have never known how the English ritual could be acceptable to any but a Christian Brother, and it must be evident that those who have been able to surmount this difficulty in the past are the proper persons to point out wherein any alteration is desirable. Any proposed modification could be easily examined, and if fundamentally injurious, disallowed.

We are quite prepared to find that those who have for years imagined there were Hindoo Lodges under the English Constitution, and have hitherto not offered objection to the purely imaginary fact, will find fault with our proposal. We expect this. But it is surely possible to officially enquire of Hindoos whether there is anything in the teaching of orthodox English Masonry that conflicts with their belief, *or whether they can accept the Bible as containing God's Law?* If they cannot accept it, it is obviously more consistent that they should have some volume which they can accept as the Light of *their part* of the system of Freemasonry.

The only important question appears to be, can Lodges which have some Great Light, other than the Bible, exist under the English Constitution? Here again we must point out that their existence has all along been assumed as a matter of course. Our own conviction is that no Lodge can consistently exist under the English Constitution if it ignores or supplants the

Bible by adopting some other book as its Great Light. Whether we be right or wrong, it would still be within the power of the Constitution to place the matter on a clearer and more consistent basis than it is at present.

We conceive that it is always in the power of a Grand Lodge to deal with difficulties which were not originally foreseen; what we have drawn attention to is of this nature, and, if we be correct, can be dealt with. It could not have been anticipated either in 1717, or in 1813 at the Union, that two hundred millions of Asiatics, with various religions, regarding many of which little, if any, knowledge then existed in Europe, would become subjects of the British Crown in 1859. We have shown that the Constitutions prove that in the first instance it was never intended that an Institution, which is now asserted to be universally applicable, should spread beyond the confines of the Cities of London and Westminster.

We do not believe that, according to the spirit of the Masonic system, any one Constitution can be universal. In the case of the English Constitution a curious difficulty has arisen owing to the expansion of the Empire; instead of closing our eyes to this, it would be far preferable to face it manfully. It would not be inconsistent if to the original English Constitution there were attached a supplementary one, recognising in the fullest manner that there are now subjects of the Empire who cannot agree with the strict teaching of English Masonry, formulated, as it was, without a thought being given to them.

If some such course should be adopted, the Sacred Volume of the non-Christian Mason will take, not a place of mere equality with other books in a Lodge, but will assume that position which it is imperative the Great Light of Masonry should take, *i.e.*, the highest.

One objection will readily occur to some readers; which is, will the State regard a Mahommedan or other non-Christian Lodge with a favourable eye? The right

of visitation does away with any objection which may be raised on this head. The Grand Lodge of England has always insisted on this right of visitation, as a landmark of our Institution, and so long as every Lodge is open to visitation by all—the Christian Lodge by the Hindoo and *vice versâ*—there can be no danger to the State. This, however, can hardly be a Masonic objection, for, as we have shown, this danger must have been supposed to exist in the past.

It has been urged in this work that any Lodge can have but one Great Light, and that this should be derived from the Constitution. The religion of a country might govern some cases, but not all; India is a case in point. If the religion of that country be decided on the numerical strength of a sect,* the Bible cannot be used as the Light of any Lodge in India. If the Constitution govern the case the Bible can remain, but, inasmuch as no one can believe that the Almighty has revealed contradictory doctrines, it is manifestly impossible that sound Masonic law should decide that an Indian Lodge can have a number of sacred volumes.

It is the office of Masonry to dispense Light, not to receive it; it cannot therefore be swayed by every

---

* We have before remarked that India, if considered as a whole, would be Hindoo in belief, but not so if dealt with in detail. There are some curious circumstances to which attention may be drawn in passing. In Europe the religion of the State is commonly the religion of a large portion of the people; instances to the contrary can be found in India. Cashmere is a State, or Kingdom, the recognised religion of which is Hindoo, whilst the vast majority of the people are Mahommedans. What is the religion of such a country on the basis of the old Constitutions? It would be a very bold Mason who dared to start a Masonic Lodge in Cashmere on a Mahommedan basis—the subsequent proceedings would doubtless be secret enough, with Hindoos well represented when the infliction of penalties was in question. The Punjab was also Mahommedan by an enormous majority when conquered by the British, but the religion of the State was Sikh, although the Sikhs were then, as now, only one twentieth of the population. Who knew these facts in the last century when so much discussion occurred about the religion of countries? Masons were enjoined to be of the religion of a country, and yet to do nothing which could bring them into conflict with the State—the very thing which their first act of Masonic compliance would in all probability have entailed.

doctrine proffered by initiates in a state of Masonic darkness. There is no more reason now than there was when Preston wrote, for a Lodge to change its belief in order to curry favour with individuals.

Our proposal carries with it no injustice. We in no way dispute the status of any present or future Brother. We, in fact, wish to place the non-Christian Brother on a footing which must improve his position in the Craft. It may be considered that the multiplication of offices offers an objection to our proposal, as, if the recognition of the non-Christian element increased the number of members of the Institution, in course of time Hindoo or other District Grand Lodges would be a necessity. We ourselves believe this necessity would very speedily arise, from the healthy stimulus which would be given to Masonry by a proper recognition of its genuine principles. It is not conceivable that the Grand Lodge or other governing body, would grant this opportunity for promotion before circumstances justified such a course.

An important fact to be remembered is, that whilst the non-Christian Masons are not as yet very strong in point of numbers in Upper India, their thoroughness and attention make up for this deficiency. Their earnestness will inevitably lead them to follow up their success in Bombay, and to seize upon every relaxation of the Englishman in order to secure a still better position for their own sacred volumes. And all honour to them for their consistency.

Whilst the Englishman is getting into doubt as to whether English Masonry has any definite sacred volume at all, and whilst in Masonic papers it has been discussed whether the English Book of Constitutions might not take the place of the Bible in a Lodge, the Indian Brother has shown a grasp of the situation by introducing, and obtaining recognition for, his sacred writings. To whatever extent he may be right or wrong

in his acceptance of our Degrees, there can be no question as to the respect he is entitled to, for the consistent perseverance with which he upholds in Masonry what he deems to be due to his religion.

We fear our opinions are feebly expressed, but they are strongly held, and we trust more to the fervency of our convictions than to our literary talents to influence the minds of our readers. If, however, we have succeeded in making any of them think more seriously of the religious import of Freemasonry, the object of this book will have been attained.

CPSIA information can be obtained
at www.ICGtesting.com
Printed in the USA
BVHW011726190819
556217BV00018B/2038/P

9 781498 011303